Jane Austen: *Emma*

Casebook Series

Jane Austen: *Emma*   DAVID LODGE

John Osborne: *Look Back in Anger*   J. RUSSELL TAYLOR

Pope: *The Rape of the Lock*   JOHN DIXON HUNT

Shakespeare: *Antony and Cleopatra*   J. RUSSELL BROWN

Shakespeare: *Hamlet*   JOHN JUMP

Shakespeare: *The Tempest*   D. J. PALMER

Shakespeare: *The Winter's Tale*   KENNETH MUIR

Yeats: *Last Poems*   JON STALLWORTHY

IN PREPARATION

William Blake: *'Songs of Innocence' and 'Songs of Experience'*
   MARGARET BOTTRALL

Emily Brontë: *Wuthering Heights*   MIRIAM ALLOTT

Joseph Conrad: *The Secret Agent*   IAN WATT

Charles Dickens: *Bleak House*   A. E. DYSON

T. S. Eliot: *Four Quartets*   BERNARD BERGONZI

T. S. Eliot: *The Waste Land*   C. B. COX AND A. HINCHLIFFE

E. M. Forster: *A Passage to India*   MALCOLM BRADBURY

D. H. Lawrence: *Sons and Lovers*   GEMINI SALGADO

D. H. Lawrence: *'The Rainbow' and 'Women in Love'*
   COLIN CLARKE

Milton: *'Comus' and 'Samson Agonistes'*   STANLEY FISH

Shakespeare: *Henry IV* Parts I and II   G. K. HUNTER

Shakespeare: *Macbeth*   JOHN WAIN

Shakespeare: *Richard II*   NICHOLAS BROOKE

Shakespeare: *The Merchant of Venice*   JOHN WILDERS

Tennyson: *In Memoriam*   JOHN DIXON HUNT

Wordsworth: *The Prelude*   W. J. HARVEY

Wordsworth: *Lyrical Ballads*   ALUN JONES

Jane Austen

Emma

A CASEBOOK

EDITED BY

DAVID LODGE

Aurora Publishers Incorporated

NASHVILLE/LONDON

FOR MY GRANDMOTHER

FIRST PUBLISHED 1969 BY
MACMILLAN AND COMPANY LIMITED
LONDON, ENGLAND

COPYRIGHT © 1970 BY
AURORA PUBLISHERS INCORPORATED
NASHVILLE, TENNESSEE 37219
STANDARD OF CONGRESS CATALOG CARD NUMBER: 76-127565
STANDARD BOOK NUMBER: 87695-036-5
MANUFACTURED IN THE UNITED STATES OF AMERICA

CONTENTS

SOURCES
AND ACKNOWLEDGEMENTS

PART I

Correspondence concerning *Emma*, from *Jane Austen's Letters to her sister Cassandra and others*, ed. R. W. Chapman (1932); opinions of *Emma*, from *Plan of a Novel by Jane Austen* (1926) pp. 20–3; review by Sir Walter Scott, in *Quarterly Review*, XIV (1815) 188–201; *British Critic*, NS VI (1816) 96; *Monthly Review*, LXXX (1816) 320; *Gentleman's Magazine*, LXXXVI (1816) 248–9.

PART 2

Susan Ferrier, *Memoir and Correspondence of Susan Ferrier*, ed. John A. Doyle (1898); Mary Russell Mitford's letter, from A. G. L'Estrange, *Life* (1870) I 331; John Henry Newman, *Letters*, ed. Anne Mozley (1891) II 223; Charlotte Brontë's letter, from Clement K. Shorter, *The Brontës: Life and Letters* (1908) II 127–8; 'Trollope on *Emma*: an unpublished note', in *Nineteenth-century Fiction*, IV (1949) 145–7 (© The Regents of the University of California 1949); Richard Simpson, 'Jane Austen', in *North British Review*, LII (1870) 129–52; 'Jane Austen and her novels', in *Dublin Review*, XV (1870) 430–45; Lord Brabourne's letter, from *Letters of Jane Austen*, ed. Lord Brabourne (1884) I 89–90; Mrs Charles Malden, *Jane Austen* (1889) pp. 128–9; Walter Herries Pollock, *Jane Austen, an essay in criticism* (1889) pp. 90–1; William Dean Howells, *Heroines of Fiction* (1901); Reginald Farrer, 'Jane Austen, *ob.* July 18, 1817', in *Quarterly Review*, CCXXVIII (July 1917) 24–8; D. W. Harding, 'Regulated Hatred: an aspect of the work of Jane Austen', in *Scrutiny*, VIII

(March 1940) 346–62 (Cambridge University Press); E. N. Hayes, '*Emma*: a dissenting opinion', in *Nineteenth-century Fiction*, IV (1949) 3–7 (© The Regents of the University of California 1949); Richard Poirier, 'Mark Twain, Jane Austen and the imagination of society', in *In Defense of Reading* (E. P. Dutton & Co. Inc.) pp. 282–309 (© Reuben A. Brower and Richard Poirier 1962); extracts from *The Dream and the Task* (Gerald Duckworth & Co. Ltd, W. W. Norton & Co. Inc.; © Graham Hough 1963).

PART 3

Arnold Kettle, 'Jane Austen: *Emma*', from *An Introduction to the English Novel*, I (Hutchinson Publishing Group Ltd); Professor Marvin Mudrick, 'Irony as Form: *Emma*', from *Jane Austen: Irony as Defense and Discovery*; Edgar F. Shannon, '*Emma*: Character and Construction', in *PMLA* LXXI (1956) (The Modern Language Association); Lionel Trilling, '*Emma* and the Legend of Jane Austen', originally published as an introduction to the Riverside Edition of *Emma* (Houghton Mifflin Co.); 'The Humiliation of Emma Woodhouse', in *Literary Review*, summer 1959 (Professor Mark Schorer and Fairleigh Dickinson University, New Jersey); R. E. Hughes, 'The Education of Emma Woodhouse', in *Nineteenth-century Fiction*, XVI (1961) 69–74 (© The Regents of the University of California 1961); Wayne Booth, 'Control of Distance in Jane Austen's *Emma*', from *The Rhetoric of Fiction* (University of Chicago Press); 'Jane Austen's *Emma*', in the *Critical Quarterly*, 1962 (Dr Malcolm Bradbury); W. J. Harvey, 'The Plot of *Emma*', in *Essays in Criticism*, XVII (1967) (The Editor).

GENERAL EDITOR'S PREFACE

EACH of this series of Casebooks concerns either one well-known and influential work of literature or two or three closely linked works. The main section consists of critical readings, mostly modern, brought together from journals and books. A selection of reviews and comments by the author's contemporaries is also included, and sometimes comments from the author himself. The Editor's Introduction charts the reputation of the work from its first appearance until the present time.

What is the purpose of such a collection? Chiefly, to assist reading. Our first response to literature may be, or seem to be, 'personal'. Certain qualities of vigour, profundity, beauty or 'truth to experience' strike us, and the work gains a foothold in our mind. Later, an isolated phrase or passage may return, to haunt or illuminate. Where did we hear that? we wonder – it could scarcely be better put.

In these and similar ways appreciation begins, but major literature prompts to very much more. There are certain facts we need to know if we are to understand properly. Who were the author's original readers, and what assumptions did he share with them? What was his theory of literature? Was he committed to a particular historical situation, or to a set of beliefs? We need historians as well as critics to help us with this. But there are also more purely literary factors to take account of: the work's structure and rhetoric; its symbols and archetypes; its tone, genre and texture; its use of language; the words on the page. In all these matters critics can inform and enrich our individual responses by offering imaginative recreations of their own.

For the life of a book is not, after all, merely 'personal'; it is more like a tripartite dialogue, between a writer living 'then', a reader living 'now', and whatever forces of survival and honour link the two. Criticism is the public manifestation of this dialogue, a witness to the continuing power of literature to arouse and excite. It illuminates the possibilities and regards of the dialogue, pushing 'interpretation' as far forward as it can go.

And here, indeed, is the rub: how far can it go? Where does 'interpretation' end and nonsense begin? Why is one interpretation superior to another, and why does each age need to interpret for itself? The critic knows that his insights have value only in so far as they serve the text, and that he must take account of views differing sharply from his own. He knows that his own writing will be judged as well as the work he writes about, so that he cannot simply assert inner illumination or a differing taste.

The critical forum is a place of vigorous conflict and disagreement, but there is nothing in this to cause dismay. What is attested is the complexity of human experience and the richness of literature, not any chaos or relativity of taste. A critic is better seen, no doubt, as an explorer than as an 'authority', but explorers ought to be, and usually are, well equipped. The effect of good criticism is to convince us of what C. S. Lewis called 'the enormous extension of our being which we owe to authors'. A Casebook will be justified only if it helps to promote the same end.

A single volume can represent no more than a small selection of critical opinions. Some critics have been excluded for reasons of space, and it is hoped that readers will follow up the further suggestions in the Select Bibliography. Other contributions have been severed from their original context, to which some readers may wish to return. Indeed, if they take a hint from the critics represented here, they certainly will.

                                                        A. E. DYSON

INTRODUCTION

'I AM going to take a heroine whom no one but myself will much like,' said Jane Austen, on commencing the composition of *Emma*.[1] Today one is inclined to interpret this remark as the recognition of a problem that was to be successfully overcome, rather than as an accurate prediction. Readers like the author's niece, Fanny Knight, who 'could not bear Emma herself' (see below, p. 33) have been in the minority. Most readers, if they respond to Jane Austen's work at all, have liked Emma Woodhouse and the novel that bears her name. There has been considerable disagreement as to *why* we like her; but that we do, despite all her faults, is one of the most common tributes paid to Jane Austen's skill as a novelist.

Although *Emma* has never been the most widely popular of Jane Austen's novels (that distinction must belong to *Pride and Prejudice*[2]) there has been a growing measure of agreement through the years among her more devoted and discriminating readers that it is her most perfect and fully representative work. It happily combines all the qualities for which she has been most admired: irony, wit, realism, vivid characterisation, moral seriousness and faultless control of tone and narrative method. No other novel presents us so strikingly with the paradox – never

[1] 'She was very fond of Emma but did not reckon on her being a general favourite; for, when commencing that work, she said: "I am going to take ..." ' James Edward Austen-Leigh, *A Memoir of Jane Austen* (1870).

[2] A check of the British Museum catalogue shows that up to 1953 *Pride and Prejudice* w as reprinted approximately twice as many times as *Emma*. Most of the people whose opinions Jane Austen collected (see below, p. 33) seem to have preferred *Pride and Prejudice* or *Mansfield Park* to *Emma*.

inseparable from our reading of Jane Austen – of rich meanings extracted from superficially slight materials. Modern criticism, in particular, has focused attention on *Emma* as the classic example of Jane Austen's art; while its first publication in 1816 marked the peak of the modest fame she attained in her own lifetime.

Jane Austen was born in 1775, at Steventon, Hampshire, where her father was rector, and where she lived until he retired to Bath in 1801. After an unsettled period following Mr Austen's death in 1805, she lived with her mother and sister Cassandra at Chawton, also in Hampshire, from 1809 to 1817. In the latter year she became seriously ill and moved, for medical attention, to Winchester, where she died on 18 July. Although she never married, Jane Austen belonged to a large and lively family, and her life was full of human interest and incident. It was not, however, in any sense a public life: her friends and relations took a keen interest in her writings, but she never moved in literary circles, and her novels were published anonymously in her own lifetime.

The six major novels were published in the following order: *Sense and Sensibility* (1811), *Pride and Prejudice* (1813), *Mansfield Park* (1814), *Emma* (1816) and (posthumously) *Persuasion* with *Northanger Abbey* (1818). As regards composition, however, *Northanger Abbey* should be grouped with *Pride and Prejudice* and *Sense and Sensibility*: these three novels were evidently first written in the 1790s, and substantially revised before their eventual publication. The three 'mature' novels were written in order of publication, but probably Jane Austen had not finished working on the manuscript of *Persuasion* when she died. *Emma* is therefore the last novel which she completed to her own satisfaction and personally saw through the press.

Modern scholarship has uncovered a good deal of information about the composition, publication and initial reception of *Emma*.[1]

---

[1] See especially Charles Beecher Hogan, 'Jane Austen and her Early Public', in *Review of English Studies*, NS I (1950) pp. 44–7, and R. W. Chapman's *Jane Austen: Facts and Problems* (Oxford, 1948) and *Jane Austen: a Critical Bibliography* (Oxford, 1953). The editor is greatly indebted to both these writers.

A memorandum in the author's own hand has survived, recording that the novel was begun in January 1814, and completed on 29 March 1815. Jane Austen was therefore no doubt thinking of her own work in progress when she wrote in September 1814 to her niece Anna, an aspirant novelist, that '3 or 4 Families in a Country Village is the very thing to work on'.[1] In May 1814 *Mansfield Park* had been published, and the edition was sold out by November: Jane Austen's reputation was growing. In 1815 she heard indirectly that the Prince Regent (later George IV) was an admirer of her novels, and 'kept a set of them in every one of his residences'.[2] The prince's librarian, James Stanier Clarke, introduced himself to Jane Austen when she was in London, and indicated that she might dedicate her next book to the prince. Though she had no respect for his personal character, Jane Austen accepted the compliment to her literary merit, and *Emma* appeared with a dedication to the prince. In the ensuing correspondence Clarke, a well-meaning but somewhat conceited and fatuous man, who might have stepped from the pages of one of Jane Austen's own novels, provoked one of her most characteristic letters by suggesting that she try her hand at a historical romance 'illustrative of the history of the august House of Cobourg'. Her reply, written (perhaps not fortuitously) on April Fool's Day, is a masterpiece of politely disguised irony, and also a serious, perceptive attempt at artistic self-definition (see below, p. 31).

Emma appeared on 29 December 1815, though the title page is dated 1816. It was published, in an edition of 2000 copies, by John Murray, to whom Jane Austen had turned perhaps because her previous publisher, Egerton, had failed to produce a second edition of *Mansfield Park*. (Murray published a second edition of this novel early in 1816.) Henry Austen, who handled his sister's business affairs, rejected on her behalf Murray's offer of £450 for the copyrights of *Sense and Sensibility*, *Mansfield Park*, and *Emma*, and the latter two novels were published on a

---

[1] *Jane Austen's Letters to her sister Cassandra and others*, collected and edited by R. W. Chapman (Oxford, 1932) p. 401.

[2] Chapman, *Facts and Problems*, p. 138.

profit-sharing basis. A note made by Jane Austen towards the end of her life records a figure of £39 as 'first profits of *Emma*'.[1]

Whatever its financial advantages, the publication of *Emma* by Murray indirectly brought its author a considerable gain in reputation. For Murray was the founder of the influential *Quarterly Review*, and his reader was the editor of that journal, William Gifford. Gifford was greatly impressed by the new novel – 'Of *Emma* I have nothing but good to say', he wrote after reading the manuscript[2] – and he suggested that the book deserved a prominent review in the *Quarterly*. Murray accordingly asked his most distinguished contributor, Sir Walter Scott, if he had 'any fancy to dash off an article on *Emma*'? Scott's review, a long article of some 5000 words, which also discussed *Pride and Prejudice* and *Sense and Sensibility*, appeared in March 1816, unsigned, as was the custom.

Even without Scott's signature, the extensive and generally favourable discussion of her work in the *Quarterly* was an important milestone in Jane Austen's literary career, the first significant recognition that she was a novelist of unusual distinction. It is not known whether she was privately told of the identity of her anonymous reviewer. We know from a letter that she was aware that Scott was the author of the enormously successful *Waverley* (1814), although this novel and its successors were published anonymously and Scott was at this time known to the general public as a poet.[3] In retrospect, there seems a nice irony in the fact that the first important tribute to Jane Austen's fiction was made by the arch-practitioner of the historical romance, a literary form which, she told James Stanier Clarke, 'I could not sit down seriously to write . . . under any other motive than to save my life.'

One of the great merits of Scott's review is that he attempts to place Jane Austen in relation to existing fictional traditions. 'In its first appearance,' he suggests, 'the novel was the legitimate child of the romance', and it honoured its parentage by offering the reader heightened narrative interest and idealised sentiment.

---

[1] Chapman, *Facts and Problems*, p. 156.   [2] Hogan, *RES* ns I 45.
[3] *Letters*, ed. Chapman, p. 404.

But, he suggests, 'these excitements ... had lost much of their poignancy by the repeated and injudicious use of them' and in consequence a 'style of novel has arisen in the last fifteen or twenty years' which instead exploits 'the art of copying from nature as she really exists in the common walks of life, and presenting to the reader, instead of the splendid scenes of an imaginary world, a concrete and striking representation of that which is daily taking place around him'. Jane Austen is the prime exemplar of this new kind of novel.

Scott's argument perhaps underestimates the realistic, anti-romantic quality of much eighteenth-century fiction, especially Richardson's; and his attempt to see Jane Austen as representing a current literary trend somewhat obscures the highly individual character of her work. For Jane Austen's realism does not merely offer alternative diversions to those of an exhausted romance tradition: it implicitly discredits the false patterns imposed upon experience by literary conventions – including those that Scott himself relied upon. That Scott was half-aware of this challenge is suggested by the conclusion of his article, where he defends, somewhat self-indulgently, the code of romantic love. But Scott is both generous and perceptive in his praise of Jane Austen's art, and is fully alive to the difficulties over which it triumphs. His detailed account of *Emma* shows that he had read it with attentive appreciation. Other contemporary reviewers were generally favourable, but only Scott shows any consciousness of dealing with a literary masterpiece.[1]

It was in fact a long time before Jane Austen was generally acknowledged to be a major novelist. In her lifetime, and immediately afterwards, she suffered the penalties of being an

[1] Scott's respect for Jane Austen was not diminished with the passing of time. In 1826 he noted in his journal: 'That young lady had a talent for describing the involvements, and feelings, and characters of ordinary life which is to me the most wonderful thing I ever met with. The big Bow-wow strain I can do myself like any now going; but the exquisite touch, which renders ordinary commonplace things and characters interesting, from the truth of the description and the sentiment, is denied to me. What a pity such a gifted creature died so early!'

anti-romantic writer in an age of romanticism. Coleridge and Southey held her work in high esteem it is true,[1] but no comment is recorded from Byron, Shelley or Keats, and Wordsworth characteristically remarked that 'though he admitted that her novels were an admirable copy of life, he could not be interested in productions of that kind; unless the truth of nature were presented to him clarified, as it were, by the pervading light of the imagination, it had scarce any attractions in his eyes'.[2] It has often been remarked that the Oxford Movement was a child of the Romantic Revival, and it is not surprising to find John Henry Newman in 1837 qualifying his admiration for *Emma* with some regrets for the lack of 'body' and 'romance' in the story (see below, p. 49). Charlotte Brontë, whose own fiction is the antithesis of Jane Austen's, puts the romantic case against her with typical vehemence (see below, p. 50). Anthony Trollope, a novelist who had rather more in common with Jane Austen, responds to the ironic characterisation of Emma, but he sees the novel, rather condescendingly, as essentially a 'period-piece' (see below, p. 51).

Jane Austen always had enthusiastic admirers in the decades following her death – Archbishop Whately, Macaulay and George Lewes, for example, all compared her skill in characterisation to Shakespeare's[3] – but it was not until 1833 that her novels were reprinted; and when her nephew James Edward Austen-Leigh published his *Memoir* in 1871 it was his opinion that 'Seldom has any literary reputation been of such slow growth as that of Jane Austen.' By that date, however, the reputation *was* established, if the wide interest shown in the *Memoir* is any evidence. Among the many long articles it provoked in the periodical press was one of the finest studies of Jane Austen ever written: Richard Simpson's essay in the *North British Review* (see below, p. 52).

[1] See Chapman, *Bibliography*, p. 25.

[2] Chapman, *Bibliography*, p. 25.

[3] See Chapman, *Bibliography*, pp. 23, 27 and 29. The comparison may surprise the modern reader, but nineteenth-century critics tended to see Shakespeare as above all the master of realistic characterisation.

Before Simpson's article – and for a long time afterwards – tributes to Jane Austen concentrated monotonously on her skill in conveying an illusion of life. 'Real' and 'natural' were the most common epithets of praise bestowed upon her work, the art of which was seen to consist principally of investing fictitious characters and actions with the kind of interest that we take in people and events within our own actual experience. Such was the response of Jane Austen's own circle, as we see from the 'Opinions' she collected, and it was one she indulged privately by providing sequels to her stories.[1] It is a natural response, and one which we can never entirely suppress – probably we should not try to. But as a way of interpreting and evaluating Jane Austen it has severe limitations. Under its influence, criticism very easily degenerates into gossip, at which level it is incapable of explaining why we should consider Jane Austen an important writer. The most hostile critics of her work – Charlotte Brontë, for example, or E. N. Hayes (see below, p. 74) have acknowledged that she gives a marvellously life-like rendering of the world she knew: their objection has been that she does nothing else, and that the world she knew was too narrow in its scope and too superficial in its values to provide the stuff of great literature.

It is the great virtue of Simpson's essay that he shows how Jane Austen's 'miniatures' of middle-class Regency society mediate a complex and challenging vision of experience, and he does so in terms which remarkably anticipate the conclusions of the most sophisticated modern criticism. That Jane Austen had an essentially critical and ironic vision, defined initially by parodic contrast with literary stereotypes; that her fiction was not thrown off by a kind of effortless knack, but 'worked up by incessant labour into its perfect form'; that her novels, arranged in order of composition, reveal a coherent pattern of development; that she was a subtle and unsentimental moralist, particularly concerned with the processes of self-discovery and the attain-

[1] According to tradition, she predicted that Mr Woodhouse would live for two years after his daughter's marriage, and that Mrs Frank Churchill would die young. See R. W. Chapman, *Facts and Problems*, pp. 123 and 186.

ment of maturity through personal relations – all these points, made by Simpson, reappear in such modern critics as Dr and Mrs Leavis, Marvin Mudrick and Lionel Trilling.

Criticism in the decades following Simpson's article, however, failed to maintain the standard he had set. The first two full-length studies of Jane Austen, Mrs Charles Malden's *Jane Austen* (1889) and Goldwin Smith's *Life of Jane Austen* (1890) rarely rise above the level of chatty paraphrase. The extract from Walter Herries Pollock's *Jane Austen: an essay in criticism* (1899) given below (see p. 61) concerning an inconsistency in *Emma*, is characteristic of the tendency of 'Janeites'[1] to concern themselves with minutiae. It was evidently the growth of a cosy, undiscriminating cult of Jane Austen at this period that provoked Henry James's outburst against 'the body of publishers, editors, illustrators, producers of the present twaddle of magazines, who have found their "dear", our dear, everybody's dear, Jane so infinitely to their material purpose'.[2] The meagreness of James's recorded comments on Jane Austen – meagre both in quantity and praise – is one of the great puzzles and disappointments of literary history, for of all earlier English novelists she seems closest to him in spirit and in concern for formal artistry – in particular the narrative method of *Emma* has been picked out as anticipating James's experiments with 'point of view'.[3] William Dean Howells, James's compatriot and friend, was more sympathetic, as his sensitive character-sketch of Emma shows (see below, p. 62). American critics are now among the most enthusiastic and perceptive readers of Jane Austen; but as Richard Poirier suggests in his comparison of *Emma* and *Huckleberry Finn* (see below, p. 78), her art concentrates all the qualities that characterise English literary culture and distinguish it from the

[1] This term for devotees of Jane Austen was coined by Rudyard Kipling in a story called 'The Janeites' (1924) and has had a somewhat equivocal currency ever since.

[2] Henry James, 'The Lesson of Balzac', in *The Question of Our Speech* (Boston, 1905) p. 60.

[3] See, for instance, R. W. Chapman, 'Jane Austen's Methods', in *Times Literary Supplement*, 9 Feb 1922, p. 82; and F. R. Leavis, *The Great Tradition* (1948) p. 19 n.

American. She has always been a peculiarly 'English' classic. Though her novels were translated into French throughout the nineteenth century, no major French novelist up to and including Proust makes reference to her, and it has been said that 'from the point of view of the European tradition of the novel she might as well never have existed'.[1]

In English criticism of the late nineteenth and early twentieth centuries, *Emma* is more and more frequently cited as the supreme example of Jane Austen's art. Mrs Oliphant, Mrs Malden, Goldwin Smith, A. C. Bradley and George Saintsbury all reach this verdict.[2] For Reginald Farrer, writing in 1917, it was 'the Book of Books'. Farrer's perceptive analysis of *Emma* anticipated much subsequent criticism of the novel in stressing the control of tone and narrative method by which Jane Austen maintains a delicate balance of sympathetic identification and critical detachment in our response to her heroine (see below, p. 64).

The twenties and thirties of this century saw a revolution in English studies, a sudden expansion and intensification of critical activity marked by the development of 'close reading' techniques and the application to literary texts of such disciplines as psychology, sociology and anthropology. But the new criticism concerned itself initially with poetry and poetic drama, and the study of the novel was comparatively late in feeling its effects. As far as Jane Austen is concerned, this period was dominated by the scholarship of R. W. Chapman, who provided definitive editions of the novels (in 1923), the *Letters* (in 1932) and much previously unpublished minor work. By the end of the thirties, most of the extant materials for the study of Jane Austen were generally available, and since then books and articles about her have streamed from the presses in ever-increasing numbers.

In 1939 Mary Lascelles published *Jane Austen and her Art*,

[1] Joseph Cady and Ian Watt, 'Jane Austen's Critics', in *Critical Quarterly*, V (1963) 55. This is the best survey known to the editor.

[2] Margaret Oliphant, *A Literary History of England* (1882) III 206; Goldwin Smith, *Life of Jane Austen* (1890) p. 118; A. C. Bradley, *Essays and Studies*, II (1911) 22; George Saintsbury, *The English Novel* (1913) p. 198.

which is still in many ways the soundest and most helpful full-length study (though it does not lend itself to representation in extracts). In the 1940s, the highly influential school of critics associated with F. R. Leavis and the journal *Scrutiny* defined Jane Austen as a living classic who answered to the most rigorous demands of modern criticism. Dr Leavis, though he has published no extended work on Jane Austen, placed her firmly at the beginning of his 'Great Tradition' of English novelists (the other members being George Eliot, Henry James, Joseph Conrad and D. H. Lawrence), and characteristically stressed her 'intense moral preoccupation'. 'When we examine the formal perfection of *Emma*,' he says, 'we find that it can be appreciated only in terms of the moral preoccupations that characterise the novelist's peculiar interest in life.'[1] This emphasis has been challenged by Graham Hough, who cites Leavis and Malcolm Bradbury on *Emma* in the course of a polemic against 'moral' criticism. Hough argues that the formal perfection of *Emma* consists of such things as its limited and clearly defined subject, its selective narrative method, its stylised dialogue, its consistency and truth to social reality, none of which have 'much to do with Jane Austen's moral preoccupations' (see below, p. 81). The present writer has suggested that this vexed question of the relationship between formal and moral value might be resolved by inverting Leavis's formulation to read: 'When we examine the moral preoccupations that characterise Jane Austen's peculiar interest in life as manifested in *Emma*, we find that they can be appreciated only in terms of the formal perfection of the novel.' In other words, the kind of interests aroused by *Emma* are fundamentally moral, but their literary value inheres in the formal artistry through which they are communicated.[2]

Two *Scrutiny* articles of particular interest are D. W. Harding's 'Regulated Hatred: an aspect of the work of Jane Austen' and Q. D. Leavis's 'A Critical Theory of Jane Austen's Writings'. Mrs Leavis emphasised Jane Austen's painstaking, dedicated

[1] Leavis, *The Great Tradition*, p. 17.
[2] David Lodge, 'The Critical Moment, 1964', in *Critical Quarterly*, VI (1964) 268–9.

craftsmanship by arguing that the major novels went through several drafts before she was satisfied with them, and suggested that their sources could be detected in the early minor work. According to this theory, *Emma* (where, Mrs Leavis says, 'we see [Jane Austen] at the climax of her art and in completest possible control over her writing') was worked up out of an unfinished story called *The Watsons*, begun probably in 1803, but not published until 1927.[1] Harding's article was a less technical and more radical exercise in reappraisal, and its influence has been profound, though controversial. This was the most forthright attack to date on the 'Janeites'. So far from being a gentle, consoling writer, comfortably confirming the values of her own *milieu*, Jane Austen, Harding argued, was in many ways fiercely hostile to her social environment, and writing was her way of 'finding some mode of existence for her critical attitudes'. Her 'hatred' is 'regulated' so successfully that most readers contrive to overlook it, but to do so is to misunderstand her. *Emma* is interesting precisely for its recognition that 'even a heroine is likely to have assimilated many of the more unpleasant possibilities of the human being in society' (see below, p. 69).

Modern criticism of Jane Austen is concerned less with defending her status as a classic (this is generally taken for granted, and 'dissenting opinions', such as that of E. N. Haynes, are rare) than with defining the precise nature of her achievement and her importance. In this debate *Emma* has occupied a central position, and the essays collected in the second part of this selection have been chosen not only for their intrinsic quality, but as illustrations of the diversity of approach and interpretation this novel continues to provoke. *Emma*, says Edmund Wilson, 'is with Jane Austen what *Hamlet* is with Shakespeare. It is the novel about which her readers are likely to disagree most.'[2] But in all the conflict of opinion we can isolate certain recurrent issues, of which the most

[1] Q. D. Leavis, 'A Critical Theory of Jane Austen's Writings', in *Scrutiny*, x (1941–2) 75 ff.

[2] Edmund Wilson, 'A Long Talk About Jane Austen', in *New Yorker*, 13 Oct 194.

important are: the character of Emma and our response to her, the nature of the adjustment she makes to her world, and the relationship of the world of *Emma* to the world of actuality. These are questions of meaning, but they involve at every point questions of form, since it is only by careful attention to the structure and texture of the novel that we can determine what it means.

Most of the contributors agree that Jane Austen gave an important clue to the meaning of *Emma* when she said she was going to take a heroine 'whom no-one but myself will much like', but it was evidently an ambiguous one. To Marvin Mudrick, clearly writing under the influence of D. W. Harding, Emma is indeed in many ways an unlikeable heroine, a latent Lesbian, who is essentially incapable of committing herself in normal human relationships, and who finally triumphs only 'because in "her social milieu charm conquers, even as it makes every cruel and thoughtless mistake; because . . . it finds committed to it even the good and the wise, even when it is known and evaluated" '. Emma's 'reformation', and the marriage to Mr Knightley which rewards it are, Mudrick suggests, built on shaky foundations, and the fact that most readers have accepted them at face value is the ultimate irony of a novel steeped in irony: '*Emma* is a novel admired, even consecrated, for qualities which it in fact subverts or ignores.'[1]

Mudrick's essay is perhaps more provocative than persuasive, and Edgar F. Shannon's conservative reading of *Emma* makes some telling points against him. Shannon's argument that Emma's reformation is genuine, and is meant to be interpreted as such, gains considerable weight from his sensitive demonstration of the pattern of counterpointed motifs that invite us to contrast the mature with the immature Emma. Malcolm Bradbury analyses the structure of the novel to much the same effect.

If, however, we interpret *Emma* as essentially the story of a flawed and self-deceived heroine who finally comes to a state of true self-awareness, it is clear that, in Bradbury's words, 'the

[1] Marvin Mudrick, *Jane Austen: Irony as Defense and Discovery* (Princeton, 1952) p. vii.

artistic problem of the book is . . . to make us care for Emma in such a way that we care about her fate, and like her, but that we in no way subdue our moral feelings about her faults'. This is essentially a problem of narrative method, of the 'point of view' from which the story is told; and no one has done fuller justice to this aspect of the novel than Wayne Booth. He shows how Jane Austen ensures our sympathetic identification with the heroine by making her the primary centre of consciousness, through which most of the experience of the novel is mediated, but controls and checks such identification by discreet authorial interventions, ironic deflations of Emma, and well-timed comments from the most morally reliable character in the book, Mr Knightley.

In one respect Booth's analysis has been pertinently challenged by W. J. Harvey. Booth suggested that the ironic distancing of Emma was sacrificed to some extent to the author's desire for mystification, particularly concerning the relationship between Frank Churchill and Jane Fairfax, so that it is only on the second reading of the novel that we fully appreciate the scale of Emma's self-deception. Harvey argues, justly I think, that the 'mystification' is not just an end in itself, but a response 'appropriate to the world of surmise, speculation, misunderstandings and cross-purposes that the novel depicts', without which the ironies would be 'ponderous and schematic'. Even on second reading, 'our attention is so diversified by the thick web of linguistic nuance that we do not concentrate single-mindedly on the ironic results of the mystification'. One might add that we never seem to exhaust the subtle ironies of *Emma*, and this perhaps explains why we can never assume a position of detached superiority towards the heroine. Becoming aware, at each re-reading, of what we 'missed' in previous readings, we are compelled to acknowledge, like Emma herself, the fallibility of our understanding.

Mark Schorer, who approaches the novel through a close analysis of its linguistic texture, comes closer to Mudrick than most of the contributors in stressing that its significance is much more ambivalent and 'open' than its elegant design suggests.

Although Jane Austen is not given to overtly figurative expression, Schorer demonstrates that her language is saturated with dead or buried metaphors drawn from commerce and property, the counting-house and the inherited estate, creating the sense of a world of peculiarly *material* values, against which the world of the action, concerned with refinement of sensibility and moral discrimination, is ironically juxtaposed. The novel is concerned with the adjustment of these two scales of value in the fate of the heroine, but it is an *adjustment*, not a victory of one over the other. This is Jane Austen's 'moral realism'. R. E. Hughes makes a similar case in plotting Emma's progress from an immature conception of love divorced from material values, to an equally immature concern with material values divorced from love, to a mature reconciliation of the two in her final self-awareness and marriage to Knightley. This reading, if somewhat over-schematic, has the advantage of bringing out the relationship of *Emma* to its historical context.

Hughes makes the interesting suggestion that views of Jane Austen's novels may be divided into the 'microscopic' (which sees them as self-sufficient renderings of a particular, limited milieu) and the 'microcosmic' (which sees them as symbolic structures having analogical relationship to the world at large, and thus conveying a timeless and universal meaning). In practice, it would be difficult to maintain either position in an absolute sense, for the kind of fiction Jane Austen writes makes its effects through the illusion of realistic particularity, but just because it is fiction, and not history, our efforts to interpret it inevitably suggest its analogical relation to a larger, more generalised 'reality'. However, as a distinction of emphasis, it is a useful one. Arnold Kettle, for instance, has difficulty in arguing away his doubts about the major significance of *Emma* because he is a 'microscopic' reader. 'We do not get from *Emma* a condensed and refined sense of a larger entity', he says. 'Neither is it a symbolic work suggesting references far beyond its surface meaning.' *Emma* is about living in Highbury, not about Life, and it is 'as convincing as our own lives'. But, as a critic with strong social – indeed, socialist – interests, Kettle is troubled by the exclusion of so much contemporary social reality from the novel. Many readers of Jane Austen have had the same misgivings, but few have faced them as honestly as Kettle, or tested them against as sensitive a reading. Given a 'microscopic' reading of *Emma*, a Leavisian emphasis on moral intelligence is one way of accounting for its 'universal' significance. This is Bradbury's conclusion: 'We have been persuaded . . . of the importance of true regard for the self and for others, persuaded to see the full human being as full, fine, morally serious, totally responsible, entirely involved, and to consider every human action as a crucial, committing act of self-definition.'

Perhaps the boldest solution to the constantly debated question of the relationship between the world of *Emma* and the world of actuality is that of Lionel Trilling, who identifies the novel generically as a combination of comedy and idyll. It is an error to suppose that 'Jane Austen's world really did exist', but a pardonable one, because it is a tribute to the moving and elevating power of her myth, the 'extraordinary promise' and 'rare hope' it holds out to us of 'controlling the personal life, of becoming acquainted with ourselves, of creating a community of "intelligent love" '. In the course of his characteristically thoughtful, suggestive and eloquent essay, Trilling makes two remarks with which I should like to conclude this introduction.

It may be felt that a casebook of this kind submerges the living text in a welter of critical commentary, and that it confuses rather than assists the reader by the diversity of interpretation it reveals. On the latter point I would invoke Trilling's observation that *Emma* 'is like a person – not to be comprehended fully and finally by any other person'; and on the former, his remark that 'it is possible to say of Jane Austen, as perhaps we can say of no other writer, that the opinions which are held of her work are almost as interesting, and almost as important to think about, as the work itself'. In fact, these statements seem to me to be applicable to any significant writer or work, and to constitute the ultimate justification of the activity we call criticism. Without a doubt, they apply to Jane Austen's *Emma*.

DAVID LODGE

PART ONE

Earlier Comments,
1815-16

Some Correspondence concerning *Emma*

To James Stanier Clarke, from Jane Austen, 11 Dec 1815

Dear Sir

My *Emma* is now so near publication that I feel it right to assure you of my not having forgotten your kind recommendation of an early copy for Carlton House, and that I have Mr. Murray's promise of its being sent to His Royal Highness, under cover to you, three days previous to the work being really out. I must make use of this opportunity to thank you, dear Sir, for the very high praise you bestow on my other novels. I am too vain to wish to convince you that you have praised them beyond their merits. My greatest anxiety at present is that this fourth work should not disgrace what was good in the others. But on this point I will do myself the justice to declare that, whatever may be my wishes for its success, I am strongly haunted with the idea that to those readers who have preferred *Pride and Prejudice* it will appear inferior in wit, and to those who have preferred *Mansfield Park* inferior in good sense. Such as it is, however, I hope you will do me the favour of accepting a copy. Mr. Murray will have directions for sending one. I am quite honoured by your thinking me capable of drawing such a clergyman as you gave the sketch of in your note of Nov. 16th. But I assure you I am *not*. The comic part of the character I might be equal to, but not the good, the enthusiastic, the literary. Such a man's conversation must at times be on subjects of science and philosophy, of which I know nothing; or at least be occasionally abundant in quotations and allusions which a woman who, like me, knows only her own mother tongue, and has read little in that, would be totally without the power of giving. A classical education, or at any

* James Stanier Clarke was Librarian to the Prince Regent, to whom *Emma* was dedicated. See Introduction, p. 13.

rate a very extensive acquaintance with English literature, ancient and modern, appears to me quite indispensable for the person who would do any justice to your clergyman; and I think I may boast myself to be, with all possible vanity, the most unlearned and uninformed female who ever dared to be an authoress.

Believe me, dear Sir,

Your obliged and faithful hum^{bl} Ser^t.

Jane Austen

To Jane Austen, from the Countess of Morley, 27 Dec 1815

Madam

I have been most anxiously waiting for an introduction to Emma, & am infinitely obliged to you for your kind recollection of me, which will procure me the pleasure of her acquaintance some days sooner than I sh^d otherwise have had it. — I am already become intimate in the Woodhouse family, & feel that they will not amuse & interest me less than the Bennetts, Bertrams, Norriss & all their admirable predecessors. — I *can* give them no higher praise —

I am

Madam

Y^r much obliged

F. Morley

To the Countess of Morley, from Jane Austen, 31 Dec 1815

Madam

Accept my thanks for the honour of your note, & for your kind disposition in favour of Emma. In my present state of doubt as to her reception in the World, it is particularly gratifying to me to receive so early an assurance of your Ladyship's approbation. — It encourages me to depend on the same share of general good opinion which Emma's predecessors have experienced, &

to believe that I have not yet – as almost every Writer of Fancy does sooner or later – overwritten myself. – I am Madam,

Your obliged & faith[l] Serv[t]

J. Austen

To Jane Austen, from James Stanier Clarke, 27 March 1816

Dear Miss Austen,

I have to return you the thanks of His Royal Highness, the Prince Regent, for the handsome copy you sent him of your last excellent novel. Pray, dear Madam, soon write again and again. Lord St. Helens and many of the nobility, who have been staying here, paid you the just tribute of their praise.

The Prince Regent has just left us for London; and having been pleased to appoint me Chaplain and Private English Secretary to the Prince of Cobourg, I remain here with His Serene Highness and a select party until the marriage. Perhaps when you again appear in print you may chuse to dedicate your volumes to Prince Leopold: any historical romance, illustrative of the history of the august House of Cobourg, would just now be very interesting.

Believe me at all times,
Dear Miss Austen,
Your obliged friend,
J. S. Clarke.

To James Stanier Clarke, from Jane Austen, 1 April 1816

My dear Sir

I am honoured by the Prince's thanks and very much obliged to yourself for the kind manner in which you mention the work. I have also to acknowledge a former letter forwarded to me from Hans Place. I assure you I felt very grateful for the friendly tenor of it, and hope my silence will have been considered, as it was truly meant, to proceed only from an unwillingness to tax your time with idle thanks. Under every interesting circumstance which your own talents and literary labours have placed you in, or the favour of the Regent bestowed, you have my best wishes. Your recent appointments I hope are a step to something still better. In my opinion, the service of a court can hardly be too well paid, for immense must be the sacrifice of time and feeling required by it.

You are very kind in your hints as to the sort of composition which might recommend me at present, and I am fully sensible that an historical romance, founded on the House of Saxe Cobourg, might be much more to the purpose of profit or popularity than such pictures of domestic life in country villages as I deal in. But I could no more write a romance than an epic poem. I could not sit seriously down to write a serious romance under any other motive than to save my life; and if it were indispensable for me to keep it up and never relax into laughing at myself or at other people, I am sure I should be hung before I had finished the first chapter. No, I must keep to my own style and go on in my own way; and though I may never succeed again in that, I am convinced that I should totally fail in any other.

> I remain, my dear Sir,
> Your very much obliged, and sincere friend,
> J. Austen

To John Murray, from Jane Austen, 1 April 1816

Dear Sir

I return you the *Quarterly Review* with many thanks. The Authoress of *Emma* has no reason, I think, to complain of her treatment in it, except in the total omission of *Mansfield Park*. I cannot but be sorry that so clever a man as the Reviewer of *Emma* should consider it as unworthy of being noticed. You will be pleased to hear that I have received the Prince's thanks for the *handsome* copy I sent him of *Emma*. Whatever he may think of *my* share of the work, yours seems to have been quite right. . . .

OPINIONS OF *EMMA*, COLLECTED BY JANE AUSTEN

Captn Austen. – liked it extremely, observing that though there might be more Wit in P & P – & an higher Morality in M P – yet altogether, on account of it's peculiar air of Nature throughout, he preferred it to either.

Mrs F. A. – liked & admired it very much indeed, but must still prefer P. & P.

Mrs J. Bridges – preferred it to all the others.

Miss Sharp – better than M P. – but not so well as P. & P. – pleased with the Heroine for her Originality, delighted with Mr K – & called Mrs Elton beyond praise. – dissatisfied with Jane Fairfax.

Cassandra – better than P. & P. – but not so well as M. P. –

Fanny K. – not so well as either P. & P. or M P. – could not bear *Emma* herself. – Mr Knightley delightful. – Should like J. F. – if she knew more of her. –

Mr & Mrs J. A. – did not like it so well as either of the 3 others. Language different from the others; not so easily read. –

Edward – preferred it to M P. – *only*. – Mr K. liked by every body.

Miss Bigg – not equal to either P & P. – or M P. – objected to the sameness of the subject (Match-making) all through. – Too much of Mr Elton & H. Smith. Language superior to the others. –

My Mother – thought it more entertaining than M P. – but not so interesting as P. & P. – No characters in it equal to Ly Catherine & Mr Collins. –

Miss Lloyd – thought it as *clever* as either of the others, but did not receive so much pleasure from it as from P. & P. – & M P. –

Mrs & Miss Craven – liked it very much, but not so much as the others. –

Fanny Cage – liked it very much indeed & classed it between P & P. – & M P. –

Mr Shean – did not think it equal to either M P – (which he liked the best of all) or P & P. – Displeased with my pictures of Clergymen. –

Miss Bigg – on reading it a second time, liked Miss Bates much better than at first, & expressed herself as liking all the people of Highbury in general, except Harriet Smith – but cd not help still thinking *her* too silly in her Loves.

The family at Upton Gray – all very much amused with it. – Miss Bates a great favourite with Mrs Beaufoy.

Mr & Mrs Leigh Perrot – saw many beauties in it, but cd not think it equal to P. & P. – Darcy & Elizth had spoilt them for anything else. – Mr K. however, an excellent Character; Emma better luck than a Matchmaker often has. – Pitied Jane Fairfax – thought Frank Churchill better treated than he deserved. –

Countess Craven – admired it very much, but did not think it equal to P & P. – which she ranked as the very first of its sort. –

Mrs Guiton – thought it too natural to be interesting.

Mrs Digweed – did not like it so well as the others, in fact if she had not known the Author, could hardly have got through it.

Miss Terry – admired it very much, particularly Mrs Elton.

Henry Sanford – very much pleased with it – delighted with Miss Bates, but thought Mrs Elton the best-drawn Character in the Book. – Mansfield Park however, still his favourite.

Mr Haden – *quite* delighted with it. Admired the Character of Emma. –

Miss Isabella Herries – did not like it – objected to my exposing the sex in the character of the Heroine – convinced that I had meant Mrs & Miss Bates for some acquaintance of theirs – People whom I never heard of before. –

Miss Harriet Moore – admired it very much, but M. P. still her favourite of all. –

Countess Morley – delighted with it. –

Mr Cockerell – liked it so little, that Fanny wd not send me his opinion. –

Mrs Dickson – did not much like it – thought it *very* inferior to P. & P. – Liked it the less, from there being a Mr. & Mrs Dixon in it. –

Mrs Brandreth – thought the 3d vol: superior to anything I had ever written – quite beautiful! –

Mr B. Lefroy – thought that if there had been more Incident, it would be equal to any of the others. – The Characters quite as well drawn & supported as in any, & from being more everyday ones, the more entertaining. – Did not like the Heroine so well as any of the others. Miss Bates excellent, but rather too much of her. Mr & Mrs Elton admirable & John Knightley a sensible Man. –

Mrs B. Lefroy – rank'd *Emma* as a composition with S & S. – not so *Brilliant* as P. & P – nor so *equal* as M P. – Preferred Emma herself to all the heroines. – The Characters like all the others admirably well drawn & supported – perhaps rather less strongly marked than some, but only the more natural for that reason. – Mr Knightley Mrs Elton & Miss Bates her favourites. – Thought one or two of the conversations too long. –

Mrs Lefroy – preferred it to M P – but liked M P. the least of all.

Mr Fowle – read only the first & last Chapters, because he had heard it was not interesting. –

Mrs Lutley Sclater – liked it very much, better than M P – & thought I had 'brought it all about very cleverly in the last volume'. –

Mrs C. Cage wrote thus to Fanny – 'A great many thanks for the loan of *Emma*, which I am delighted with. I like it better than any. Every character is thoroughly kept up. I must enjoy reading it again with Charles. Miss Bates is incomparable, but I was nearly killed with those precious treasures! They are Unique, & really with more fun than I can express. I am at Highbury all day, & I can't help feeling I have just got into a new set of acquaintance. No one writes such good sense. & so very comfortable.'

Mrs Wroughton – did not like it so well as P. & P. – Thought the Authoress wrong, in such times as these, to draw such Clergymen as Mr Collins & Mr Elton.

Sir J. Langham – thought it much inferior to the others. –

Mr Jeffery (of the *Edinburgh Review*) was kept up by it three nights.*

Miss Murden – certainly inferior to all the others.

Capt. C. Austen wrote – 'Emma arrived in time to a moment. I am delighted with her, more so I think than even with my favourite Pride & Prejudice, & have read it three times in the Passage.'

Mrs D. Dundas – thought it very clever, but did not like it so well as either of the others.

* This was perhaps the most significant of all the 'Opinions'. Judge Francis Jeffrey (1773–1850), editor of the *Edinburgh Review* at this time, could be a harsh critic.

CONTEMPORARY REVIEWS

SIR WALTER SCOTT *Quarterly Review*, 'Oct. 1815' (actually appeared March 1816)

THERE are some vices in civilized society so common that they are hardly acknowledged as stains upon the moral character, the propensity to which is nevertheless carefully concealed, even by those who most frequently give way to them; since no man of pleasure would willingly assume the gross epithet of a debauchee or a drunkard. One would almost think that novel-reading fell under this class of frailties, since among the crowds who read little else, it is not common to find an individual of hardihood sufficient to avow his taste for these frivolous studies. A novel, therefore, is frequently 'bread eaten in secret;' and it is not upon Lydia Languish's toilet alone that *Tom Jones* and *Peregrine Pickle* are to be found ambushed behind works of a more grave and instructive character. And hence it has happened, that in no branch of composition, not even in poetry itself, have so many writers, and of such varied talents, exerted their powers. It may perhaps be added, that although the composition of these works admits of being exalted and decorated by the higher exertions of genius; yet such is the universal charm of narrative, that the worst novel ever written will find some gentle reader content to yawn over it, rather than to open the page of the historian, moralist, or poet. We have heard, indeed, of one work of fiction so un-utterably stupid, that the proprietor, diverted by the rarity of the incident, offered the book, which consisted of two volumes in duodecimo, handsomely bound, to any person who would declare, upon his honour, that he had read the whole from beginning to end. But although this offer was made to the passengers on board an Indiaman, during a tedious outward-bound voyage, the *Memoirs of Clegg the Clergyman*, (such was the title of this unhappy composition,) completely baffled the most dull and determined student on board, and bid fair for an exception to the general rule above-mentioned, – when the love of glory prevailed with the boatswain, a man of strong and solid parts, to hazard the attempt, and he actually conquered and carried off the prize!

The judicious reader will see at once that we have been pleading our own cause while stating the universal practice, and preparing him for a display of more general acquaintance with this fascinating department of literature, than at first sight may seem consistent with the graver studies to which we are compelled by duty: but in truth, when we consider how many hours of languor and anxiety, of deserted age and solitary celibacy, of pain even and poverty, are beguiled by the perusal of these light volumes, we cannot austerely condemn the source from which is drawn the alleviation of such a portion of human misery, or consider the regulation of this department as beneath the sober consideration of the critic.

If such apologies may be admitted in judging the labours of ordinary novelists, it becomes doubly the duty of the critic to treat with kindness as well as candour works which, like this before us, proclaim a knowledge of the human heart, with the power and resolution to bring that knowledge to the service of honour and virtue. The author is already known to the public by the two novels announced in her title-page, and both, the last especially, attracted, with justice, an attention from the public far superior to what is granted to the ephemeral productions which supply the regular demand of watering-places and circulating libraries. They belong to a class of fictions which has arisen almost in our own times, and which draws the characters and incidents introduced more immediately from the current of ordinary life than was permitted by the former rules of the novel.

In its first appearance, the novel was the legitimate child of the romance; and though the manners and general turn of the composition were altered so as to suit modern times, the author remained fettered by many peculiarities derived from the original style of romantic fiction. These may be chiefly traced in the conduct of the narrative, and the tone of sentiment attributed to the fictitious personages. . . .

Here, therefore, we have two essential and important circumstances, in which the earlier novels differed from those now in fashion, and we were more nearly assimilated to the old romances. And there can be no doubt that, by the studied involution and extrication of the story, by the combination of incidents new, striking and wonderful beyond the course of ordinary life, the former authors opened that obvious and strong sense of interest which arises from curiosity; as by the pure, elevated, and romantic cast of the sentiment, they conciliated those better propensities of our nature which loves to contemplate the picture of virtue, even when confessedly unable to imitate its excellences.

But strong and powerful as these sources of emotion and interest may be, they are, like all others, capable of being exhausted by habit. . . . And thus in the novel, as in every style of composition which appeals to the public taste, the more rich and easily worked mines being exhausted, the adventurous author must, if he is desirous of success, have recourse to those which were disdained by his predecessors as unproductive, or avoided as only capable of being turned to profit by great skill and labour.

Accordingly a style of novel has arisen, within the last fifteen or twenty years, differing from the former in the points upon which the interest hinges; neither alarming our credulity nor amusing our imagination by wild variety of incident, or by those pictures of romantic affection and sensibility, which were formerly as certain attributes of fictitious characters as they are of rare occurrence among those who actually live and die. The substitute for these excitements, which had lost much of their poignancy by the repeated and injudicious use of them, was the art of copying from nature as she really exists in the common walks of life, and presenting to the reader, instead of the splendid scenes of an imaginary world, a correct and striking representation of that which is daily taking place around him.

In adventuring upon this task, the author makes obvious sacrifices, and encounters peculiar difficulty. He who paints from

le beau idéal, if his scenes and sentiments are striking and interesting, is in a great measure exempted from the difficult task of
reconciling them with the ordinary probabilities of life: but he
who paints a scene of common occurrence, places his composition
within that extensive range of criticism which general experience
offers to every reader. The resemblance of a statue of Hercules
we must take on the artist's judgment; but every one can criticize
that which is presented as the portrait of a friend, or neighbour.
Something more than a mere sign-post likeness is also demanded.
The portrait must have spirit and character, as well as resemblance; and being deprived of all that, according to Bayes, goes
'to elevate and surprize,' it must make amends by displaying
depth of knowledge and dexterity of execution. We, therefore,
bestow no mean compliment upon the author of *Emma*, when
we say that, keeping close to common incidents, and to such
characters as occupy the ordinary walks of life, she has produced
sketches of such spirit and originality, that we never miss the
excitation which depends upon a narrative of uncommon events,
arising from the consideration of minds, manners, and sentiments, greatly above our own. In this class she stands almost
alone; for the scenes of Miss Edgeworth are laid in higher life,
varied by more romantic incident, and by her remarkable power
of embodying and illustrating national character. But the author
of *Emma* confined herself chiefly to the middling classes of
society; her most distinguished characters do not rise greatly
above well-bred country gentlemen and ladies; and those which
are sketched with most originality and precision, belong to a
class rather below that standard. The narrative of all her novels is
composed of such common occurrences as may have fallen under
the observation of most folks; and her dramatis personæ conduct
themselves upon the motives and principles which the readers may
recognize as ruling their own and that of most of their acquaintances. The kind of moral, also, which these novels inculcate,
applies equally to the paths of common life. . . .

    Emma has even less story than either of the preceding novels.
Miss Emma Woodhouse, from whom the book takes its name,
is the daughter of a gentleman of wealth and consequence

residing at his seat in the immediate vicinage of a country village called Highbury. The father, a good-natured, silly valetudinary, abandons the management of his household to Emma, he himself being only occupied by his summer and winter walk, his apothecary, his gruel, and his whist table. The latter is supplied from the neighbouring village of Highbury with precisely the sort of persons who occupy the vacant corners of a regular whist table, when a village is in the neighbourhood, and better cannot be found within the family. We have the smiling and courteous vicar, who nourishes the ambitious hope of obtaining Miss Woodhouse's hand. We have Mrs. Bates, the wife of a former rector, past every thing but tea and whist; her daughter, Miss Bates, a good-natured, vulgar, and foolish old maid; Mr. Weston, a gentleman of a frank disposition and moderate fortune, in the vicinity, and his wife an amiable and accomplished person, who had been Emma's governess, and is devotedly attached to her. Amongst all these personages, Miss Woodhouse walks forth, the princess paramount, superior to all her companions in wit, beauty, fortune, and accomplishments, doated upon by her father and the Westons, admired, and almost worshipped by the more humble companions of the whist table. The object of most young ladies is, or at least is usually supposed to be, a desirable connection in marriage. But Emma Woodhouse, either anticipating the taste of a later period of life, or, like a good sovereign, preferring the weal of her subjects of Highbury to her own private interest, sets generously about making matches for her friends without thinking of matrimony on her own account. We are informed that she had been eminently successful in the case of Mr. and Mrs. Weston; and when the novel commences she is exerting her influence in favour of Miss Harriet Smith, a boarding-school girl without family or fortune, very good humoured, very pretty, very silly, and, what suited Miss Woodhouse's purpose best of all, very much disposed to be married.

In these conjugal machinations Emma is frequently interrupted, not only by the cautions of her father, who had a particular objection to any body committing the rash act of matrimony, but also by the sturdy reproof and remonstrances of

Mr. Knightley, the elder brother of her sister's husband, a sensible country gentleman of thirty-five, who had known Emma from her cradle, and was the only person who ventured to find fault with her. In spite, however, of his censure and warning, Emma lays a plan of marrying Harriet Smith to the vicar; and though she succeeds perfectly in diverting her simple friend's thoughts from an honest farmer who had made her a very suitable offer, and in flattering her into a passion for Mr. Elton, yet, on the other hand, that conceited divine totally mistakes the nature of the encouragement held out to him, and attributes the favour which he found in Miss Woodhouse's eyes to a lurking affection on her own part. This at length encourages him to a presumptuous declaration of his sentiments; upon receiving a repulse, he looks abroad elsewhere, and enriches the Highbury society by uniting himself to a dashing young woman with as many thousands as are usually called ten, and a corresponding quantity of presumption and ill breeding.

While Emma is thus vainly engaged in forging wedlock-fetters for others, her friends have views of the same kind upon her, in favour of a son of Mr. Weston by a former marriage, who bears the name, lives under the patronage, and is to inherit the fortune of a rich uncle. Unfortunately Mr. Frank Churchill had already settled his affections on Miss Jane Fairfax, a young lady of reduced fortune; but as this was a concealed affair, Emma, when Mr. Churchill first appears on the stage, has some thoughts of being in love with him herself; speedily, however, recovering from that dangerous propensity, she is disposed to confer him upon her deserted friend Harriet Smith. Harriet has, in the interim, fallen desperately in love with Mr. Knightley, the sturdy, advice-giving bachelor; and, as all the village supposes Frank Churchill and Emma to be attached to each other, there are cross purposes enough (were the novel of a more romantic cast) for cutting half the men's throats and breaking all the women's hearts. But at Highbury Cupid walks decorously, and with good discretion, bearing his torch under a lanthorn, instead of flourishing it around to set the house on fire. All these entanglements bring on only a train of mistakes and embarrassing situations, and dialogues at balls and parties of pleasure, in which the author displays her peculiar powers of humour and knowledge of human life. The plot is extricated with great simplicity. The aunt of Frank Churchill dies; his uncle, no longer under her baneful influence, consents to his marriage with Jane Fairfax. Mr. Knightley and Emma are led, by this unexpected incident, to discover that they had been in love with each other all along. Mr. Woodhouse's objections to the marriage of his daughter are overpowered by the fears of house-breakers, and the comfort which he hopes to derive from having a stout son-in-law resident in the family; and the facile affections of Harriet Smith are transferred, like a bank bill by indorsation, to her former suitor, the honest farmer, who had obtained a favourable opportunity of renewing his addresses. Such is the simple plan of a story which we peruse with pleasure, if not with deep interest, and which perhaps we might more willingly resume than one of those narratives where the attention is strongly riveted, during the first perusal, by the powerful excitement of curiosity.

The author's knowledge of the world, and the peculiar tact with which she presents characters that the reader cannot fail to recognize, reminds us something of the merits of the Flemish school of painting. The subjects are not often elegant, and certainly never grand; but they are finished up to nature, and with a precision which delights the reader. This is a merit which it is very difficult to illustrate by extracts, because it pervades the whole work, and is not to be comprehended from a single passage. . . . [In] a dialogue between Mr. Woodhouse, and his elder daughter Isabella, who shares his anxiety about health, and has, like her father, a favourite apothecary. . . . [and who] with her husband, a sensible, peremptory sort of person, had come to spend a week with her father. . . . the reader may collect . . . both the merits and faults of the author. The former consists much in the force of a narrative conducted with much neatness and point, and a quiet yet comic dialogue, in which the characters of the speakers evolve themselves with dramatic effect. The faults, on the contrary, arise from the minute detail which the author's plan comprehends. Characters of folly or simplicity, such as those of old Woodhouse and Miss Bates, are ridiculous when first presented, but if too often brought forward or too long dwelt upon, their prosing is apt to become as tiresome in fiction as in real society. Upon the whole, the turn of this author's novels bears the same relation to that of the sentimental and romantic cast, that cornfields and cottages and meadows bear to the highly adorned grounds of a show mansion, or the rugged sublimities of a mountain landscape. It is neither so captivating as the one, nor so grand as the other, but it affords to those who frequent it a pleasure nearly allied with the experience of their own social habits; and what is of some importance, the youthful wanderer may return from his promenade to the ordinary business of life, without any chance of having his head turned by the recollection of the scene through which he has been wandering.

One word, however, we must say in behalf of that once powerful divinity, Cupid, king of gods and men, who in these times of revolution, has been assailed, even in his own kingdom of romance, by the authors who were formerly his devoted priests. We are quite aware that there are few instances of first attachment being brought to a happy conclusion, and that it seldom can be so in a state of society so highly advanced as to render early marriages among the better class, acts, generally speaking, of imprudence. But the youth of this realm need not at present be taught the doctrine of selfishness. It is by no means their error to give the world or the good things of the world all for love; and before the authors of moral fiction couple Cupid indivisibly with calculating prudence, we would have them reflect, that they may sometimes lend their aid to substitute more mean, more sordid, and more selfish motives of conduct, for the romantic feelings which their predecessors perhaps fanned into too powerful a flame. Who is it, that in his youth has felt a virtuous attachment, however romantic or however unfortunate, but can trace back to its influence much that his character may possess of what is honourable, dignified, and disinterested? If he recollects hours wasted in unavailing hope, or saddened by doubt and disappointment; he may also dwell on many which have been snatched from folly or libertinism, and dedicated to studies which might render him worthy of the object of his affection, or pave the way perhaps to that distinction necessary to raise him to an equality with her. Even the habitual indulgence of feelings totally unconnected with ourselves and our own immediate interest, softens, graces, and amends the human mind; and after the pain of disappointment is past, those who survive (and by good fortune those are the greater number) are neither less wise nor less worthy members of society for having felt, for a time, the influence of a passion which has been well qualified as the 'tenderest, noblest and best.'

British Critic, July 1816

WHOEVER is fond of an amusing, inoffensive and well principled novel, will be well pleased with the perusal of *Emma*. It rarely happens that in a production of this nature we have so little to find fault with.

In few novels is the unity of place preserved; we know not of one in which the author has sufficient art to give interest to the circle of a small village. The author of *Emma* never goes beyond the boundaries of two private families, but has contrived in a very interesting manner to detail their history, and to form out of so slender materials a very pleasing tale. The characters are well kept up to the end. The valetudinarian fathers, the chattering village belles, are all preserved to the life. . . .

We are not the less inclined to speak well of this tale, because it does not dabble in religion; of fanatical novels and fanatical authoresses we are already sick.

Monthly Review, July 1816

IF this novel can scarcely be termed a composition, because it contains but one ingredient, *that one* is, however, of sterling worth; being a strain of genuine natural humour, such as is seldom found conjointly with the complete purity of images and ideas which is here conspicuous. The character of Mr. Woodhouse, with his 'habits of gentle selfishness,' is admirably drawn, and the dialogue is easy and lively. The fair reader may also glean by the way some useful hints against forming romantic schemes, or indulging a spirit of patronage in defiance of sober reason; and the work will probably become a favourite with all those who seek, for harmless amusement, rather than deep pathos or appalling horrors, in works of fiction.

Gentleman's Magazine, Sept 1816

Dulce est desipere in loco; and a good Novel is now and then an agreeable relaxation from severer studies. Of this description was *Pride and Prejudice*; and from the entertainment which those volumes afforded us, we were desirous to peruse the present work; nor have our expectations been disappointed. If *Emma* has not the highly-drawn characters in superior life which are so interesting in *Pride and Prejudice*; it delineates with great accuracy the habits and the manners of a middle class of gentry; and of the inhabitants of a country village at one degree of rank and gentility beneath them. Every character throughout the work, from the heroine to the most subordinate, is a portrait which comes home to the heart and feelings of the Reader; who becomes familiarly acquainted with each of them, nor loses sight of a single individual till the completion of the work. The unities of time and place are well preserved; the language is chaste and correct; and if *Emma* be not allowed to rank in the very highest class of modern Novels, it certainly may claim at least a distinguished degree of eminence in that species of composition. It is amusing, if not instructive; and has no tendency to deteriorate the heart.

PART TWO

Some Opinions and Criticism, 1816-1964

SOME OPINIONS AND CRITICISM

SUSAN FERRIER: 'Excellent'

I have been reading *Emma*, which is excellent; there is no story whatever, and the heroine is no better than other people; but the characters are all so true to life, and the style so piquant, that it does not require the adventitious aids of mystery and adventure.

(from a letter to Miss Clavering, 1816)

MARY RUSSELL MITFORD: 'Delightful'

By-the-way, how delightful is her *Emma*! the best, I think, of all her charming works.   (from a letter to Sir William Elford, 1816)

JOHN HENRY NEWMAN: 'The Most Interesting of all her Heroines'

I have been reading *Emma*. Everything Miss Austen writes is clever, but I desiderate something. There is a want of *body* to the story. The action is frittered away in over-little things. There are some beautiful things in it. Emma herself is the most interesting to me of all her heroines. I feel kind to her whenever I think of her. But Miss Austen has no romance – none at all. What vile creatures her parsons are! she has not a dream of the high Catholic ἦθος. That other woman, Fairfax, is a dolt – but I like Emma.*   (from a letter to Mrs John Mozley, 1837)

* The editor of Newman's letters, Anne Mozley, makes the following footnote at this point: 'In inserting this critique on Miss Austen's masterpiece the Editor has a sense almost of disloyalty to this delightful writer. But Miss Austen's novels are a battlefield and the reader has a right to the opinion here given. The ethos, as Mr Newman calls it, of a

CHARLOTTE BRONTË: 'Nothing Profound'

I have . . . read one of Miss Austen's works – *Emma* – read it
with interest and with just the degree of admiration which Miss
Austen herself would have thought sensible and suitable. Anything like warmth or enthusiasm – anything energetic, poignant,
heart-felt is utterly out of place in commending these works: all
such demonstration the authoress would have met with a well-
bred sneer, would have calmly scorned as outre and extravagant.
She does her business of delineating the surface of the lives of
genteel English people curiously well. There is a Chinese
fidelity, a miniature delicacy in the painting. She ruffles her reader
by nothing vehement, disturbs him by nothing profound. The
passions are perfectly unknown to her; she rejects even a speaking
acquaintance with that stormy sisterhood. Even to the feelings
she vouchsafes no more than an occasional graceful but distant
recognition – too frequent converse with them would ruffle the
smooth elegance of her progress. Her business is not half so
much with the human heart as with the human eyes, mouth,
hands, and feet. What sees keenly, speaks aptly, moves flexibly,
it suits her to study; but what throbs fast and full, though
hidden, what the blood rushes through, what is the unseen seat
of life and the sentient target of death – this Miss Austen ignores.
She no more, with her mind's eye, beholds the heart of her race
than each man, with bodily vision, sees the heart in his heaving
breast. Jane Austen was a complete and most sensible lady, but a
very incomplete and rather insensible (*not senseless*) woman. If
this is heresy, I cannot help it. If I said it to some people (Lewes
for instance) they would directly accuse me of advocating
exaggerated heroics, but I am not afraid of your falling into any
such vulgar error.   (from a letter to W. S. Williams, 1850)

---

book came always foremost in his critical estimation. He condoned a
good deal when this satisfied him. Miss Austen described parsons as
she saw them, and did not recognise it as in her province to preach to
them, except indirectly by portraying the Mr Collinses and Mr Eltons
of the day.'

ANTHONY TROLLOPE: 'Miss Austen's Timidity'*

Emma is undoubtedly very tedious; – thereby shewing rather the patience of readers in the authors day than any incapacity on her part to avoid the fault. The dialogues are too long and some of them are unnecessary.

But the story shews wonderful knowledge of female character, and is severe on the little foibles of women with a severity which no man would dare to use. Emma, the heroine, is treated almost mercilessly. In every passage of the book she is in fault for some folly, some vanity, some ignorance, – or indeed for some meanness. Her conduct to her friend Harriett, – her assumed experience and real ignorance of human nature – are terribly true; but nowadays we dare not make our heroines so little. Her weaknesses are all plain to us, but of her strength we are only told; and even at the last we hardly know why Mr Knightley loves her.

The humour shewn in some of the female characters in *Emma* is very good. Mrs Elton with her loud Bath-begotten vulgarity is excellent; and Miss Bates, longwinded, self-denying, ignorant, and eulogistic has become proverbial. But the men are all weak. There is nothing in *Emma* like Mr Bennet and Mr Collins the immortal heroes of *Pride and Prejudice*. Mr Woodhouse, the malade imaginaire, is absurd, and the Knightleys and Westons are simply sticks. It is as a portrait of female life among ladies in an English village 50 years ago that Emma is to be known and remembered.

We have here, given to us unconsciously, a picture of the clerical life of 1815 which we cannot avoid comparing with the clerical life of 1865. After a modest dinner party, when the gentlemen join the ladies, the parson of the parish, a young man, is noticed as having taken too much wine. And no one else has done so. But allusion is made to this, not because he is a clergyman, nor is he at all a debauched or fast-living clergyman. It

* Anthony Trollope wrote these comments on the end papers of his copy of *Emma*, in 1865. He was then engaged on his sequence of 'Barsetshire' novels about clerical life – hence his interest in Mr Elton.

simply suits the story that he should be a little flushed & free of speech. The same clergyman, when married, declines to dance because he objects to the partner proposed to him; and special mention is made of card parties at this clergyman's house. How must the mouths of young parsons water in these days as they read these details, if they are now ever allowed to read such books as *Emma*.

I cannot but notice Miss Austens timidity in dealing with the most touching scenes which come in her way, and in avoiding the narration of those details which a bolder artist would most eagerly have seized. In the final scene between Emma and her lover, – when the conversation has become almost pathetic, – she breaks away from the spoken dialogue, and simply tells us of her hero's success. This is a cowardice which robs the reader of much of the charm which he has promised himself –

RICHARD SIMPSON: 'The Platonic Idea'*

IT is clear that she began, as Shakespeare began, with being an ironical censurer of her contemporaries. After forming her prentice hand by writing nonsense, she began her artistic self-education by writing burlesques. One of her works, *Northanger Abbey*, still retains the traces and the flavour of these early essays. By it we may learn that her parodies were designed not so much to flout at the style as at the unnaturalness, unreality, and fictitious morality, of the romances she imitated. She began by being an ironical critic; she manifested her judgment of them not by direct censure, but by the indirect method of imitating and exaggerating the faults of her models, thus clearing the fountain by first stirring up the mud. This critical spirit lies at the foundation of her artistic faculty. Criticism, humour, irony, the judgment not of one that gives sentence but of the mimic who quizzes while he mocks, are her characteristics. . . .

The paramount activity of the critical faculty is clearly seen in

* Richard Simpson (1820–76) was one of the 'Oxford converts' who followed Newman into the Church of Rome. He edited the *Rambler*, and was a Shakespeare scholar of some distinction.

the didactic purpose and even nomenclature of her novels. *Pride and Prejudice* and *Sense and Sensibility* are both evidently intended to contrast, and by the contrast to teach something about, the qualities or acts named in the titles. In *Persuasion* the risks and advantages of yielding to advice are set forth. *Northanger Abbey* exhibits the unreality of the notions of life which might be picked out of Mrs Radcliffe's novels; and *Mansfield Park* and *Emma*, though too many-sided and varied to be easily defined by a specific name, are in reality just as didactic as the rest. This didactic intention is even interwoven with the very plots and texture of the novel. The true hero, who at last secures the heroine's hand, is often a man sufficiently her elder to have been her guide and mentor in many of the most difficult crises of her youth. Miss Austen seems to be saturated with the Platonic idea that the giving and receiving of knowledge, the active formation of another's character, or the more passive growth under another's guidance, is the truest and strongest foundation of love. *Pride and Prejudice, Emma,* and *Persuasion* all end with the heroes and heroines making comparisons of the intellectual and moral improvement which they have imparted to each other. The author has before her eyes no fear of the old adage, 'Wise lovers are the most absurd.'. . . [Emma], like Marianne Dashwood and Catharine Morland, is a young lady full of preconceived ideas, which she has not, however, like Marianne and Catharine, borrowed from the traditional romance of poets and novelists, but which are the product of her own reflections upon her own mental powers. Her prejudices are natural, not artificial; she fancies herself cleverer than she is, with an insight into other hearts which she does not possess, and with a talent for management which is only great enough to produce entanglements, but not to unravel them. These ideas of hers govern the plot; and she is cured of them by the logic of events. At the same time, her esteem for the mentor who stands by her and tries to guide her through her difficulties gradually ripens into love; the scholar gratefully marries her master; and the novel ends, as usual, with a retrospect in which both teacher and taught find themselves equal gainers each from the other, even intellectually, and the

Platonic ideal is realized, not merely through the heart, but through the intelligence. . . .

There is a decided growth in the general intention of Miss Austen's novels; she goes over the same ground, trying other ways of producing the same effects, and attempting the same ends by means less artificial, and of more innate origin. The same may be said of the details of her works – for instance, of the characters. . . . Her biographer refers to her fools as a class of characters in delineating which she has quite caught the knack of Shakespeare. It is a natural class, better defined than most natural classes are, and less difficult to analyse. It ought therefore to serve very well to test her manner of working. In reality her fools are not more simple than her other characters. Her wisest personages have some dash of folly in them, and her least wise have something to love. And there is a collection of absurd persons in her stultifera navis, quite sufficient to make her fortune as a humourist. She seems to have considered folly to consist in two separate qualities: first, a thorough weakness either of will or intellect, an emptiness or irrelevancy of thought, such as to render it impossible to know what the person would think of any given subject, or how he would act under it; and often, secondly, in addition to this, fixed ideas on a few subjects, giving the whole tone to the person's thoughts so far as he thinks at all, and constituting the ground of the few positive judgments arrived at, even in subject-matter to which the ideas in question are scarcely related. . . . [In] *Emma*, where perhaps Miss Austen perfects her processes for painting humorous portraits, the negative fool is . . . represented in Miss Bates. Miss Bates has enough of womanly kindness and other qualities to make her a real living person, even a good Christian woman. But intellectually she is a negative fool. She has not mind enough to fall into contradictions. There is a certain logical sequence and association between two contradictories, which it requires mind to discover: Miss Bates's fluent talk only requires memory. She cannot distinguish the relations between things. If she is standing in a particular posture when she hears a piece of news, her posture becomes at once a part of the event which it is her duty to hand down to tradition: 'Where could you possibly hear it? For it is not five minutes since I received Mrs Cole's note – no, it cannot be more than five – or at least ten – for I had got my bonnet and spencer on just ready to come out – I was only gone down to speak to Patty again about the pork – Jane was standing in the passage – were you not, Jane? – for my mother was so afraid that we had not any salting-pan large enough', etc. etc. for it might go on for ever. Any reader can see that here is the same fortuitous concourse of details which makes up Mrs Quickly's description of Falstaff's promising her marriage – the sea-coal fire, and the green wound, and the dish of prawns – in the speech which Coleridge so justly contrasts with Hamlet's equally episodical, but always relevant, narrative of his voyage towards England.

The fool simple is soon exhausted; but when a collection of fixed ideas is grafted upon him he becomes a theme for endless variations. Mrs Bennet, in *Pride and Prejudice*, Miss Austen's earliest work, is one of this kind. . . .

However good [such] characters may be, it cannot be denied that they have in them much of the element of farce. Miss Austen in her later series of novels has given us new and improved versions of them; for example, Mr Woodhouse in *Emma*, a mere white curd of asses' milk, but still a man with humanity enough in him to be loveable in spite of, nay partly because of, his weakness and foolishness. His understanding is mean enough. His invalid's fixed ideas, which divide all that is into two kinds, wholesome and unwholesome, his notion of the superiority of his own house and family to all other houses and families, his own doctor to all other doctors, and his pork to all other pork, and his judgment of all proposals and events by their effect in bringing persons nearer to, or driving them further off from, the centre of happiness which he enjoys, show that the portrait is one of the same kind as that of Mrs Bennet, but improved by the addition of a heart. . . . Miss Austen, in constructing her chief characters, sometimes lets her theory run away with her. For instance, Darcy, in *Pride and Prejudice*, is the proud man; but he is a gentleman by birth and education, and a gentleman in feeling. Would it be possible for such a man, in making a proposal of marriage to a lady whose only fault in his eyes is that some of her connections are vulgar, to do so in the way in which Darcy makes his overtures to Elizabeth? It is true that great pains are taken to explain this wonderful lapse of propriety. But, all the explanations notwithstanding, an impression is left on the reader that either Darcy is not so much of a gentleman as he is represented, or that his conduct is forced a little beyond the line of nature in order the better to illustrate the theory of his biographer. The same criticism is applicable to the most elaborate of the novels, *Emma*. The heroine's suspicions about the relations between Miss Fairfax and Mr Dixon may be natural; but her decision in believing without proof what she suspected, and her open and public reproaches to the lady, are violently opposed to the general notion of feminine grace and good-nature which the character is intended to embody. Here again, theory seems to be pushed a little beyond the line not of possibility but of consistency....

Hints given in Miss Mitford's letters, however strenuously controverted, seem to show that in early days there was something offensive in Miss Austen's manner and conduct. It may be that both Emma and Darcy contain autobiographical elements. There is an air of confession in the conception of each. We find in the novels a theory that, as love is educated by contradiction, so is love the great educator of the mind through sorrow and contradiction. Dante describes philosophy as the amoroso uso de sapienza: wisdom without it talks but does not act wisely. He who acts without love acts at haphazard; love alone shows him how and where to apply his principles, chiefly by the agony it gives him when he wounds it by wrong applications of them. Emma's wisdom nearly ruins her happiness, till she finds that wisdom is nothing unless it is directed by love. Darcy too by his similar love of managing almost ruins the prospects of his friend and himself. With all the importance which Miss Austen attributes to education, she never forgets its double aspect, theoretical and practical. But the practice must be directed by love. Love is however only a tardy teacher; it teaches as the conscience teaches, or as the dæmon of Socrates taught him, by the penalties it exacts for error. Πάθει μάθος, as Æschylus says.

If Miss Austen ever was a flirt, as Mrs Mitford reported, it was most likely rather in Emma's style; not with any idea of engaging men's hearts in order to disappoint them, but with a view to show her disengaged manners, and the superiority of which she was conscious. The shade of priggishness with which her earlier novels are tinged is perhaps most easily explicable on this supposition.

But in any case, after all possible deductions, Miss Austen must always have been a woman as charming in mind as she was elegant in person. What defects she had only prevented her being so good as to be good for nothing.

(from *North British Review*, 1870)

Dublin Review: 'Miss Austen's Superiority'

IT is in respect of her portraiture of women that Miss Austen is so superior to almost every other novelist among those who preceded her, to such of her contemporaries as are remembered, and to most subsequent writers of fiction. The heroic type would have been as much out of her line of execution as it was anti-pathetic to her taste; but with all Scott's domestic heroines hers may be compared to her advantage, in those respects in which any comparison is to be instituted. If we pass by the numerous novelists since Scott, and come to the novelists of this age, selecting a few of the representative ones, we shall not find any surpass or equal her in this important regard. Thackeray, Dickens, Mrs Gaskell, and Mr Anthony Trollope suggest them-selves at once. Miss Brontë's coarse and repulsive pictures of women, though undeniably clever, serve only to indicate the exact opposites in taste and appreciation. A society composed of Jane Eyres, Shirleys, and Lucy Snowes would be a lamentable spectacle to gods and men; whereas a society in which such women as Emma Woodhouse, Jane Fairfax, Elinor Dashwood, Jane Bennet, and above all Anne Elliot should abound, would present a picture of pure, rational, intellectual, and actual happi-ness and respectability without room for an 'ism' or toleration for any of those aberrations, whether of passion or conceit, which tend to make men sad and women ridiculous. Miss Austen's Fanny Price is as submissive, as simple-minded, and as jealous as Mr Thackeray's Amelia; she is as little understood and as much snubbed, and she has an antagonist as brilliant, if less base; but she is charming, rational, and ladylike, while Amelia is silly, insipid, and underbred, though Mr Thackeray frequently assures us of her humility and gentility. He *calls* Amelia a lady; Miss Austen *makes* Fanny Price one. Again, Mrs Newcome is a capital picture of purse-proud patronizing vulgarity, but she is not so clever a picture as Mrs Elton, who is indeed unsurpassed, we believe unequalled, and who is indispensable to the story of *Emma*, while Mrs Newcome is not indispensable to that of *The Newcomes*. Calling her 'Virtue', and keeping her dingy gloves perpetually before us, is Mr Thackeray's method of enforcing Mrs Newcome's self-importance and ill-breeding. Mrs Elton is introduced in a few lines of description, never repeated or referred to, but a fresh touch is added to every sentence she speaks, and she is so real as to be positively irritating, but not positively tiresome, as Mrs Newcome is, as Clive Newcome's mother-in-law is, as Mrs Baynes is – (she is indeed a replica of the Old Soldier, as Charlotte Baynes is a copy of Rosy, and Philip a cheap edition of Clive) – as all Mr Thackeray's vulgar people are. Miss Austen was too consummate an artist to produce any such effect. She can make us understand how Mr Woodhouse wearied his clear-headed, decisive, selfish son-in-law, and how the ceaseless stream of Miss Bates's talk was too much for Emma's charity and endurance; but she makes us love Mr Woodhouse, and we are sure nobody ever read Miss Bates's monologues once without turning to them again. Mrs Nickleby is Miss Bates in caricature – how inferior to the original will be seen by comparing her absurd remarks to Kate about her early reminiscences, as they are sitting together in the arbour, with Miss Bates's infliction of all the details of Jane Fairfax's letter upon Emma Woodhouse, with her ramblings to pork and roast apples, or her endless eulogium of the delights and splendours of the ball at the Crown. In this branch of her art, we regard Miss Bates as the author's masterpiece. She is highly ridiculous, but most estimable and respectable, and while the reader laughs at her, he feels for her all the friendly regard which she has long enjoyed in her native town of Highbury, and tastes with pleasure the delicate flavour of serious moral interest with which Miss Austen invests the poor, simple old maid's humble, laborious, estimable life. She adjusts this flavour so dexterously, she presents it so adroitly. In Mrs Gaskell's last work, *Wives and Daughters*, unhappily unfinished at the time of her death, there is some resemblance to Miss Austen's men and women. The canvas is larger, the manipulation is bolder, but there are shades and touches like those of the master-hand. . . .

Cranford is worthy of comparison with the miniature portrait of Highbury, Emma's home. Mrs Gaskell's microcosmic performance has more breadth of plan and of feeling; Miss Austen's has more sharpness and superior humour.   (1870)

LORD BRABOURNE: 'Too Respectable to be A Hero'

I FRANKLY confess that I never could endure Mr Knightley. He interfered too much, he judged other people rather too quickly and too harshly, he was too old for Emma, and being the elder brother of her elder sister's husband, there was something incongruous in the match which I could never bring myself to approve. To tell the truth, I always wanted Emma to marry Frank Churchill, and so did Mr and Mrs Weston. Mr Knightley, however, is an eminently respectable hero – too respectable, in fact, to be a hero at all; he does not seem to rise above the standard of respectability into that of heroism; and I should have disputed his claim to the position had he not satisfactorily established it beyond all possible doubt by marrying the heroine. But I have never felt satisfied with the marriage, and feel very sure that Emma was not nearly so happy as she pretended. I am certain that he frequently lectured her, was jealous of every agreeable man that ventured to say a civil word to her, and evinced his intellectual superiority by such a plethora of eminently suitable conversations, as either speedily hurried her to an untimely grave, or induced her to run away with somebody possessed of an inferior intellect, but more endearing qualities.

(from *Letters of Jane Austen*, 1884)

MRS CHARLES MALDEN: 'A Thorough English Gentleman'

MOST readers of Jane Austen will agree in thinking that in *Emma* she reached the summit of her literary powers. She has given us quite as charming individual characters both in earlier and later writings, but it is impossible to name a flaw in *Emma*; there is not a page that could with advantage be omitted, nor could any additions improve it. It has all the brilliancy of *Pride and Prejudice*, without any immaturity of style, and it is as carefully finished as *Mansfield Park*, without the least suspicion of prolixity. In *Emma*, too, as has been already noticed, she worked into perfection some characters which she had attempted earlier with less success, and she gave us two or three, such as Mr Weston, Mrs Elton, and Miss Bates, which we find nowhere else in her writings. Moreover, in *Emma*, above all her other works, she achieved a task in which many a great writer has failed; for she gives us there the portrait of a thorough English gentleman, drawn to the life. Edmund Bertram, indeed, is, in the best sense of the word, a gentleman, but he is a very young one; Mr Darcy and Henry Tilney at times are on the verge of not being quite thorough-bred; but Mr Knightley is from head to foot a gentleman, and we feel that he never could have said or done a thing unworthy of one. Jane Austen herself classed him with Edmund Bertram in her speech already given, as 'far from being what I know English gentlemen often are'. I think she was unjust to both her heroes, but, above all, to Mr Knightley, for it is difficult to see how he could be surpassed.* The man, who, in the full vigour of health and strength, was always patient and forbearing towards a fussy, fidgety invalid; who would not propose to the woman he loved because he believed that another younger and more attractive man was on the verge of doing so; then was ready to help and comfort her without any *arrière pensée* of advantage to himself, when she was deserted by her supposed lover; who

* Mrs Malden was evidently insensitive to irony.

took with indifference any annoyance or impertinence to himself, but whose righteous indignation was instantly roused by any slight to those whose position made them defenceless; who was refined in thought and language, sincere to friends and foes, and uncompromisingly straightforward in every transaction; surely this is a very real type of English gentleman, and few writers have drawn it so successfully. Emma Woodhouse, too, is very good. Her faults, follies, and mistakes are completely those of a warm-hearted, rather spoilt girl, accustomed to believe in herself, and to be queen of her own circle. She deserves the amount of punishment she gets, but we are glad it is no worse; and, with Mr. Knightley to look after her, she will do very well.

(from *Jane Austen*, 1889)

WALTER HERRIES POLLOCK: 'One Slip in Miss Austen's Accuracy'

THE one slip in Miss Austen's accuracy in observation and description of features in landscape . . . occurs in *Emma*, where, to quote . . . from my father's article in *Fraser*,* at almost midsummer

Strawberries are described as being eaten from the beds at Donwell Abbey, while the orchard is in blossom at the neighbouring Abbey Mill Farm – an anachronism which we have never met with any horticulturist able to explain by bringing together even the earliest and latest varieties of apple and strawberry.

The passage in question runs thus: Emma, when the party are on their way to see the view of Abbey Mill Farm from Donwell, perceives 'Mr Knightley and Harriet distinct from the rest, quietly leading the way'. There had been a time when Harriet Smith and Mr Knightley were not likely to be companions, and when Emma would have been sorry Harriet should see so favourable a view of Abbey Mill Farm. However, a young

* The reference is to Sir William Frederick Pollock's 'British Novelists – Richardson, Miss Austen, Scott', in *Fraser's*, LXI (1860) 20–38.

farmer wishes to marry, and finally does marry, Harriet Smith; but at first this is a most displeasing idea to Emma, who has 'taken up' Harriet, and thinks, foolishly, that she ought to do better. 'Now' Abbey Mill Farm 'might be safely viewed with all its appendages of prosperity and beauty, its rich pastures, spreading flocks, *orchard* in *blossom*, and light column of smoke ascending.' With regard to this I find, on the fly-leaf at the end of the volume in which the article on 'British Novelists' is bound up, the following copy, in my father's handwriting, of a letter written by Miss Caroline Austen, niece to Jane:

Ferog Firle.

MY DEAREST CHARLOTTE, – There is a tradition in the family respecting the apple-blossom as seen from Donwell Abbey on the occasion of the strawberry party, and it runs thus – That the first time my uncle Knight [this was the first Mr Edward Knight of Chawton House] saw his sister after the publication of *Emma* he said, 'Jane, I wish you would tell me where you get those apple-trees of yours that come into bloom in July.' In truth she did make a mistake – there is no denying it – and she was speedily apprised of it by her brother – but I suppose it was not thought of sufficient consequence to call for correction in a later edition.

Mr W. Austen Leigh writes to me that 'the *Charlotte* to whom my aunt wrote must, we think, have been Charlotte Warren – a school friend. She afterwards became Mrs Roberts, and was the mother of the Margaret Roberts who wrote *Mademoiselle Mori*'.

(from *Jane Austen, an essay in criticism,* 1899)

WILLIAM DEAN HOWELLS: 'Her Most Boldly Imagined Heroine'

EMMA WOODHOUSE, in the story named after her, is one of the most boldly imagined of Jane Austen's heroines. Perhaps she is the very most so, for it took supreme courage to portray a girl, meant to win and keep the reader's fancy, with the characteristics frankly ascribed to Emma Woodhouse. We are indeed allowed to know that she is pretty; not formally, but casually, from the words of a partial friend: 'Such an eye! – the true hazel eye – and so brilliant! – regular features, open countenance, with a complexion – ah, what a bloom of full health, and such a pretty height and size; such a firm and upright figure.' But, before we are allowed to see her personal beauty we are made to see in her some of the qualities which are the destined source of trouble for herself and her friends. In her wish to be useful she is patronizing and a little presumptuous; her self-sufficiency early appears, and there are hints of her willingness to shape the future of others without having past enough of her own to enable her to do it judiciously. The man who afterwards marries her says of her: 'She will never submit to anything requiring industry and patience, and a subjection of the fancy to the understanding. . . . Emma is spoiled by being the cleverest of her family. At ten years old she had the misfortune of being able to answer questions which puzzled her sister at seventeen. She was always quick and assured . . . and ever since she was twelve Emma has been mistress of the house and you all.'

An officious and self-confident girl, even if pretty, is not usually one to take the fancy, and yet Emma takes the fancy. She manages the delightful and whimsical old invalid her father, but she is devotedly and unselfishly good to him. She takes the destiny of Harriet Smith unwarrantably into her charge, but she breaks off the girl's love-affair only in the interest of a better match. She decides that Frank Churchill, the stepson of her former governess, will be in love with her, but she never dreams that Mr Elton, whom she means for Harriet Smith, can be so. She is not above a little manœuvring for the advantage of those she wishes to serve, but the tacit insincerity of Churchill is intolerable to her. She is unfeelingly neglectful of Jane Fairfax and cruelly suspicious of her, but she generously does what she can to repair the wrong, and she takes her punishment for it meekly and contritely. She makes thoughtless and heartless fun of poor, babbling Miss Bates, but when Knightley calls her to account for it, she repents her unkindness with bitter tears. She will not be advised against her pragmatical schemes by Knightley, but she is humbly anxious for his good opinion. She is charming in the very degree of her feminine complexity, which is finally an endearing single-heartedness.

Her character is shown in an action so slight that the novel of *Emma* may be said to be hardly more than an exemplification of Emma. In the placid circumstance of English country life where she is the principal social figure the story makes its round with a a few events so unexciting as to leave the reader in doubt whether anything at all has happened. . . . Duels and abductions, of course, there are none; for Jane Austen had put from her all the machinery of the great and little novelists of the eighteenth century, and openly mocked at it. This has not prevented its being frequently used since, and she shows herself more modern than all her predecessors and contemporaries and most of her successors, in the rejection of the major means and the employment of the minor means to produce the enduring effects of *Emma*. Among her quiet books it is almost the quietest, and so far as the novel can suggest that repose which is the ideal of art *Emma* suggests it, in an action of unsurpassed unity, consequence, and simplicity.   (from *Heroines of Fiction*, 1901)

REGINALD FARRER: 'The Book of Books'

BUT now we come to the Book of Books, which is the book of Emma Woodhouse.* And justly so named, with Jane Austen's undeviating flair for the exact title. For the whole thing *is* Emma; there is only one short scene in which Emma herself is not on the stage; and that one scene is Knightley's conversation about her with Mrs Weston. Take it all in all, *Emma* is the very climax of Jane Austen's work; and a real appreciation of *Emma* is the final test of citizenship in her kingdom. For this is not an easy book to read; it should never be the beginner's primer, nor be published without a prefatory synopsis. Only when the story has been thoroughly assimilated, can the infinite delights and

---

* [Farrer's note:] 'Heavens, let me not suppose that she dares go about Emma-Woodhouseing me!' – *Emma*, ch. 33 – a typical instance of a remark which, comic in itself, has a second comic intention, as showing Emma's own ridiculousness.

subtleties of its workmanship begin to be appreciated, as you realise the manifold complexity of the book's web, and find that every sentence, almost every epithet, has its definite reference to equally unemphasised points before and after in the development of the plot. Thus it is that, while twelve readings of *Pride and Prejudice* give you twelve periods of pleasure repeated, as many readings of *Emma* give you that pleasure, not repeated only, but squared and squared again with each perusal, till at every fresh reading you feel anew that you never understood anything like the widening sum of its delights. But, until you know the story, you are apt to find its movement dense and slow and obscure, difficult to follow, and not very obviously worth the following.

For this is *the* novel of character, and of character alone, and of one dominating character in particular. And many a rash reader, and some who are not rash, have been shut out on the threshold of Emma's Comedy by a dislike of Emma herself. Well did Jane Austen know what she was about, when she said, 'I am going to take a heroine whom nobody but myself will much like.' And, in so far as she fails to make people like Emma, so far would her whole attempt have to be judged a failure, were it not that really the failure, like the loss, is theirs who have not taken the trouble to understand what is being attempted. Jane Austen loved tackling problems; her hardest of all, her most deliberate, and her most triumphantly solved, is Emma.

What is that problem? No one who carefully reads the first three opening paragraphs of the book can entertain a doubt, or need any prefatory synopsis; for in these the author gives us quite clear warning of what we are to see. We are to see the gradual humiliation of self-conceit, through a long self-wrought succession of disasters, serious in effect, but keyed in Comedy throughout. Emma herself, in fact, *is never to be taken seriously*. And it is only those who have not realised this who will be 'put off' by her absurdities, her snobberies, her misdirected mischievous ingenuities. Emma is simply a figure of fun. To conciliate affection for a character, not because of its charms, but in

C

defiance of its defects, is the loftiest aim of the comic spirit; Shakespeare achieved it with his besotted old rogue of a Falstaff, and Molière with Celimène. It is with these, not with 'sympathetic' heroines, that Emma takes rank, as the culminating figure of English high-comedy. And to attain success in creating a being whom you both love and laugh at, the author must attempt a task of complicated difficulty. He must both run with the hare and hunt with the hounds, treat his creation at once objectively and subjectively, get inside it to inspire it with sympathy, and yet stay outside it to direct laughter on its comic aspects. And this is what Jane Austen does for Emma, with a consistent sublimity so demure that indeed a reader accustomed only to crude work might be pardoned for missing the point of her innumerable hints, and actually taking seriously, for example, the irony with which Emma's attitude about the Coles' dinner-party is treated, or the even more convulsing comedy of Emma's reflexions after it. But only Jane Austen is capable of such oblique glints of humour; and only in *Emma* does she weave them so densely into her kaleidoscope that the reader must be perpetually on his guard lest some specially delicious flash escape his notice, or some touch of dialogue be taken for the author's own intention.

Yet, as Emma really does behave extremely ill by Jane Fairfax, and even worse by Robert Martin, merely to laugh would not be enough, and every disapproval would justly be deepened to dislike. But, when we realise that each machination of Emma's, each imagined piece of penetration, is to be a thread in the snare woven unconsciously by herself for her own enmeshing in disaster, then the balance is rectified again, and disapproval can lighten to laughter once more. For this is another of Jane Austen's triumphs here – the way in which she keeps our sympathies poised about Emma. Always some charm of hers is brought out, to compensate some specially silly and ambitious naughtiness; and even these are but perfectly natural, in a strong-willed, strong-minded girl of only twenty-one, who has been for some four years unquestioned mistress of Hartfield, unquestioned Queen of Highbury. Accordingly, at every turn we are kept so dancing up and down with alternate rage and delight at Emma that finally, when we see her self-esteem hammered bit by bit into collapse, the nemesis would be too severe, were she to be left in the depths. By the merciful intention of the book, however, she is saved in the very nick of time, by what seems like a happy accident, but is really the outcome of her own unsuspected good qualities, just as much as her disasters had been the outcome of her own most cherished follies.

In fact, Emma is intrinsically honest (it is not for nothing that she is given so unique a frankness of outlook on life); and her brave recognition of her faults, when confronted with their results, conduces largely to the relief with which we hail the solution of the tangle, and laugh out loud over 'Such a heart, such a Harriet'! The remark is typical, both of Emma and of Emma's author. For this is the ripest and kindliest of all Jane Austen's work. Here alone she can laugh at people, and still like them; elsewhere her amusement is invariably salted with either dislike or contempt. *Emma* contains no fewer than four silly people, more or less prominent in the story; but Jane Austen touches them all with a new mansuetude, and turns them out as candidates for love as well as laughter. Nor is this all that must be said for Miss Bates and Mr Woodhouse. They are actually inspired with sympathy. Specially remarkable is the treatment of Miss Bates, whose pathos depends on her lovableness, and her lovableness on her pathos, till she comes so near our hearts that Emma's abrupt brutality to her on Box Hill comes home to us with the actuality of a violent sudden slap in our own face. But then Miss Bates, though a twaddle, is by no means a fool; in her humble, quiet, unassuming happiness, she is shown throughout as an essentially wise woman. For Jane Austen's mood is in no way softened to the second-rate and pretentious, though it is typical of *Emma* that Elton's full horror is only gradually revealed in a succession of tiny touches, many of them designed to swing back sympathy to Emma; even as Emma's own bad behaviour on Box Hill is there to give Jane Fairfax a lift in our sympathy at her critical moment, while Emma's repentance afterwards is just what is wanted to win us back to Emma's side again, in time for the coming catastrophe. And even Elton's 'broad handsome face,' in which 'every feature works', pales before that of the lady who 'was, in short, so very ready to have him'. 'He called her Augusta; how delightful!'

Jane Austen herself never calls people she is fond of by these fancy names, but reserves them for such female cads or cats as Lydia Bennet, Penelope Clay, Selina Suckling, and 'the charming Augusta Hawkins'. It is characteristic, indeed, of her methods in *Emma*, that, though the Sucklings never actually appear, we come to know them (and miss them) as intimately as if they did. Jane Austen delights in imagining whole vivid sets of people, never on the stage, yet vital in the play; but in *Emma* she indulges herself, and us, unusually lavishly, with the Sucklings at Maple Grove, the Dixons in Ireland, and the Churchills at Enscombe. As for Frank, he is among her men what Mary Crawford is among her women, a being of incomparable brilliance, moving with a dash that only the complicated wonderfulness of the whole book prevents us from lingering to appreciate. In fact, he so dims his cold pale Jane by comparison that one wonders more than ever what he saw in her. The whole Frank–Jane intrigue, indeed, on which the story hinges, is by no means its most valuable or plausible part. But Jane Fairfax is drawn in dim tones by the author's deliberate purpose. She had to be dim. It was essential that nothing should bring the secondary heroine into any competition with Emma. Accordingly Jane Fairfax is held down in a rigid dulness so conscientious that it almost defeats another of her *raisons d'être* by making Frank's affection seem incredible.

But there is very much more in it than that. Emma is to behave so extremely ill in the Dixon matter that she would quite forfeit our sympathy, unless we were a little taught to share her unregenerate feelings for the 'amiable, upright, perfect Jane Fairfax'. Accordingly we are shown Jane Fairfax always from the angle of Emma; and, despite apparently artless words of eulogy, the author is steadily working all the time to give us just that picture of Jane, as a cool, reserved, rather sly creature, which is demanded by the balance of emotion and the perspective of the

picture.* It is curious, indeed, how often Jane Austen repeats a
favourite composition; two sympathetic figures, major and minor,
set against an odious one. In practice, this always means that,
while the odious is set boldly out in clear lines and brilliant
colour, the minor sympathetic one becomes subordinate to the
major, almost to the point of dulness. The respective positions of
Emma, Jane, and Mrs Elton shed a flood of light back on the
comparative paleness of Eleanor Tilney, standing in the same
minor relation to Catherine, as against Isabella Thorpe; and the
trouble about *Sense and Sensibility* is that, while Marianne and
Elinor are similarly set against Lucy, Elinor, hypothetically the
minor note to Marianne, is also, by the current and intention of
the tale, raised to an equal if not more prominent position, thus
jangling the required chord, so faultlessly struck in *Northanger
Abbey*, and in *Emma* only marred by the fact that Jane Fairfax's
real part is larger than her actual sound-value can be permitted to
be.   (from *Quarterly Review*, 1917)

D. W. HARDING: 'Regulated Hatred'

THE impression of Jane Austen which has filtered through to
the reading public, down from the first-hand critics, through
histories of literature, university courses, literary journalism and
polite allusion, deters many who might be her best readers from
bothering with her at all. How can this popular impression be
described? In my experience the first idea to be absorbed from
the atmosphere surrounding her work was that she offered
exceptionally favourable openings to the exponents of urbanity.
... I was given to understand that her scope was of course
extremely restricted, but that within her limits she succeeded
admirably in expressing the gentler virtues of a civilised social
order. She could do this because she lived at a time when, as a
sensitive person of culture, she could still feel that she had a place
in society and could address the reading public as sympathetic

* [Farrer's note:] Remember, also, that Jane Austen did herself
personally hate everything that savoured of reserve and disingenuous-
ness, 'trick and littleness'.

equals; she might introduce unpleasant people into her stories, but she could confidently expose them to a public opinion that condemned them. Chiefly, so I gathered, she was a delicate satirist, revealing with inimitable lightness of touch the comic foibles and amiable weaknesses of the people whom she lived amongst and liked.

All this was enough to make me quite certain I didn't want to read her. And it is, I believe, a seriously misleading impression. Fragments of the truth have been incorporated in it but they are fitted into a pattern whose total effect is false. And yet the wide currency of this false impression is an indication of Jane Austen's success in an essential part of her complex intention as a writer: her books are, as she meant them to be, read and enjoyed by precisely the sort of people whom she disliked; she is a literary classic of the society which attitudes like hers, held widely enough, would undermine.

In order to enjoy her books without disturbance, those who retain the conventional notion of her work must always have had slightly to misread what she wrote at a number of scattered points, points where she took good care (not wittingly perhaps) that the misreading should be the easiest thing in the world. Unexpected astringencies occur which the comfortable reader probably overlooks, or else passes by as slight imperfections, trifling errors of tone brought about by a faulty choice of words. ... In *Emma* ... Jane Austen seems to be on perfectly good terms with the public she is addressing and to have no reserve in offering the funniness and virtues of Mr Woodhouse and Miss Bates to be judged by the accepted standards of the public. She invites her readers to be just their natural patronising selves. But this public that Jane Austen seems on such good terms with has some curious things said about it, not criticisms, but small notes of fact that are usually not made. They almost certainly go unnoticed by many readers, for they involve only the faintest change of tone from something much more usual and acceptable.

When she says that Miss Bates 'enjoyed a most uncommon degree of popularity for a woman neither young, handsome, rich, nor married', this is fairly conventional satire that any reading public would cheerfully admit in its satirist and chuckle over. But the next sentence must have to be mentally rewritten by the greater number of Jane Austen's readers. For them it probably runs, 'Miss Bates stood in the very worst predicament in the world for having much of the public favour; and she had no intellectual superiority to make atonement to herself, or compel an outward respect from those who might despise her.' This, I suggest, is how most readers, lulled and disarmed by the amiable context, will soften what in fact reads, '. . . and she had no intellectual superiority to make atonement to herself, or frighten those who might hate her into outward respect'. Jane Austen was herself at this time 'neither young, handsome, rich, nor married', and the passage perhaps hints at the functions which her unquestioned intellectual superiority may have had for her.

This eruption of fear and hatred into the relationships of everyday social life is something that the urbane admirer of Jane Austen finds distasteful; it is not the satire of one who writes securely for the entertainment of her civilised acquaintances. And it has the effect, for the attentive reader, of changing the flavour of the more ordinary satire amongst which it is embedded.

Emma is especially interesting from this point of view. What is sometimes called its greater 'mellowness' largely consists in saying quietly and undisguisedly things which in the earlier books were put more loudly but in the innocuous form of caricature. Take conversation, for instance. Its importance and its high (though by no means supreme) social value are of course implicit in Jane Austen's writings. But one should beware of supposing that a mind like hers therefore found the ordinary social intercourse of the period congenial and satisfying. In *Pride and Prejudice* she offers an entertaining caricature of card-table conversation at Lady Catherine de Bourgh's house.

Their table was superlatively stupid. Scarcely a syllable was uttered that did not relate to the game, except when Mrs Jenkinson expressed her fears of Miss de Bourgh's being too hot or too cold, or having too much or too little light. A great deal more passed at the other table. Lady Catherine was generally speaking – stating the mistakes of the three others, or relating some anec-

dote of herself. Mr Collins was employed in agreeing to everything her ladyship said, thanking her for every fish he won, and
apologising if he thought he won too many. Sir William did not
say much. He was storing his memory with anecdotes and noble
names.

This invites the carefree enjoyment of all her readers. They can
all feel superior to Lady Catherine and Mr Collins. But in *Emma*
the style changes: the talk at the Coles' dinner party, a pleasant
dinner party which the heroine enjoyed, is described as '. . . the
usual rate of conversation; a few clever things said, a few down-
right silly, but by much the larger proportion neither the one nor
the other – nothing worse than everyday remarks, dull repetitions, old news, and heavy jokes'. 'Nothing worse'! – that phrase
is typical. It is not mere sarcasm by any means. Jane Austen
genuinely valued the achievements of the civilisation she lived
within and never lost sight of the fact that there might be something vastly worse than the conversation she referred to. 'Nothing
worse' is a positive tribute to the decency, the superficial friendli-
ness, the absence of the grosser forms of insolence and self-
display at the dinner party. At least Mrs Elton wasn't there. And
yet the effect of the comment, if her readers took it seriously
would be that of a disintegrating attack upon the sort of social
intercourse they have established for themselves. It is not the
comment of one who would have helped to make her society
what it was, or ours what it is.

To speak of this aspect of her work as 'satire' is perhaps misleading. She has none of the underlying didactic intention
ordinarily attributed to the satirist. Her object is not missionary;
it is the more desperate one of merely finding some mode of
existence for her critical attitudes. To her the first necessity was
to keep on reasonably good terms with the associates of her
everyday life; she had a deep need of their affection and a genuine
respect for the ordered, decent civilisation that they upheld. And
yet she was sensitive to their crudenesses and complacencies and
knew that her real existence depended on resisting many of
the values they implied. The novels gave her a way out of
this dilemma. This, rather than the ambition of entertaining

a posterity of urbane gentlemen, was her motive force in writing. . . .

Whether or not Jane Austen realised what she had been doing, at all events the production of *Mansfield Park* enabled her to go on next to the extraordinary achievement of *Emma*, in which a much more complete humility is combined with the earlier unblinking attention to people as they are. The underlying argument has a different trend. She continues to see that the heroine has derived from the people and conditions around her, but she now keeps clearly in mind the objectionable features of those people; and she faces the far bolder conclusion that even a heroine is likely to have assimilated many of the more unpleasant possibilities of the human being in society. And it is not that society has spoilt an originally perfect girl who now has to recover her pristine good sense, as it was with Catherine Morland, but that the heroine has not yet achieved anything like perfection and is actually going to learn a number of serious lessons from some of the people she lives with.

Consider in the first place the treatment here of the two favourite themes of the earlier novels. The Cinderella theme is now relegated to the sub-heroine, Jane Fairfax. Its working out involves the discomfiture of the heroine, who in this respect is put into the position of one of the ugly sisters. Moreover the Cinderella procedure is shown in the light of a social anomaly, rather a nuisance and requiring the excuse of unusual circumstances.

The associated theme of the child brought up in humble circumstances whose inborn nature fits her for better things is frankly parodied and deflated in the story of Harriet Smith, the illegitimate child whom Emma tries to turn into a snob. In the end, with the insignificant girl cheerfully married to a deserving farmer, 'Harriet's parentage became known. She proved to be the daughter of a tradesman, rich enough to afford her the comfortable maintenance which had ever been hers, and decent enough to have always wished for concealment. Such was the blood of gentility which Emma had formerly been so ready to vouch for!'

Thus the structure of the narrative expresses a complete change in Jane Austen's outlook on the heroine in relation to others. And the story no longer progresses towards her vindication or consolation; it consists in her gradual, humbling self-enlightenment. Emma's personality includes some of the tendencies and qualities that Jane Austen most disliked – self-complacency, for instance, malicious enjoyment in prying into embarrassing private affairs, snobbery, and a weakness for meddling in other people's lives. But now, instead of being attributed in exaggerated form to a character distanced into caricature, they occur in the subtle form given them by someone who in many ways has admirably fine standards.

We cannot say that in _Emma_ Jane Austen abandons the Cinderella story. She so deliberately inverts it that we ought to regard _Emma_ as a bold variant of the theme and a further exploration of its underlying significance for her.

(from _Scrutiny_, 1940)

E. N. HAYES: _Emma_: A Dissenting Opinion

THE material which Jane Austen uses in _Emma_ is singularly confined. All the fully developed characters of the novel are of the same social and economic group, the upper middle class; the two possible exceptions, Miss Harriet Smith and Miss Bates, really 'belong', for the first aspires to a position in that group, and the second has once been a prosperous member of it. The scene of the novel is Highbury, a large and populous village sixteen miles from London, and most of the incidents of the book occur in the drawing rooms and gardens of the characters, the streets of the town, Ford's clothing establishment, and several rural spots near the village. The rest of the village is quite neglected, although Emma does once journey to the poorer section in order to relieve the distress of the sick and needy. The subject of the novel is courtship culminating in marriage: more specifically, of Miss Harriet Smith and Mr Robert Martin; of Miss Hawkins and Mr Elton; of Mr Frank Churchill and Miss Jane Fairfax; and of Miss Emma Woodhouse and Mr George Knightley.

It is essential to note what is omitted from this sketch of English life in the early years of the nineteenth century, for I take the initial function of a novel to be the description of human nature and values in a particular social setting. The aristocracy does not appear; Mrs Churchill, a woman of mighty descent and mightier selfishness, is talked about but never seen; the reaction of Emma and the Westons to reports of Mrs Churchill's character reveals a class attitude which charges those above them with pride and malice. The lower middle class receives similar treatment from the novelist; Robert Martin, a young farmer, is allowed to make his appearance in only two or three scenes, and Emma's remarks about him are those of a snob – she does not even consider him of sufficiently high social standing to marry a bastard daughter of the gentry. The poor are admitted into the novel only in the scene already mentioned, and then simply to show that Emma is kindhearted. What is of major significance is that Jane Austen again and again hints at a class conflict which is never allowed to develop in the pages of this pleasant romance. There are frequent suggestions that the middle class is struggling for position in a world until then dominated by the aristocracy, and that the struggle is being won by the bourgeoise's adopting the social attitudes and habits of the upper classes. For example, although Mr Woodhouse and the Knightleys derive their money directly or indirectly from commerce, the attitude of Emma is that of an aristocrat – trade is degrading; of Mr Hawkins she thinks that 'merchant, of course, he must be called'. The author's unwillingness or inability to develop this theme constitutes one of the major inadequacies of the novel, an inadequacy which could have been avoided only by her enlarging her view of society. She does not completely understand the gentry, because she does not see their essential relationship to the rest of England.

One of the consequences of this emphasis on the social rather than the economic activities of the middle class is that the world described is one of idle pleasure, of vacation play. In this respect the novel bears comparison to *The Sun Also Rises* – as it also does in the use of dramatic scene; and if Hemingway's people are vicious and immoral because unproductive, we must remark the same of Jane Austen's in *Emma*. However, Jane Austen is incapable of arriving at the conclusion that elegance, 'nice' manners, and simpering performances on the piano are stupid and wasteful. Her view is too narrow, her understanding too limited, her ethic too much bound to that of her class to understand the true nature of the lives of these people.

Of the limitations of scene little need be said, for an author has the privilege of restricting the action to whatever background he thinks appropriate, and certainly as much can be said about the world and society in terms of Highbury as in terms of any other place. As Thomas Hardy confined the action of his novels to an area of only a few hundred square miles, and Emily Brontë that of *Wuthering Heights* to even less, we have no grounds for criticizing Jane Austen for limiting the events of *Emma* to a small village.

The limitations of subject, however, are of more importance. We have remarked that the novel is about courtship culminating in marriage, and thus we have every right to expect that the author will speak of love and its effect on the minds and thoughts of the characters. She does devote a great many pages to the manner in which a young lady of 1814 should find and 'seize' a husband, but of the passion of love little is said, I think for the obvious reason that Jane Austen knew nothing of it firsthand. If her men and women feel the thrill of love, certainly the reader is never aware of the fact.

At this point we run the obvious risk of criticizing not Jane Austen but her characters, of condemning not her attitudes and feelings but those actually apparent in the society in which she lived; for English men and women of the middle class during the early years of the nineteenth century were reticent in matters of sex, and abided by conventions which today we consider foolish. The point is, however, that the novelist should rise above the particularities of her time and show her characters totally and in relation to mankind, and this is precisely what Jane Austen does not do. For example, much of the plot centers on the problem of a secret engagement – a gross sin in the eyes of Mrs Weston and the others, – and the reader is expected to take the matter seriously. Now it is legitimate for the novelist to say that the question of a secret engagement was important to Mrs Weston, but not that it is of the same importance to her. We expect the novelist to deal with more basic problems: of birth, death, love, work, leisure.

Perhaps a comparison will be useful at this point. *Clarissa Harlowe* begins as a tract on the necessity of filial devotion and obedience; had not the heroine disobeyed her father, she would not have been carried to a house of prostitution by the villainous lover. Now similar problems exist in our time, but not in the same terms and not in the same manner, and an entire novel devoted to an eighteenth-century version of the matter would be dull in the extreme except to a historian. However, Richardson soon expands the theme of the fiction to that of the eternal relationship between a man and a woman, and to the manner in which a society helps or hinders that relationship. We read the novel today not for the initial problem, but for the larger, more universal one. Had Jane Austen been similarly able to expand her view of the affair between Jane Fairfax and Frank Churchill, we might now be better able to enjoy the novel.

To return for a moment to the theme of courtship, we note that the same hints of social and economic conflict occur here as well. Harriet cannot marry Elton because she is illegitimate and has no money; Jane is forbidden to Frank because she is not of the proper station in life. Here an ambiguity of the novelist is revealed, for Jane Austen seems not quite sure what she should think on these matters. Although she ends the novel with suitable, conventional marriages for the main characters, and although her spokesman, Emma, is certainly bound to the accepted views of the age in most respects, yet several times, particularly in Emma's conversations with Harriet, there is apparent a certain freedom of opinion which is surprising. And when the true parentage of Harriet is discovered, when Emma learns that her father was a tradesman, she thinks (or is it Jane Austen?): 'Such was the blood of gentility which Emma had formerly been so ready to vouch for! It was likely to be as untainted, perhaps, as the blood of many a gentleman.' However, it is impossible to conclude precisely what were Jane Austen's opinions on these matters.

Summing up these limitations of substance, we can say that the intellectual and psychological understanding is so superficial and the range of characters so small that the novel has little meaning beyond the particularities of bourgeois courtship and marriage in England at the beginning of the nineteenth century. There is revealed in the book no attitude toward the major political, economic, psychological, or philosophical problems with which most novelists of importance since Richardson have more or less been concerned in their books. And if irony is the tone of *Emma*, the voice with which the author addresses her reader, it never carries any conception of the essential nature of man and society, which I take to be the ultimate subject of any good novel.

(from *Nineteenth-century Fiction*, IV (1949))

RICHARD POIRIER: Emma and Huck Finn

IN part, the objections to Jane Austen by Mark Twain* and American writers of roughly similar prejudice can be explained as a blindness to society as she imagines it. Their prejudice gets between even these illustrious readers and what in fact the work of Jane Austen does express about society and artifice. They are apparently unable to see, so alien to them is her positive vision of social experience, that she is fully aware of the dangers *in* society which for them are the dangers *of* it. The capacity to imagine society as including the threat of conformity and artificiality and as offering, nevertheless, beneficial opportunities for self-discovery is never evident in Emerson, only sporadically in James, and in Twain mostly in the works before *Huckleberry Finn* and inferior to it.

* In *Following the Equator* (1897) Mark Twain remarked of a ship's library: 'Jane Austen's books . . . are absent from this library. Just that one omission alone would make a fairly good library out of a library that hadn't a book in it.' His low opinion was developed at greater length in an unpublished manuscript entitled 'Jane Austen', described by Ian Watt in his Introduction to *Jane Austen: a collection of twentieth-century views* (New York, 1963) p. 7.

The contrast to Jane Austen, so obvious in a general way, can be meaningfully particularized. In *Emma*, for example, Mrs Elton imagines a party at Knightley's which will be held out of doors so that everything may be as 'natural and simple as possible'. ('I shall wear a large bonnet, and bring one of my little baskets hanging on my arm . . . a sort of gipsy party.') Knightley's reply, typically direct and restrained, affirms how much for Jane Austen, as for him, words like 'simple' and 'natural' can be defined very adequately by an uncomplicated observation of unfussy social habits:

'Not quite. My idea of the simple and the natural will be to have the table spread in the dining-room. The nature and simplicity of gentlemen and ladies, with their servants and furniture, I think is best observed by meals within doors. When you are tired of eating strawberries in the garden, there shall be cold meat in the house.'

The dramatic issue of the novel is in a sense whether or not Emma, as she herself fears just before the episode at Box Hill, is to be considered 'of Mrs Elton's party'. This, like every phrase in the episode, has an unmistakable resonance. To be 'of Mrs Elton's party' is a metaphor for submitting to social forms in which Mrs Elton's false, affected, and pretentious ideas of the 'natural' predominate, much as similar ideas fully control the society of *Huckleberry Finn*. Indeed, to be thought 'natural' by society in Twain's novel means that you must have acted artificially or imitated a prescribed role. The stakes for Jane Austen and her heroine are very high indeed – to prevent society from *becoming* what it is condemned for *being* in *Huckleberry Finn*.

Mark Twain cannot imagine a society in which his hero has any choice, if he is to remain in society at all, but to be 'of Tom Sawyer's party'. The evidence for such a comparative limitation on the hero – and, indeed, a justification for making a comparison to the greater freedom allowed Emma – is in the similarity between the situations of the two characters at the central crisis in each book. Beside the famous picnic scene at Box Hill in *Emma*, when the heroine insults Miss Bates, we can place the corresponding scene in *Huckleberry Finn* when, in chapter 15, Huck also insults a social inferior who is at the same time a trusting friend. The process by which each of these insults comes about is roughly the same. Emma gradually surrenders what is called her 'self-command' at Box Hill to the theatrical urgings and flatteries of Frank Churchill, much as Huck often acts in imitation of the 'style' of Tom Sawyer even when it ill befits his own feelings and necessities. Emma literally forgets who she is and therefore the identity of Miss Bates in relation to her, and her witty retort to one of the older lady's simplicities expresses not her true relationship to Miss Bates so much as the theatrical and self-aggrandizing role which Churchill has encouraged her to play to the whole group. Her social and psychological situation – and the literary problem thus created – is much like Huck's at the similar moment when imitation of Tom's role has led to his violation of the bond between him and Jim. The central character in each novel has violated a social contract by being artificial. Both recognize what has happened and both make amends. But at this point there appears an important and essential difference between the situations of these two, and the difference is indicative of the problem in American nineteenth-century fiction of imagining personal relationships within the context of social manners. Huck's recognition cannot involve a choice, as can Emma's, against some forms of social expression in favor of others: against the Frank Churchills, Mrs Eltons (and Tom Sawyers) of this world, and for the Mr Knightleys. Mark Twain simply cannot provide Huck with an alternative to 'games' that has any social viability or acceptance within the society of the novel. Huck's promise to do Jim 'no more mean tricks' is, in effect, a rejection of the only modes of expression understood by that society. At a similar point Emma recognizes and rejects social artifice and is then in a position to accept her natural place in society as Knightley's wife.

Huck chooses at the end 'to light out for the Territory ahead of the rest', while Emma, joined to Knightley in 'the perfect happiness of the union', is both more firmly within the social group and yet saved from all the false kinds of undiscriminating 'amiability' practised at Box Hill. The ceremony is witnessed, significantly, not by the whole community but by a 'small band of true friends'. 'Marriageableness', as Emerson scornfully puts it, emphatically is Jane Austen's subject. Marriage represents for her what he cannot imagine – not merely the act of choice within society but, more importantly, the union of social with natural inclinations. Naturalness and social form are fused in her work in a way that I do not think Emerson, Mark Twain of *Huckleberry Finn*, or even Henry James were able to recognize. It is no wonder that Mark Twain's difficulties begin at a comparable point where Jane Austen most brilliantly succeeds. *Huckleberry Finn* cannot dramatize the meanings accumulated at the moment of social crisis because the crisis itself reveals the inadequacy of the terms by which understandings can be expressed between the hero and the other members of his society. There is no publicly accredited vocabulary which allows Huck to reveal his inner self to others.

(from 'Mark Twain, Jane Austen and the
Imagination of Society', 1962)

GRAHAM HOUGH: *Emma* and 'Moral' Criticism

'MORAL' becomes the password at which all gates are to open; and it becomes the only password. I can illustrate this from a remark of Dr Leavis on Jane Austen's *Emma* [in *The Great Tradition*]:

When we examine the formal perfections of *Emma* we find that it can be appreciated only in terms of the moral preoccupations that characterise the novelist's peculiar interest in life.

Now we don't, I think, find anything so simple as this. This judgment may just mean that moral preoccupations are what Dr Leavis wants to talk about; if so, well enough, for a critic has the right to choose his own terms. It may be hortatory in intention – meant to persuade us to consider only moral preoccupations. We may or may not be persuaded. But take the thing at its face value, as a considered critical judgment, and it is manifestly quite inadequate. Let me list shortly some of the things we mean when we talk about the formal perfection of *Emma*. We mean first, I think, that the novel has a limited and clearly defined subject; that it deals with the small-scale problems of a narrow closed society, to which it is reasonable to expect a solution within the limits of the book. You could hardly expect to find solutions to the problems posed by Dostoievski's *The Possessed*; and it is *formally* less perfect in consequence. And contained within the idea of formal perfection is precisely a very successful, deliberate *formalisation*; the dialogue, though preserving its delightful air of naturalness, is in fact slightly stylised, in diction, in syntax, and general ordering. The handling of the scenes and incidents is very selective; all the more vulgar incidents and many material pre-occupations are excluded. We could not derive the same sense of refined economy from the sort of realist novel that feels obliged to include a mass of physical detail simply because it happens to be there. Last and most important, we must include consistency, in presentation of character, narrative mode, and relation to social reality. Lawrence's *Kangaroo*, for example, suffers a formal breakdown because it begins in one mode – shrewd and lively social portraiture – and then shifts uneasily to another, to symbolic mythology in the portrayal of Kangaroo himself. In *Emma*, as in all Jane Austen, there is a beautiful coherence of interest and consistency of surface. These considerations are banal enough; but they are some of the things we have to con-sider if we really want to examine the formal perfection of *Emma*. None of them has much to do with Jane Austen's moral pre-occupations, important as these are. . . .

The first error, and the worst, lay at her door. It was foolish, it was wrong, to take so active a part in bringing any two people together. It was adventuring too far, assuming too much, making light of what ought to be serious – a trick of what ought to be simple. She was quite concerned and ashamed, and resolved to do such things no more.

This is Emma Woodhouse, reflecting on her own conduct; and throughout Jane Austen's fiction we are required to par-ticipate in such acts of moral judgment.

However, when the moral judgments are as explicit as this, it is hard to see what there is for criticism to do except to dot the i's and cross the t's. It can go a little further, and sort out the moral code that emerges from a multiplicity of such judgments, as Mr Malcolm Bradbury does in a recent article on Jane Austen's *Emma*.* He points out that some of the values are merely social, some are moral in a deeper sense, and that there is sometimes conflict between the two. He anatomises the whole book as an account of Emma's moral education. This is fair enough. But it hardly says more than is said with considerable clarity in the text itself. And since there is so much more in *Emma* than this structure of moral judgments, such criticism goes a long way to substitute a thin abstraction for the actual work of art.

Mr Bradbury concludes:

We have been persuaded in fact of the importance of true regard for self and others, persuaded to see the full human being as full, fine, morally serious, totally responsible, entirely involved, and to consider every human action as a crucial, committing act of self-definition.

Well, perhaps we have; but I am inclined to think that Mr Bradbury has allowed his ethical enthusiasm to run away with him. These are not at any rate the reflections that impose themselves most strongly upon me after reading *Emma*. This is not what the experience of reading the book *feels* like. Even if we grant something of this sort is implicit in the action, it is only implicit; and when it is extracted and set on its own in this way to represent the significant essence of the novel, much is lost and some violence is done to the book's real nature. And I am not at all sure that I have been 'persuaded', as Mr Bradbury puts it, of these admirable moral propositions. I have seen a rather presumptuous young woman make several mistakes, involving herself and others, some of which might have been serious; but by the help of intelligence, a good disposition and good friends she gets out of them, and things turn out well after all. This is a different

* This article, published in the *Critical Quarterly*, 1962, is reprinted in this volume, pp. 217–31.

set of abstractions from Mr Bradbury's, but quite as true to the facts. And neither of them gives much sense of the actual quality of the novel, of the actual flavour of reading it.

As it happens, *Emma* is a comedy. In Mr Bradbury's summation it might be a Christian-existentialist introduction to the devout life. Let us look at a bit of it in the concrete – the last few pages, for example. Emma and Mr Knightley are to be married, but the wedding is delayed because Mr Woodhouse, Emma's invalidish father cannot reconcile himself to her change of condition, even though the young couple are to continue living with him. However, some poultry houses in the neighbourhood are robbed; turkeys are stolen by wicked men. This suggests housebreaking to Mr Woodhouse's apprehensive mind; he immediately becomes sensible of the advantages of having a solid reliable son-in-law on the premises, and all his objections disappear. The wedding takes place, and it goes off very well. But we are permitted to see it for a moment through the eyes of Mrs Elton, the vulgar pretentious parson's wife whom Emma cordially dislikes:

She thought it all extremely shabby, and very inferior to her own. 'Very little white satin, very few lace veils; a most pitiful business! Selina would stare when she heard of it.' But in spite of these deficiencies, the wishes, the hopes, the confidence, the predictions of the small band of true friends who witnessed the ceremony, were fully answered in the perfect happiness of the union.

With these words the book ends. Why should it end with these accidental and trivial particulars? We can put the thing through the moral juice-extractor if we will. The irony at the expense of Mr Woodhouse's timid selfishness is there to throw the integrity and devotion of Emma and her husband into higher relief. The closing sentences indicate the contrast between the false social values of Mrs Elton and the deeper moral values of Emma and her friends. But surely this won't do. We have known all about Mr Woodhouse from the first chapter. The vulgarity of Mrs Elton against the straightforward good breeding of Emma has been abundantly established long ago. And do we really need to be taught that the happiness of a marriage does not depend on the finery at the ceremony? This sort of explanation completely alters the tone and balance of the passage; Mr Woodhouse and Mrs Elton are comic elements in the scene, in keeping with the domestic high-comedy of the whole book. It is to end with happiness, but happiness of a very uninflated kind. There is nothing passionate, exalted or transcendental about this eminently satisfactory marriage. To the last it is dependent on trivialities, surrounded by absurd accidents and foolish comments. This dense atmosphere of the contingent, the small-scale and the ludicrous surrounds all the serious issues in *Emma* and forms an essential part of its nature. To distil the pure moral elixir gives no idea of this.

At one point in the story Emma is cruelly witty at the expense of Miss Bates, a poor, kind, ridiculous, chattering old spinster. She bitterly regrets it, and though the incident is trivial, the moral concern is not. To put it in the austere language of a firmer theology than Emma's, her thoughtless speech is a sin against charity. But we are not to suppose that this is the prime reason for Miss Bates's presence in the book. She is not there as a moral try-your-strength machine for Emma to measure herself against. She exists for her own sake; and the same is true of the whole closely particularised texture of Highbury life; the mere contingent facts interest, amuse, delight – not only the moral pattern that is seen behind them. Many novels, beside an infinite number of sermons and tracts, can persuade us to see the human being as being full, fine, morally serious, deeply committed and all the rest of it. But only these particular characters, incidents and scenes make *Emma* the novel that it is.

Are we to suppose that Miss Bates's affectionate amiable rattle, Mrs Elton's sublime vulgarities, the moon-struck little Harriet cherishing the court-plaster from Mr Elton's cut finger – are we to suppose that they are just jam to sweeten the pill? For that is what moral criticism seems to reduce them to. And is Jane Austen's morality, abstracted and in itself, so very remarkable a thing after all? Surely not. Jane Austen's ethical system represents the best standards of the society that she actually knew; that is to say an English middle-class version of Christian morals – Christian morals with all the heroism, all the asceticism, all the *contemptus mundi* left out. It is an eminently practical system, and within its limits an admirable one; but it is not this that gives her her distinction as a novelist, indeed it is not this that makes her a novelist at all. The reasons she is admired and loved as a writer are that her temperate and unremarkable scale of values is so fully embodied in character and circumstance, that the conditions of a certain way of living are so faithfully observed, with so much sharpness, amusement, affection – and more than that, with a gratuitous abundance of what I was going to call life, until the sultry shadow of D. H. Lawrence interposed his special claim to that overworked word. Life in the Lawrentian sense, the life of the blood and the passions is indeed conspicuously absent in Jane Austen; but she has another quality with as good a claim to the title – a slightly effervescent responsiveness, a continuous enjoyment of the detail and texture of those parts of existence that come under her notice. And we as readers are brought to share in her temperate exhilaration.

(from *The Dream and the Task*, 1964)

PART THREE

Recent Studies

Arnold Kettle

EMMA (1951)

> My strong point is those little things which are more impor-
> tant than big ones, because they make up life. It seems that big
> ones do not do that, and I daresay it is fortunate.
>
> I. COMPTON-BURNETT: *A Family and a Fortune*

THE subject of *Emma* is marriage. Put that way the statement
seems ludicrously inadequate, for *Emma* – we instinctively feel –
is not about anything that can be put into one word. And yet it is
as well to begin by insisting that this novel does have a subject.
There is no longer, especially after Mrs Leavis's articles, any
excuse for thinking of Jane Austen as an untutored genius or
even as a kind aunt with a flair for telling stories that have
somehow or other continued to charm. She was a serious and
conscious writer, absorbed in her art, wrestling with its problems. Casting and re-casting her material, transferring whole
novels from letter to narrative form, storing her subject-matter
with meticulous economy, she had the great artist's concern with
form and presentation. There is nothing soft about her.[1]

Emma is about marriage. It begins with one marriage, that of
Miss Taylor, ends with three more and considers two others by the
way. The subject is marriage; but not marriage in the abstract.
There is nothing of the moral fable here; indeed it is impossible
to conceive of the subject except in its concrete expression, which
is the plot. If, then, one insists that the subject of *Emma* is important it is not in order to suggest that the novel can be read in the
terms of *Jonathan Wild*, but rather to counteract the tendency to
treat plot or story as self-sufficient. If it is not quite adequate to
say that *Emma* is about marriage it is also not adequate to say it is
about Emma.

The concrete quality of the book, that is what has to be

emphasized. We have no basic doubts about *Emma*. It is there, a living organism, and it survives in the vibrations of its own being. In *Clarissa* time and again our attention is shifted in a particular direction not because it *must* be so directed but because Richardson wishes to give his reader an 'exquisite sensation'; in *Tom Jones* the happenings are too often contrived, so that we sense Fielding's presence behind the scenes, pulling a string. But *Emma* lives with the inevitable, interlocking logic of life itself; no part of it is separable from any other part. Even those episodes of the plot which seem at first mere contrivances to arouse a little suspense and keep the story going (such as the mystery of the pianoforte, Jane's letters at the post office, the confusion as to whether Harriet referred to Mr Knightley or to Frank Churchill), such passages all have a more important purpose. They reveal character, or they fail to reveal it. This latter function is subtle and important.

Jane Austen, like Henry James, is fascinated by the complexities of personal relationships. What is a character *really* like? Is Frank Churchill *really* a bounder? She conveys the doubt, not in order to trick, but in order to deepen. The more complex characters in *Emma*, like people in life, reveal themselves gradually and not without surprises. Putting aside for the moment certain minor faults which we will return to, it is not an exaggeration to say that *Emma* is as convincing as our own lives and has the same kind of concreteness.

It is for this reason that the subject of *Emma*, its generalized significance, is not easily or even usefully abstracted from the story. Just as in real life 'marriage' (except when we are considering it in a very theoretical and probably not very helpful way) is not a problem we abstract from the marriages we know, so marriage in *Emma* is thought of entirely in terms of actual and particular personal relationships. If we learn more about marriage in general from Jane Austen's novel it is because we have learned more – that is to say experienced more – about particular marriages. We do, in fact, in reading *Emma* thus enrich our experience. We become extremely closely involved in the world of Highbury so that we experience the precise quality of, say, Mr

Woodhouse's affection for his daughters, or Harriet's embarrassment at meeting the Martins in the draper's. When Emma is rude to Miss Bates on Box Hill we *feel* the flush rise to Miss Bates's cheek.

The intensity of Jane Austen's novels is inseparable from their concreteness, and this intensity must be stressed because it is so different from the charming and cosy qualities with which these novels are often associated. Reading *Emma* is a delightful experience, but it is not a soothing one. On the contrary our faculties are aroused, we are called upon to participate in life with an awareness, a fineness of feeling, and a moral concern more intense than most of us normally bring to our everyday experiences. Everything matters in *Emma*. When Frank Churchill postpones his first visit to Randalls it matters less finely to Mr Weston than to his wife, but the reader gauges precisely the difference in the two reactions and not only appreciates them both but makes a judgment about them. We do not 'lose ourselves' in *Emma* unless we are the kind of people who lose ourselves in life. For all the closeness of our participation we remain independent.

Jane Austen does not demand (as Richardson tends to) that our subjective involvement should prejudice our objective judgment. On the contrary a valid objective judgment is made possible just because we have been so intimately involved in the actual experience. This seems to me a very valuable state of mind. How can we presume to pass judgment on the Emma Woodhouses of the world unless we have known them, and how can we valuably know them without bringing to bear our critical intelligence?

Because the critical intelligence is everywhere involved, because we are asked continuously, though not crudely, to judge what we are seeing, the prevailing interest in *Emma* is not one of mere 'aesthetic' delight but a moral interest. And because Jane Austen is the least theoretical of novelists, the least interested in Life as opposed to living, her ability to involve us intensely in her scene and people is absolutely inseparable from her moral concern. The moral is never spread on top; it is bound up always in the quality of feeling evoked.

Even when a moral conclusion is stated explicitly, as Mr Knightley states it after the Box Hill incident or while he reads Frank Churchill's letter of explanation, its force will depend not on its abstract 'correctness' but on the emotional conviction it carries, involving of course our already acquired confidence in Mr Knightley's judgment and character. Some of Mr Knightley's remarks, out of their context, might seem quite intolerably sententious. 'My Emma, does not everything serve to prove more and more the beauty of truth and sincerity in all our dealings with one another?' (III xv).[2] The sentiment, abstracted, might serve for the conclusion of one of Hannah More's moral tales. In fact, in the novel, it is a moment of great beauty, backed as it is (even out of context the 'my Emma' may reveal something of the quality) by a depth of feeling totally convincing.

How does Jane Austen succeed in thus combining intensity with precision, emotional involvement with objective judgment? Part of the answer lies, I think, in her almost complete lack of idealism, the delicate and unpretentious materialism of her outlook. Her judgment is based never on some high-falutin irrelevancy but always on the actual facts and aspirations of her scene and people. The clarity of her social observation (the Highbury world is scrupulously seen and analysed down to the exact incomes of its inmates) is matched by the precision of her social judgments and all her judgments are, in the broadest sense, social. Human happiness not abstract principle is her concern. Such precision – it is both her incomparable strength and her ultimate limitation – is unimaginable except in an extraordinarily stable corner of society. The precision of her standards emerges in her style. Each word – 'elegance', 'humour', 'temper', 'ease' – has a precise unambiguous meaning based on a social usage at once subtle and stable. Emma is considering her first view of Mrs Elton:

She did not really like her. She would not be in a hurry to find fault, but she suspected that there was no elegance; – ease, but not elegance. – She was almost sure that for a young woman, a stranger, a bride, there was too much ease. Her person was rather good; her face not unpretty; but neither feature, nor air, nor

voice, nor manner, were elegant. Emma thought at least it would
turn out so.   (II xiv)

The exquisite clarity, the sureness of touch, of Jane Austen's
prose cannot be recaptured because in a different and quickly
changing society the same sureness of values cannot exist.

But to emphasize the stability and, inevitably too, the narrowness of Jane Austen's society may lead us to a rather narrow and
mechanical view of the novels. *Emma* is *not* a period-piece. It is
not what is sometimes called a 'comedy of manners'. We read it
not just to illuminate the past, but also the present. And we must
here face in both its crudity and its importance the question:
exactly what relevance and helpfulness does *Emma* have for us
today? In what sense does a novel dealing (admittedly with great
skill and realism) with a society and its standards dead and gone
for ever have value in our very different world today? The question itself – stated in such terms – is not satisfactory. If *Emma*
today captures our imagination and engages our sympathies (as
in fact it does) then either it has some genuine value for us, or
else there is something wrong with the way we give our sympathy, and our values are pretty useless.

Put this way, it is clear that anyone who enjoys *Emma* and
then remarks 'but of course it has no relevance today' is in fact
debasing the novel, looking at it not as the living work of art
which he has just enjoyed, but as something he does not even
think it is – a mere dead picture of a past society. Such an attitude
is fatal both to art and to life. The more helpful approach is to
enquire why it is that this novel does in fact still have the power
to move us today.

One has the space only to suggest one or two lines of consideration. The question has, I hope, been partly answered
already. An extension of human sympathy and understanding is
never irrelevant and the world of *Emma* is not presented to us (at
any rate in its detail) with complacency. Emma faced with what
she has done to Harriet, the whole humiliating horror of it, or
Emma finding – the words are not minced – that, save for her
feeling for Mr Knightley, 'every other part of her mind was dis-

gusting': these are not insights calculated to decrease one's moral awareness. And in none of the issues of conduct arising in the novel is Jane Austen morally neutral. The intensity with which everything matters to us in *Emma* is the product of this lack of complacency, this passionate concern of Jane Austen for human values. Emma is the heroine of this novel only in the sense that she is its principal character and that it is through her consciousness that the situations are revealed; she is no heroine in the conventional sense. She is not merely spoilt and selfish, she is snobbish and proud, and her snobbery leads her to inflict suffering that might ruin happiness. She has, until her experience and her feeling for Mr Knightley brings her to a fuller, more humane understanding, an attitude to marriage typical of the ruling class. She sees human relationships in terms of class snobbery and property qualifications: Harriet, for the sake of social position, she would cheerfully hand over to the wretched Elton and does in fact reduce to a humiliating misery; her chief concern about Mr Knightley is that his estate should be preserved for little Henry. It is only through her own intimate experiences (which we share) that she comes to a more critical and more fully human view.

The question of Jane Fairfax is relevant here. Many readers find her and her relationship with Frank Churchill less than fully convincing. Does she quite bear the full weight of admiration which clearly we are supposed to feel for her? If she is indeed the person she is intended to be, would she love Frank Churchill? Has not Jane Austen here failed, perhaps, completely to reconcile the character she has created and the plot and pattern to which she is committed?

I think it is worth pausing for a moment on these criticisms, in order to consider not only their justice (which can be fairly objectively tested by careful reading) but their relevance. May we not here be slipping into the undisciplined habit of judging a novel according to rather vague criteria of 'probability' or 'character'? We all know the old lady who doesn't like *Wuthering Heights* because its so improbable and the old gentleman who reads Trollope for the characters (not to mention the 'Janeites' whose chief interest in *Emma* is to determine how many nursemaids Isabella Knightley brought with her to Hartfield); and we all know how unsatisfactory such criteria are when it comes to the point.

It is worth emphasizing, therefore, that a just criticism of Jane Fairfax has nothing to do with the question of whether we should like to meet her at dinner or even whether we think she acted rightly or wrongly. Jane Fairfax is a character in a novel. We know nothing of her except what we gather in the course of the novel. What we learn while we read (and we learn, of course, more than mere 'facts'), is that, although unduly reserved (for reasons which when revealed make the fault pardonable) she is a young woman of singular refinement and 'true elegance', a phrase carrying great significance ('elegance of mind' involves a genuine sensibility to human values as well as the more superficial refinements of polished manner). She is, moreover, especially singled out for commendation by Mr Knightley (whose judgment is recommended as invariably sound) and warmly liked (e.g. the very, very earnest shake of the hand) by Emma herself.

Now the critical question is whether the reader can be convinced that this Jane Fairfax would in fact play her essential part in the novel and marry Frank Churchill, a young man whose total quality is a good deal less than admirable. Many readers are not convinced. Are they right?

I think they are not right. It is true that Jane Fairfax is – we have been convinced – as good as she is clever and as clever as she is beautiful. But it is also true that Jane Fairfax is an unprovided woman with no prospects in life beyond those of earning her living as governess at Mrs Smallridge's (and how well the nature of that establishment has been revealed to us through Mrs Elton!) and passing her hard-earned holidays with Miss Bates. The quality of Jane's reaction to such a future has been clearly indicated:

'I am not at all afraid [she says to Mrs Elton] of being long unemployed. There are places in town, offices, where enquiry would soon produce something – Offices for the sale – not quite of human flesh – but of human intellect.'

'Oh! my dear, human flesh! You quite shock me; if you mean a

fling at the slave-trade I assure you Mr Suckling was always
rather a friend to the abolition.'

'I did not mean, I was not thinking of the slave-trade' replied
Jane; 'governess-trade, I assure you, was all that I had in view;
widely different certainly as to the guilt of those who carry it on;
but as to the greater misery of the victims, I do not know where
it lies....'   (II xvii)

It is her horror of this alternative (notice the extraordinary
force of the word 'offices'; the sentence is broken in the sense of
degradation) that those who are unconvinced by Jane's decision
to marry Frank Churchill have, I think, overlooked. Perhaps all
this makes Jane Fairfax less 'good' than Emma thought her; but
it does not make her less convincing to us. On the contrary a
good deal of the moral passion of the book, as of her other
novels, does undoubtedly arise from Jane Austen's understanding
of and feeling about the problems of women in her society. It is
this realistic, unromantic, and indeed, by orthodox standards,
subversive concern with the position of women that gives the
tang and force to her consideration of marriage. Jane Fairfax's
marriage has not, indeed, been made in heaven, and it is unlikely
that Frank Churchill will turn out to be an ideal husband; but is
that not precisely Jane Austen's point?

More vulnerable is the marrying-off of Harriet Smith and
Robert Martin. Here it is not the probability that is to be
questioned but the manner. The treatment is altogether too glib
and the result is to weaken the pattern of the novel. Since the
experiences of Emma – her blunders and romanticisms – are the
core of the book, and what most intimately illuminate the theme
of marriage, it is essential to Jane Austen's plan that these
experiences should be in no way muffled or sentimentalized. We
must feel the whole force of them. The marriage of Harriet is
presented in a way which does, to some extent, sentimentalize.
Emma is allowed too easy a way out of her problem and the
emotional force of the situation is thereby weakened. The
objection to too conventional a sense of happy ending is not that
it is happy (we do not question that) but that it is conventional
and so lulls our feelings into accepting it too easily.

Sufficient has perhaps been said to suggest that what gives *Emma* its power to move us is the realism and depth of feeling behind Jane Austen's attitudes. She examines with a scrupulous yet passionate and critical precision the actual problems of her world. That this world is narrow cannot be denied. How far its narrowness matters is an important question.

Its *smallness* does not matter at all. There is no means of measuring importance by size. What is valuable in a work of art is the depth and truth of the experience it communicates, and such qualities cannot be identified with the breadth of the panorama. We may find out more about life in a railway carriage between Crewe and Manchester than in making a tour round the world. A conversation between two women in the butcher's queue may tell us more about a world war than a volume of despatches from the front. And when Emma says to Mr Knightley: 'Nobody, who has not been in the interior of a family, can say what the difficulties of any individual of that family may be', she is dropping a valuable hint about Jane Austen's method. The silliest of all criticisms of Jane Austen is the one which blames her for not writing about the battle of Waterloo and the French Revolution. She wrote about what she understood and no artist can do more.

But did she understand enough? The question is not a silly one, for it must be recognized that her world was not merely small but narrow. Her novels are sometimes referred to as miniatures, but the analogy is not apt. We do not get from *Emma* a condensed and refined sense of a larger entity. Neither is it a symbolic work suggesting references far beyond its surface meaning. The limitations of the Highbury world, which are indeed those of Surrey in about 1814, are likely therefore to be reflected in the total impact of the novel.

The limitation and the narrowness of the Highbury world is the limitation of class society. And the one important criticism of Jane Austen (we will suspend judgment for the moment on its truth) is that her vision is limited by her unquestioning acceptance of class society. That she did not write about the French Revolution or the Industrial Revolution is as irrelevant as that she did not write about the Holy Roman Empire; they were not her subjects. But Highbury is her subject and no sensitive contemporary reader can fail to sense here an inadequacy (again, we will suspend judgment on its validity). It is necessary to insist, at this point, that the question at issue is not Jane Austen's failure to suggest a *solution* to the problem of class divisions but her apparent failure to notice the *existence* of the problem.

The values and standards of the Highbury world are based on the assumption that it is right and proper for a minority of the community to live at the expense of the majority. No amount of sophistry can get away from this fact and to discuss the moral concern of Jane Austen without facing it would be hypocrisy. It is perfectly true that, within the assumptions of aristocratic society, the values recommended in *Emma* are sensitive enough. Snobbery, smugness, condescension, lack of consideration, unkindness of any description, are held up to our disdain. But the fundamental condescension, the basic unkindness which permits the sensitive values of *Emma* to be applicable only to one person in ten or twenty, is this not left unscathed? Is there not here a complacency which renders the hundred little incomplacencies almost irrelevant?

Now this charge, that the value of *Emma* is seriously limited by the class basis of Jane Austen's standards, cannot be ignored or written off as a nonliterary issue. If the basic interest of the novel is indeed a moral interest, and if in the course of it we are called upon to re-examine and pass judgment on various aspects of human behaviour, then it can scarcely be considered irrelevant to face the question that the standards we are called upon to admire may be inseparably linked with a particular form of social organization.

That the question is altogether irrelevant will be held, of course, by the steadily decreasing army of aesthetes. Those who try to divorce the values of art from those of life and consequently morality will not admit that the delight we find in reading *Emma* has in fact a moral basis. It is a position, I think, peculiarly hard to defend in the case of a Jane Austen novel, because of the obvious preoccupation of the novelist with social morality. If *Emma* is *not* concerned with the social values involved in and involving personal relationships (and especially marriage) it is difficult to imagine what it *is* about.

That the question though relevant is trivial will be held by those readers who consider class society either good or inevitable. Clearly, to those who think aristocracy today a morally defensible form of society, and are prepared to accept (with whatever modifications and protestations of innocence) the inevitability of a cultural *élite* whose superior standards depend on a privileged social position based on the exploitation of their inferiors, clearly such readers will not feel that Jane Austen's acceptance of class society weakens or limits her moral perspicacity. The suspicion that the true elegance which Emma so values could not exist in Highbury without the condemnation to servility and poverty of hundreds of unnamed (though not necessarily unpitied) human beings will not trouble their minds as they admire the civilized sensibility of Jane Austen's social standards. The position of such readers cannot of course be objected to on logical grounds so long as all its implications are accepted.

At the other extreme of critical attitudes will be found those readers whose sense of the limitations of Jane Austen's social consciousness makes it impossible for them to value the book at all. How can I feel sympathy, such a reader will say, for characters whom I see to be, for all their charm and politeness, parasites and exploiters? How can I feel that the problems of such a society have a relevance to me? Now if art were a matter of abstract morality it would be impossible to argue against this puritan attitude; but in truth it misses the most essential thing of all about *Emma*, that it is a warm and living work of art. To reject *Emma* outright is to reject the humanity in *Emma*, either to dismiss the delight and involvement that we feel as we read it as an unfortunate aberration, or else to render ourselves immune to its humanity by imposing upon it an attitude narrower than itself.

More sophisticated than this philistine attitude to the problem is that which will hold that *Emma* does indeed reflect the class basis and limitations of Jane Austen's attitudes, but that this really does not matter very much or seriously affect its value. This is a view, plausible at first sight, held by a surprisingly large number of readers who want to have their novel and yet eat it. Yes indeed, such a reader will say, the moral basis of Jane Austen's novels is, for us, warped by her acceptance of class society; her standards obviously can't apply in a democratic society where the Emmas and Knightleys would have to work for their living like anyone else. But, after all, we must remember when Jane Austen was writing; we must approach the novels with sympathy in their historical context. Jane Austen, a genteel bourgeoise of the turn of the eighteenth century, could scarcely be expected to analyse class society in modern terms. We must make a certain allowance, reading the book with a willing suspension of our own ideas and prejudices.

This represents a view of literature which, behind an apparently historical approach, debases and nullifies the effects of art. It invites us to read *Emma* not as a living, vital novel, relevant to our own lives and problems, but as a dead historical 'document'. A work of art which has to be read in such a way is not a work of art. The very concept of 'making allowances' of this sort for an artist is both insulting and mechanical. It has something of the puritan's contempt for those who have not seen the light, but it lacks the puritan's moral courage, for it is accompanied by a determination not to be done out of what cannot be approved. The final result is generally to come to terms with the aesthetes. For if *Emma* is morally undesirable and yet Art, then Art can have little to do with morality and some new, necessarily idealist, criteria must be found.

It is important, I believe, to realize the weakness of this pseudo-historical view of *Emma*. If, in whatever century she happened to live, Jane Austen were indeed nothing but a genteel bourgeoise 'reflecting' the views of her day, she would not be a great artist and she could not have written *Emma*. The truth is that in so far as *Emma* does reveal her as a conventional member of her class, blindly accepting its position and ideology, the value of *Emma* is indeed limited, not just relatively, but objectively and always. But the truth is also that this is not the principal or most important revelation of *Emma*.

The limitation must not be ignored or glossed over. There can be no doubt that there *is* an inadequacy here, an element of complacency that does to some extent limit the value of *Emma*. The nature of the inadequacy is fairly illustrated by by this description of Emma's visit, with Harriet, to a sick cottager:

They were now approaching the cottage, and all idle topics were superseded. Emma was very compassionate; and the distresses of the poor were as sure of relief from her personal attention and kindness, her counsel and her patience, as from her purse. She understood their ways, could allow for their ignorance and their temptations, had no romantic expectations of extra-ordinary virtue from those, for whom education had done so little, entered into their troubles with ready sympathy, and always gave her assistance with as much intelligence as good-will. In the present instance, it was sickness and poverty together which she came to visit; and after remaining there as long as she could give comfort or advice, she quitted the cottage with such an impres-sion of the scene as made her say to Harriet, as they walked away,

'These are the sights, Harriet, to do one good. How trifling they make every thing else appear! – I feel now as if I could think of nothing but these poor creatures all the rest of the day; and yet, who can say how soon it may all vanish from my mind?'

'Very true,' said Harriet. 'Poor creatures! one can think of nothing else.'

'And really, I do not think the impression will soon be over,' said Emma, as she crossed the low hedge and tottering footstep which ended the narrow, slippery path through the cottage garden, and brought them into the lane again. 'I do not think it will,' stopping to look once more at all the outward wretchedness of the place, and recall the still greater within.

'Oh! dear, no,' said her companion. They walked on. The lane made a slight bend; and when that bend was passed, Mr Elton was immediately in sight; and so near as to give Emma time only to say farther,

'Ah! Harriet, here comes a very sudden trial of our stability in good thoughts. Well, (smiling), I hope it may be allowed that if compassion has produced exertion and relief to the sufferers, it has done all that is truly important. If we feel for the wretched, enough to do all we can for them, the rest is empty sympathy, only distressing to ourselves.'

Harriet could just answer. 'Oh! dear, yes,' before the gentleman joined them.   (IX)

Now there can be no doubt about the quality of the feeling
here. Harriet's silly responses underline most potently the doubt
that Emma herself feels as to the adequacy of her own actions.
There can be no point in this passage (for it has no inevitable
bearing on the plot) save to give a sense of the darker side of the
moon, the aspect of Highbury that will not be dealt with. And it
does indeed to a great extent answer the doubt in the reader's
mind that an essential side of the Highbury world is being
conveniently ignored. But the doubt is not entirely answered.
After all, the important question is not whether Emma recognizes the existence of the poor at Highbury, but whether she
recognizes that her own position depends on their existence.
'Comfort or advice' moreover remain the positives in Emma's
attitudes and one's doubts as to their sufficiency are in fact, like
Emma's, swept away by the arrival of Mr Elton and the plot. The
essential moral issue is shelved; and it is, in general, the supreme
merit of Jane Austen, that essential moral issues are *not* shelved.

But that the inadequacy is not crippling the passage just quoted
will also suggest. That final remark of Emma's is very significant.
The parenthesized 'smiling' and the idiocy of Harriet's comment
have the effect of throwing into doubt the whole aristocratic
philosophy that Emma is expounding and that doubt, though it
does not balance the shelving of the problem, does at least
extenuate it. We are not wholly lulled.

Against the element of complacency other forces, too, are at
work. We should not look merely to the few specific references
to the poor to confirm our sense that the inadequacies of Jane
Austen's social philosophy are overtopped by other, more positive vibrations. Among these positive forces are, as we have seen,
her highly critical concern over the fate of women in her society,
a concern which involves a reconsideration of its basic values.
Positive also are her materialism and her unpretentiousness. If
aristocracy is implicitly defended it is at least on rational grounds;
no bogus philosophical sanctions are called in to preserve the

status quo from reasonable examination. And no claim is made, explicit or implicit, that we are being presented with a revelation of a fundamental truth. Highbury is offered to us as Highbury, not as Life.

And this is ultimately, I think, the strength of *Emma*: this rejection of Life in favour of living, the actual, concrete problems of behaviour and sensibility in an actual, concrete society. It is Jane Austen's sensitive vitality, her genuine concern (based on so large an honesty) for human feelings in a concrete situation, that captures our imagination. It is this concern that gives her such delicate and precise insight into the problems of personal relationships (how will a group of individuals living together best get on, best find happiness?). And the concern does not stop at what, among the ruling class at Highbury, is pleasant and easily solved.

It gives us glimpses of something Mr Woodhouse never dreamed of – the world outside the Highbury world and yet inseparably bound up with it: the world Jane Fairfax saw in her vision of offices and into which Harriet in spite of (no, *because of*) Emma's patronage, was so nearly plunged: the world for which Jane Austen had no answer. It is this vital and unsentimental concern which defeats, to such a very large extent, the limitations. So that when we think back on *Emma* we do not think principally of the narrow inadequacies of Highbury society but of the delight we have known in growing more intimately and wisely sensitive to the way men and women in a particular, given situation, work out their problems of living.

NOTES

1. Mrs Leavis has emphasized, too, how strong a part in Jane Austen's novels is played by her conscious war on the romance. She did to the romance of her day (whether the domestic romance of Fanny Burney or the Gothic brand of Mrs Radcliffe) what Cervantes had done in his. *Pride and Prejudice* is as much an anti-*Cecilia* as *Northanger Abbey* is an anti-*Udolpho*.

2. Parenthetical references are to the part and chapter numbers in the Chapman edition of *Emma* (Oxford, 1926).

Marvin Mudrick

IRONY AS FORM: *EMMA* (1952)

Emma is a throwing off of chains. The author and her characters move with a freedom and assurance unparalleled in Jane Austen's earlier work, and all the more astonishing by contrast with the uneasy stiffness of *Mansfield Park*. The new impetus is her old familiar one, but – from our first impression of *Emma* – purely assimilated to the medium as, in *Northanger Abbey* or even in *Pride and Prejudice*, it is not: the impetus is irony. In *Emma*, the sense of strain and anxiety is purged altogether. This time the author is in her novel and never out of it, never imposing upon us as in *Northanger Abbey* with her condescension or in *Pride and Prejudice* with her occasional prim moral reminders; and she is there for the comic artist's purpose only – to embody and direct our laughter.

The relaxation of an achieved technique is the very climate of *Emma*. Certainly, no other of Jane Austen's novels offers so pleasant and comfortable an atmosphere, so much the effect of an uncomplex and immediate art: wit, irony, light laughter shining in a triumph of surface. Its surface is, in fact, unmarred by a trace of self-justification, ill humor, or back-sliding into morality. The story tells itself, and nothing seems more superfluous than inquiry or deep thought about it.[1]

Emma, like *Pride and Prejudice*, is a story of self-deception, and the problem of each heroine is to undeceive herself. Yet Emma needs, not facts, but people, to help her. If Elizabeth Bennet is self-deceived under a set of special, doubtful circumstances, if she waits mainly for facts, Emma Woodhouse is a girl absolutely self-deceived, who takes and refashions whatever circumstances may arise, who can be checked only by a personality as positive as her own. We follow Emma's comic train of misunderstandings in the happy conviction that she cannot act otherwise until someone with will and intelligence takes her in hand – someone like Mr Knightley, for example. We sympathize with Emma because she *must* fall in love, and we are relaxed because we know that she will. The love story in *Emma* is, then, predetermined to a degree unimaginable in *Pride and Prejudice*; for all Elizabeth needs in order to see is to have the facts before her, while Emma – in spite of her will and intelligence – cannot even begin to see clearly or steadily until Mr Knightley tells her what is there.

Everything, it seems, is made as easy for us as for Mr Woodhouse. Emma is provided from the beginning with a man not only admirable, but indispensable to her education. We need not worry about that. We have no financial anxiety: Emma is an 'heiress of thirty thousand pounds.' Rank is no problem: Emma is herself of an 'ancient family', and her potential lover has an ancestry equally antique. Precedence is no problem: for Emma reigns alone at Hartfield and over Highbury, unencumbered by sisters, aunts, tyrannical parents or guardians, or petty nobility. Emma is, of course, habitually self-deceived; yet Mr Knightley will come to the rescue: and we can read the novel, with no discomfort and only a pleasant minimum of suspense, as the ironic portrait of a girl who falls into mild self-deception and whose trustworthy friend always and finally helps her out.

Emma likes to manage things. Brought up by a doting governess, mistress of her father's house, almost from her childhood obliged to manage her invalid father, Emma – not surprisingly – wishes to dominate elsewhere as well; and the wish to dominate, unimpeded by anxieties over wealth or rank, quickly translates itself into action. It is not surprising that, after her governess leaves to be married, Emma takes on a protégée, especially one so malleable as Harriet Smith, and that in her extension of self-conceit she persuades herself that Harriet can trap into marriage men whose rank and ambition would lead them to aspire even to Emma. It is not surprising that Emma feels confident of her ability to manage Mr Elton or Frank Churchill – everyone, in fact, except Mr Knightley.

It is Mr Knightley who sets us at ease. His acute and decisive mind circumscribes Emma always, keeps her from the gravest consequences of her mistakes, enlightens her when she commits a particularly flagrant snobbery or stupidity, as at Box Hill after her brutal insult to Miss Bates:

'Her situation should secure your compassion. It was badly done, indeed! – You, whom she had known from an infant, whom she has seen grow up from a period when her notice was an honour, to have you now, in thoughtless spirits, and the pride of the moment, laugh at her, humble her – and before her niece, too – and before others, many of whom (certainly *some,*) would be entirely guided by *your* treatment of her. – This is not pleasant to you, Emma – and it is very far from pleasant to me; but I must, I will – I will tell you truths while I can, satisfied with proving myself your friend by very faithful counsel, and trusting that you will some time or other do me greater justice than you can do now.'   (375)[2]

We know that this will bring Emma up sharply, as it very satisfactorily does. Through all of Emma's self-deceptions, we feel Mr Knightley's reassuring nearness; and we know that nothing can go crucially wrong.

Nowhere else is Jane Austen so relaxed, so certain, skilled, and exact in her effects. There is no excess; almost no sense of plot in this delicate ordering of a small calm world, the miniature world of the English rural gentry at the start of the nineteenth century. The ease of style and setting predisposes us to an easy response, prepares us for a mellowing, even a softening, of Jane Austen's newly reasserted irony. The characters of *Emma* seem our familiars at once, in what has been called – with a dangerous patness – 'the absolute triumph of that reliance on the strictly ordinary which has been indicated as Miss Austen's title to pre-eminence in the history of the novel'.[3]

Emma herself seems one of the most attractive of all heroines: beautiful, cultivated, intelligent; solicitous of her father; inclined to snobbery and to rash judgment, but appealing even in her errors and caprices. There is more, but it does not bear out our preconception. Mr Knightley is a man of integrity, of force, wit, and high sense, and – we suspect – rather too good for Emma; but this is just a suspicion. Frank Churchill is an elegant and engaging trifler, whose secret courtship of Jane Fairfax, the worthy girl in unworthy circumstances, comes finally to light as his only recommendation. The yielding Mrs Weston, as Emma's sympathetic confidante, recalls to us the yielding Miss Taylor who could only have given way before her pupil's precocious wilfulness; so that with her we add to our stock of good reasons why Emma is what she is. The author provides us with five varieties of nonentity, will-less comic foils to Emma's wilfulness: Harriet, the obliging; Mr Woodhouse, the gently querulous; Mr Weston, the congenial; Isabella, the domestic; and Miss Bates, the interminably talkative. John Knightley sets off his brother's forthrightness by presenting the same quality with a bristly manner and a touch of misanthropy. For villains – harmless enough to be only amusing – the author gives us the Eltons: Mr Elton, a pillar of meanly aspiring egotism; and his perfectly appropriate wife, Augusta, radiating that field of monomaniac affectation and self-deceit which no sarcasm or earthly judgment can penetrate.

These are Jane Austen's creatures in her new mild climate, and at the end she placidly disposes of them all: nobody left out, no strand left unwoven, nobody unhappy. The plot is fulfilled when the characters are placed where they wish to be: Emma with Mr Knightley, Frank Churchill with Jane Fairfax, Mr Elton with his Augusta, motherly Mrs Weston with her first child; everybody at Hartfield, Donwell, Randalls, and Highbury comfortably settled.

Still, as we follow her attentively, Emma comes to appear less and less an innocuous figure in a novel of simple irony. She begins as a representative young gentlewoman of her age: snobbish, half-educated, wilful, possessive; and, certainly, her consciousness of rank accounts for a good many of her prejudices and cruelties. The fact remains that Emma has unpleasant qualities, which persist in operating and having effect. Whether we try to explain these qualities on the ground of upbringing or youth or personal impulse, we cannot blind ourselves to them. They are there, embedded in the novel.

Emma is, of course, an inveterate snob. Having defined her attitude toward the yeomanry,

'precisely the order of people with whom I feel I can have nothing to do. A degree or two lower, and a creditable appearance might interest me; I might hope to be useful to their families in some way or other. But a farmer can need none of my help, and is therefore in one sense as much above my notice as in every other he is below it.'   (29)

she advises (or, more accurately, commands) Harriet to decline Robert Martin's proposal:

'Dear affectionate creature! – *You* banished to Abbey-Mill Farm! – *You* confined to the society of the illiterate and vulgar all your life! I wonder how the young man would have the assurance to ask it.'   (54)

Without having seen Mrs Elton, Emma dismisses her at once upon learning that she

brought no name, no blood, no alliance. Miss Hawkins was the youngest of the two daughters of a Bristol – merchant, of course, he must be called; but, as the whole of the profits of his mercantile life appeared so very moderate, it was not unfair to guess the dignity of his line of trade had been very moderate also.   (183)

She decides to turn down an invitation from the Coles because, though they

were very respectable in their way ... they ought to be taught that it was not for them to arrange the terms on which the superior families would visit them. This lesson, she very much feared, they would receive only from herself; she had little hope of Mr Knightley, none of Mr Weston.   (207)

Her first thought is always of rank and family. She regards Mr Knightley's possible attachment to Jane Fairfax as a 'very shameful and degrading connection'; and although here she has other reasons, yet unknown to herself, for objecting, it is significant that her first target is Jane's family. She thinks with satisfaction of the Knightleys as a 'family of ... true gentility, untainted in blood and understanding'. When Harriet turns out to be only the daughter of a tradesman, 'Such was the blood of gentility', Emma reflects, which she

had formerly been so ready to vouch for! – It was likely to be as untainted, perhaps, as the blood of many a gentleman: but what a connexion had she been preparing for Mr Knightley – or for the Churchills – or even for Mr Elton! – The stain of illegitimacy, unbleached by nobility or wealth, would have been a stain indeed. (482)

Nor are we allowed to charge these snobberies wholly to the temper of her class and age, since they draw rebukes for her not only from Mrs Weston, on the subject of Jane's suitableness for Mr Knightley, but, on her attitude toward Robert Martin as well as toward Miss Bates (375), from the impeccably pure-blooded Mr Knightley himself.

Emma has neglected the genteel feminine accomplishments, and cannot endure being reminded of her neglect. Shamed by Jane's superior playing on the piano, she detests her more unjustly than ever. She sketches a fair likeness of Harriet; and the immoderate praise of her subject and Mr Elton, though it cannot delude her, is enough to flatter her ego into silence:

She was not much deceived as to her own skill either as an artist or a musician, but she was not unwilling to have others deceived, or sorry to know her reputation for accomplishment often higher than it deserved. (44)

Yet Mr Knightley remarks, 'I do not think her personally vain. Considering how very handsome she is, she appears to be little occupied with it' (39). She lacks, that is, the customary vanity that springs from the desire to please a suitor or lover; Mr Knightley adds: 'her vanity lies another way. Mrs Weston, I am not to be talked out of my dislike of her intimacy with Harriet Smith, or my dread of its doing them both harm' (39).

It is true that much of Emma's unpleasantness can be attributed to her consciousness of rank. In her class, family is the base, property the outward symbol, and suitable marriage the goal; and family and property are the chief criteria of acceptability for Emma. Marriage, however, she dismisses as a goal for herself:

'Were I to fall in love, indeed, it would be a different thing! but I never have been in love; it is not my way, or my nature; and I do not think I ever shall. And, without love, I am sure I should be a fool to change such a situation as mine. Fortune I do not want; employment I do not want; consequence I do not want: I believe few married women are half as much mistress of their husband's house as I am of Hartfield; and never, never could I expect to be so truly beloved and important; so always first and always right in any man's eyes as I am in my father's.'   (84)

Emma deals only in measurable quantities: anything uncertain is to be dismissed, avoided; and marriage, however neatly and by a balance of tangibles she may arrange it for others, seems for her both an uncertainty and an abasement.

Emma is an arranger, a manager of other people's affairs. Accustomed to look after her father's every whim and to forestall his every possible discomfort, she tries to extend this duty over her circle of friends and acquaintances as well. Yet she prophesies only what she wills, and she is always wrong. She will never admit what she herself has not contrived, until the truth strikes her in the face. She is wrong about Mr Elton's feelings toward Harriet. She quite misconceives her own feelings toward Mr Knightley. Baffled and angered by Jane Fairfax's reserve, she creates without a shred of evidence the most outrageous slander about an affair she imagines Jane to have had with another woman's husband; and she is even ready to pass her slander on to Churchill:

I do not mean to reflect upon the good intentions of either Mr Dixon or Miss Fairfax, but I cannot help suspecting either that, after making his proposals to her friend, he had the misfortune to fall in love with *her*, or that he became conscious of a little attachment on her side. One might guess twenty things without guessing exactly the right; but I am sure there must be a particular cause for her chusing to come to Highbury instead of going with the Campbells to Ireland. Here, she must be leading a life of privation and penance; there it would have been all enjoyment.   (217)

She is wrong about Harriet's feelings toward Churchill. She complacently fabricates an entire love affair between Churchill and herself – including its decline and dissolution – with no more encouragement than the gentleman's adroit and uncommitting flirtation; yet throughout this imaginary affair she reiterates her 'resolution . . . of never marrying' (206): for though Emma can imagine everything else, she cannot imagine her own commitment. She is wrong about Mr Knightley's feelings toward both Harriet and herself. Even when she has recognized her own love for Mr Knightley and heard his declaration joyfully, she finds the duty of remaining with her father superior to the claim of love: 'a very short parley with her own heart produced the most solemn resolution of never quitting her father'. She is ready, then, to alter everyone's life but her father's, which is after all only a shadowy extension of her own.

Emma is occupied in altering, as she sees fit, the lives of others; and to this end any means will do. If, to save Harriet for gentility, Robert Martin must be made unhappy, he is merely another obstacle to be set aside with no more than a moment's uneasiness; so, after Emma's quarrel with Mr Knightley over her intervention:

'. . . I only want to know that Mr Martin is not very, very bitterly disappointed.'
 'A man cannot be more so,' was his short, full answer.
 'Ah! – Indeed I am very sorry. – Come, shake hands with me.'
                 (99)

Even death, the death of Mrs Churchill, is for Emma a means, serving to freshen her wholly fanciful hope for a match between Churchill and Harriet:

The character of Mrs Churchill, the grief of her husband – her mind glanced over them both with awe and compassion – and then rested with lightened feelings on how Frank might be affected by the event, how benefited, how freed. She saw in a moment all the possible good. Now, an attachment to Harriet Smith would have nothing to encounter.   (388)

The personal, as personal, cannot engage Emma for more than a moment: her mind cannot rest upon it without making it over altogether into a means.

Emma claims the role of adviser, but denies its responsibility. She delights in bullying anyone who will yield – poor Harriet most of all: 'Dear Harriet, I give myself joy of this. It would have grieved me to lose your acquaintance, which must have been the consequence of your marrying Mr Martin' (53) yet at the last, unwilling to face Harriet after her own disastrous series of errors in her protégée's affairs, she limits her compunction and their relationship to letters:

Harriet expressed herself very much as might be supposed, without reproaches, or apparent sense of ill usage; and yet Emma fancied there was a something of resentment, a something bordering on it in her style, which increased the desirableness of their being separate. – It might be only her own consciousness; but it seemed as if an angel only could have been quite without resentment under such a stroke.   (451)

and Emma is utterly relieved when Harriet falls into the patient arms of Robert Martin: 'She must laugh at such a close! Such an end of the doleful disappointment of five weeks back! Such a heart – such a Harriet!' (475). Far from examining the past, Emma absolves herself of it. Even when Harriet's confession of love for Mr Knightley has roused Emma to the pitch of self-analysis, Emma's outcry sinks easily into the luxury of an acknowledged defeat – 'She was most sorrowfully indignant; ashamed of every sensation but the one revealed to her – her affection for Mr Knightley. – Every other part of her mind was disgusting' (412) – the act of self-abasement that claims sin, in order to avoid the responsibility of self-knowledge.

Emma and Harriet are the most unexpected companions in all of Jane Austen's work. Nor may we pass off their intimacy – at least from Emma's side – as the effect of blind adolescent exuberance. Emma is already a worldly twenty-one; and she is aware enough of Harriet's intellectual limitations to comment ironically on Mr Elton's charade: 'Harriet's ready wit! All the better. A man must be very much in love indeed, to describe her so' (72). Emma has no intellectual ties with the unalterably sheeplike Harriet, and she can gain no material advantage from her friendship. Of course, Emma likes to manage people, and Harriet is manageable. But why Harriet, of all people; and why so tenaciously Harriet, at least until every trick has failed?

Emma observes Harriet's beauty with far more warmth than anyone else: 'She was so busy in admiring those soft blue eyes, in talking and listening, and forming all these schemes in the in-betweens, that the evening flew away at a very unusual rate' (24). This is the clever and sophisticated Emma, transported by the presence of the most insipid girl imaginable. Moreover, Emma's attention never falls so warmly upon a man; against this feeling for Harriet, her good words for Mr Knightley's appearance seem pale indeed. Emma will excuse low birth in no one else, but Harriet's parentless illegitimacy she will talk away with nonsense about gentle lineage:

'The misfortune of your birth ought to make you particularly careful as to your associates. There can be no doubt of your being a gentleman's daughter, and you must support your claim to that station by every thing within your own power, or there will be plenty of people who would take pleasure in degrading you.' (30)

To Mr Knightley, Emma maintains heatedly that since men are attracted by pretty faces Harriet will have all she wants of handsome offers:

'she is . . . a beautiful girl, and must be thought so by ninety-nine out of a hundred; and till it appears that men are much more philosophic on the subject of beauty than they are generally supposed; till they do fall in love with well-informed minds instead of handsome faces, a girl, with such loveliness as Harriet, has a certainty of being admired and sought after, of having the power of choosing from among many, consequently a claim to be nice.' (63)

Nor is she moved, except to discomfort, by Mr Knightley's natural objection:

'Miss Harriet Smith may not find offers of marriage flow in so
fast, though she is a very pretty girl. Men of sense, whatever you
may chuse to say, do not want silly wives. Men of family would
not be very fond of connecting themselves with a girl of such
obscurity – and most prudent men would be afraid of the
inconvenience and disgrace they might be involved in, when the
mystery of her parentage came to be revealed.'   (64)

Emma merely lies about her hopes for Harriet with Mr Elton,
and keeps her opinion intact. Yet – with the exception of the
young farmer, Robert Martin – not one man through the range
of the novel ever shows the slightest interest in Harriet. When
Emma tries to cool the ardent Mr Elton in the coach by asserting
that his attentions have been directed not toward her but toward
Harriet, he rejects the very notion with horror:

'Good heaven! . . . what can be the meaning of this? – Miss
Smith! – I never thought of Miss Smith in the whole course of
my existence – never paid her any attentions, but as your friend:
never cared whether she were dead or alive, but as your friend.'
                                                                  (130)

No one, it seems, is attracted by *this* pretty face except Emma.

Harriet draws her unqualified confidence as only one other
person does: Mrs Weston. Mrs Weston has been her affectionate
governess, and continued affection between them is natural
enough. But Emma's regard reaches the same noteworthy excess
as with Harriet. Emma has imagined herself to be falling in love
with Frank Churchill; now he and Mrs Weston, who is his step-
mother, come upon her together:

She was wanting to see him again, and especially to see him in
company with Mrs Weston, upon his behaviour to whom her
opinion of him was to depend. If he were deficient there, nothing
should make amends for it.   (196)

One assumes that not even imagining herself in love with him
could impel Emma to forgive Churchill's possible coolness toward his stepmother.

Emma's attitude toward young men – when she is not trying
to drive them into Harriet's arms – touches now and then upon

the thought of a suitable marriage for herself. With Churchill she can sustain the idea of marriage just as long as it remains an idea, a neat, appropriate, socially approved arrangement:

She had frequently thought—especially since her father's marriage with Miss Taylor – that if she *were* to marry, he was the very person to suit her in age, character and condition. He seemed by this connection between the families, quite to belong to her. She could not but suppose it to be a match that every body who knew them must think of.   (119)

The direct threat of marriage, however, she always thrusts aside, indignantly with Mr Elton – 'I have no thoughts of matrimony at present' – after long deliberation (which has nothing to feed on but itself), with respect to Churchill – 'Her own attachment had really subsided into a mere nothing; it was not worth thinking of' – even, for a time, in answer to Mr Knightley. Meanwhile, her involvement with Harriet – until the culminating error – remains steady and strong.

The fact is that Emma prefers the company of women, more particularly of women whom she can master and direct; the fact is that this preference is intrinsic to her whole dominating and uncommitting personality. The same tendency has been recognized by Edmund Wilson; but Mr Wilson adds that it is 'something outside the picture which is never made explicit'.[4] The tendency is certainly never made explicit; but is it for that reason external? The myth of Jane Austen's simplicity persists; and its corollary, that in her work the unexplicit is an error of tone: for surface must tell all.

Emma needs to dominate, she can of course – in her class and time – most easily dominate women; and her need is urgent enough to forgo even the pretense of sympathetic understanding. She feels affection only towards Harriet, Mrs Weston, and her father: instances, not of tenderness, but rather of satisfied control. She feels affection only toward those immediately under her command, and all of them are women. Mr Woodhouse is no exception. The effect of decayed gentlemanliness that he produces is a *tour de force* of Jane Austen's, nothing else; for Mr

Woodhouse is really an old woman, of the vacuous, mild-natured, weakly selfish sort very common to novels and (possibly) to life. He has no single masculine trait, and his only distinction lies in the transfer of sex. He is Mrs Bates elevated to the dignity of Hartfield.

As she herself admits, Emma has no tenderness:

> There is no charm equal to tenderness of heart. . . . There is nothing to be compared to it. Warmth and tenderness of heart, with an affectionate, open manner, will beat all the clearness of head in the world, for attraction. I am sure it will. It is tenderness of heart which makes my dear father so generally beloved – which gives Isabella all her popularity. – I have it not – but I know how to prize and respect it.   (269)

This last is already a misjudgment, for Emma does *not* know how to prize and respect tenderness in anyone who rejects her domination. Still, she recognizes her defect. Emma is a beautiful and clever girl, with every grace but tenderness. Without it, she exhibits the strong need to dominate, the offhand cruelty, the protective playfulness, the malice of Jane Austen, the candid Jane Austen of the letters – in which miscarriage is a joke:

> Mrs Hall, of Sherborne, was brought to bed yesterday of a dead child, some weeks before she expected, owing to a fright. I suppose she happened unawares to look at her husband.[5]

and death equally amusing:

> Only think of Mrs Holder's being dead! Poor woman, she has done the only thing in the world she could possibly do to make one cease to abuse her.[6]

recalling the more literary echo in *Emma*, on Mrs Churchill's death:

> Goldsmith tells us, that when lovely woman stoops to folly, she has nothing to do but do die; and when she stoops to be disagreeable, it is equally to be recommended as a clearer of ill fame. (387)

and marriage also, as – anticipating Emma on Churchill – she shrugs off the fading interest of an eligible young man:

This is rational enough; there is less love and more sense in it than sometimes appeared before, and I am very well satisfied. It will all go on exceedingly well, and decline away in a very reasonable manner.[7]

Emma, of course, is only an 'imaginist' and twenty-one; creating her, Jane Austen is an artist and thirty-nine. In the assurance of mastery – with a quarter-century of writing behind her, a portion of fame, and a congenial subject isolated from moral qualms[8] – Jane Austen could be freely aware of the Emma in herself, she could convert her own personal limitations into the very form of her novel. All she had to discard for the character of Emma was her own overarching artist's awareness, her unresting irony, which even in life, in her letters at least, directed and used her need to dominate, her fear of commitment: which made her coldly right where Emma is coldly wrong.

Emma is moved to play God, but without tenderness or social caution (or the artist's awareness) she falls into every conceivable mistake and misjudgment. She must feel herself to be central and centripetal, the confidante and adviser of all. Without tenderness or caution, she makes the worst of every situation: imagines evil when there is good – because Jane Fairfax is 'disgustingly reserved' or has an 'odious composure' – and good where there is nothing but an extension of self.

Mrs Elton – for all of Emma's heartfelt aversion to her – is Emma's true companion in motive. Both must dominate every situation. Both must have admirers to confirm their position. Both are profoundly wanting in altruism and sympathy. The chief difference is that Mrs Elton's motive lies bare, without ornament of intelligence, beauty, or rank. Mrs Elton is 'vulgar' (Emma's favorite word for her and her friends) – 'A little upstart, vulgar being, with her Mr E., and her *caro sposo*, and her resources, and all her airs of pert pretension and under-bred finery' (279) – and Emma is 'refined'.[9] Mrs Elton has no brake of intelligence or breeding upon her egocentrism; she can rattle on and give herself away without self-consciousness:

'I honestly said that *the world* I could give up – parties, balls, plays – for I had no fear of retirement. Blessed with so many resources within myself, the world was not necessary to *me*. I could do very well without it. To those who had no resources it was a different thing; but my resources made me quite independent. And as to smaller-sized rooms than I had been used to, I really could not give it a thought. I hoped I was perfectly equal to any sacrifice of that description. Certainly I had been accustomed to every luxury of Maple Grove; but I did assure him that two carriages were not necessary to my happiness, nor were spacious apartments.'   (277)

Since she is happy as long as she is allowed to condescend:

'My dear Jane, what is this I hear? – Going to the post-office in the rain! – This must not be, I assure you. – You sad girl, how could you do such a thing? – It is a sign I was not there to take care of you.'   (295)

Jane Fairfax's mere politeness she can accept as homage. Emma, though, is neither fatuous nor unperceptive. She must play the idol and the confidante, but she requires some evidence of idolatry; and she builds up a vindictive dislike of Jane Fairfax precisely because it is clear that Jane will worship or trust neither her nor anyone else.

Emma can fall back on the nonentities of her world, those vessels of neutral purpose that are always governed from the outside: Harriet, Mr Woodhouse, Mr Weston, Isabella, and Miss Bates. Not that they have anything to offer beyond agreeableness: Mr Weston, happy with his son, ready to be satisfied with everyone, even Mrs Elton; Isabella, dwindling pleasantly in hypochondria and her husband's shadow; Harriet, with her infinite pliancy; Miss Bates, spreading her obsessive good cheer: 'It is such a happiness when good people get together – and they always do' (175).

Mr Woodhouse has not even this recommendation. He is not agreeable. He is, in fact, an annoyance, with his gruel, his hypochondria, his often-quoted friend Perry, his feeble but effective insistence that nothing, nothing at all, be changed in his life or in the lives of the people around him; and we can sympathize with John Knightley when he looses his hot temper against the nagging solicitations of his father-in law. Mr Woodhouse – after long years of invalidism, of being coddled by his daughter, of scarcely stirring from his house or seeing a new person – is an idiot. He is quite incapable of thought or judgment. Miss Bates, Jane Fairfax, Mr Knightley, Frank Churchill – all are agreeable persons, as long as the young ladies dry their stockings after a rain and the young men do not insist on opening windows. Even on Mrs Elton, 'considering we never saw her before', he remarks that 'she seems a very obliging, pretty-behaved young lady, and no doubt will make him a very good wife. Though I think he had better not have married' (279–80). When Emma, in a rare mood of almost irritable playfulness with him, tries to point out the contradiction between his respect for brides and his dislike of marriage, she only makes him nervous without making him at all understand. (280) Anything is satisfactory as long as it does not require change; and there is no distinction between satisfactory things. As he has no taste for people, so he has no taste for food – except for thin, smooth gruel and soft-boiled eggs – or for Mr Knightley's objects of art: 'Mrs Weston had been showing them all to him, and now he would show them all to Emma; – fortunate in having no other resemblance to a child, than in a total want of taste for what he saw, for he was slow, constant, and methodical' (362). He has his habits, his advice, his fears, his small worn-out courtesies – without a touch of discriminating thought or feeling except between what is familiar and what is alien. His tenacious clinging to Emma, to his acquaintances, to the seen boundaries of his world comes to resemble the clinging of a parasitic plant, which must be now or sometime shaken off. Mr Woodhouse is the living – barely living – excuse for Emma's refusal to commit herself to the human world.

He is also, like the other governable characters and like Mrs Weston (whom Emma, at least, can govern), the kind of person whom Emma can most easily persuade of her supremacy; and it is significant that she treats them all – except one – with the utmost kindness and solicitude. The exception is Miss Bates, whom Emma mimics in company and shockingly ridicules to her face:

'Oh very well,' exclaimed Miss Bates, 'then I need not be uneasy. "Three things very dull indeed." That will just do for me, you know. I shall be sure to say three dull things as soon as ever I open my mouth, shan't I? – (looking round with the most good-humoured dependence on every body's assent) – Do not you all think I shall?'

Emma could not resist.

'Ah! ma'am, but there may be a difficulty. Pardon me – but you will be limited as to number – only three at once.'   (370)

since Miss Bates, unluckily for her, has no greater pleasure than chattering the praises of her niece, Jane Fairfax.

The only character in the story who sees Emma at all clearly is Frank Churchill. He is as egoistic and calculating as she, but he beats her at her own game because he is far less self-deluded. Emma's prodigious self-deception springs at least partly from inexperience. With experience, with the especially valuable experience of pampering a cross and dictatorial old woman, Churchill has learned to be cautious, to blunt the edge of his ego with careless charm. He has learned to use people more success-fully than Emma, but he is not less destructive. His playing at love with Emma is required, perhaps, in order to keep the secret of his engagement to Jane; but he takes cynical delight in tor-menting the latter and mystifying the former. He convinces Emma that he wholly accepts her slander about Jane and Mr Dixon, and her view that it is Mr Dixon who has sent the piano: 'Indeed you injure me if you suppose me unconvinced . . . now I can see it in no other light than as an offering of love' (218–19). Allusion to Mr Dixon and Ireland becomes, in fact, his favorite method of simultaneously hurting Jane and amusing Emma while he laughs at both. He jokes with Emma about Jane's hair-do:

'Those curls! – This must be a fancy of her own. I see nobody else looking like her! – must go and ask her whether it is an Irish fashion. Shall I? – Yes, I will – I declare I will – and you shall see how she takes it; – whether she colours.'   (222)

Concerning the gift piano, he baits Jane openly, over Emma's feeble objection:

'It is not fair,' said Emma in a whisper, 'mine was a random guess. Do not distress her.'

He shook his head with a smile, and looked as if he had very little doubt and very little mercy. Soon afterwards he began again,

'How much your friends in Ireland must be enjoying your pleasure on this occasion, Miss Fairfax. I dare say they often think of you, and wonder which will be the day, the precise day of the instrument's coming to hand.' (241)

He persists, though Emma is 'half ashamed':

Emma wished he would be less pointed, yet could not help being amused. . . .

'You speak too plain. She must understand you.'

'I hope she does. I would have her understand me. I am not in the least ashamed of my meaning.'

'But really, I am half ashamed, and wish I had never taken up the idea.'

'I am very glad you did, and that you communicated it to me. I have now a key to all her odd looks and ways. Leave shame to her. If she does wrong, she ought to feel it.' (243)

At Hartfield, Mr Knightley, with considerable suspicion of Churchill's deceit, watches the word-game in progress:

He saw a short word prepared for Emma, and given to her with a look sly and demure. He saw that Emma had soon made it out, and found it highly entertaining, though it was something which she judged it proper to appear to censure; for she said, 'Nonsense! for shame!' He heard Frank Churchill next say, with a glance towards Jane, 'I will give it to her – shall I?' – and as clearly heard Emma opposing it with eager laughing warmth. 'No, no, you must not; you shall not, indeed.'

It was done, however. This gallant young man, who seemed to love without feeling, and to recommend himself without complaisance, directly . . . handed over the word to Miss Fairfax, and, with a particular degree of sedate civility entreated her to study it. Mr Knightley's excessive curiosity to know what this word might be, made him seize every possible moment for darting his eye towards it, and it was not long before he saw it to be *Dixon*. (348)

In the strained and heavy atmosphere at Box Hill, with the company separating into small sullen parties, with Jane bitterly jealous (though no one but Churchill knows) of Churchill's attentions to Emma, he flirts defiantly with Emma and directs his scorn at everyone else: 'Our companions are excessively stupid. What shall we do to rouse them? Any nonsense will serve. They *shall* talk' (369). Through his unsuspecting dupe, Emma, Churchill recalls to Jane their meeting at a resort and baits her cruelly about her family:

'as to any real knowledge that Bath, or any public place, can give – it is all nothing; there can be no knowledge. It is only by seeing women in their own homes, among their own set, just as they always are, that you can form any just judgment. Short of that, it is all guess and luck – and will generally be ill-luck. How many a man has committed himself on a short acquaintance, and rued it all the rest of his life.'   (372)

And all the while he makes Jane sick with shame, jealousy, bitterness, and fear: uncertain of his affection, uncertain even whether she desires it, sick with the burden of a clandestine engagement,[10] bitterly resigned to sinking her talent, her taste, her intelligence into the governess-role by which – if Churchill fails her – she must live: 'There are places in town, offices, where inquiry would soon produce something – Offices for the sale – not quite of human flesh – but of human intellect' (300). Moreover, Churchill does all this consciously and with relish, enjoying his duplicity: 'I am the wretchedest being in the world at a civil falsehood' (234). He has no scruples, for he needs none: charm and wealth excuse everything. One wonders whether Emma – even under the vigilance of Mr Knightley – will not be polished into the same engaging ruthlessness after several years of marriage.

Emma accepts Mr Knightley doubtless because she loves and admires him. She has failed so discouragingly with Harriet as to give up all thought of protégées for the present; and Mr Knightley is after all a very impressive and admirable man. He is even the most likable and most heroic of Jane Austen's heroes: unlike Darcy, he is a frank and social man; he is not a prig like Edmund

Bertram, or a wary ironist like Henry Tilney. He is intelligent, perceptive, mature – but not so indivertibly as to save his judgment altogether from the effects of love:

> He had found her agitated and low. – Frank Churchill was a villain. – He heard her declare that she had never loved him. Frank Churchill's character was not desperate. – She was his own Emma, by hand and word, when they returned into the house; and if he could have thought of Frank Churchill then, he might have deemed him a very good sort of fellow. (433)

That he should continue to love Emma at all, after observing her through all her misdemeanors, is in fact a tribute to the power of love; for Mr Knightley is quite capable of recognizing and pointing out the implications of her conduct, with Harriet, with Churchill and Jane Fairfax, with Miss Bates – implications he vigorously points out to Emma herself. Success in love, though, overthrows him. As for Emma, she has been defeated. All her dreams of fruitful dominion have been at least temporarily dissipated; and, for the time being, she is willing to be dominated by a man of whom her intelligence and her snobbery can approve (though even now she accepts only on condition that he move into her father's home!). The flood of repentance has not yet subsided. Yet there is no sign that Emma's motives have changed, that there is any difference in her except her relief and temporary awareness. Later on, the story may turn back again: it is hard to think of Emma undominant for any length of time.

Emma plays God because she cannot commit herself humanly. Her compulsion operates in the absence of one quality: a quality which Emma, Frank Churchill, and Mrs Elton – the only destructive figures in the novel – are all without. The quality is tenderness. For Emma, there is no communication of feeling. She can esteem, loathe, praise, censure, grieve, rejoice – but she cannot feel like anyone else in the world. Her ego will admit nothing but itself. Frank Churchill and Mrs Elton fall under the same charge: but Mrs Elton is too transparently vulgar to be effective; and Churchill, too astute to be caught playing God, keeps his own counsel, trifles, observes, and makes use of people by the less imposing and less dangerous tactic of charm. Of the three, only Emma is both foolish enough to play God and dazzling enough to blind anyone even for a short time.

The primary large irony of the novel is, then, the deceptiveness of surface. Charm is the chief warning-signal of Jane Austen's world, for it is most often the signal of wit adrift from feeling. The brilliant façades of Emma and Frank Churchill have no door. Indeed, the only charming person in all of Jane Austen's novels whom both she and the reader fully accept is Elizabeth Bennet, and Elizabeth has obvious virtues – a clear head and good intentions – to lend depth and steadiness to her charm. The other heroines – Elinor Dashwood, Catherine Morland, Fanny Price, Anne Elliot – are presented in the quietest colors. And Willoughby, Wickham, Mary Crawford, Frank Churchill – the charming interlopers – always betray.

In *Emma*, Jane Austen has given surface the benefit of every alluring quality in the persons of the heroine and of Frank Churchill. She has given them beauty, wealth, position, and immediate circumstances most favorable to the exercise of their wills. The only results have been confusion and unhappiness, on the reduced scale appropriate to the people and the society involved.

Of course, the denouement brushes aside confusion and unhappiness, and brings Emma and Churchill into ostensibly happy marriages. *Emma* can be read as the story of a spoiled rich girl who is corrected by defeat and love, and who lives happily ever after. This is a limited vision, but it is not a false one; for Jane Austen does succeed on her primary levels in achieving her 'ripest and kindliest',[11] her most perfect love comedy. On these levels, Emma is 'faultless in spite of all her faults' (433), Frank Churchill's frivolity will be tempered by the sense and grave sweetness of his wife, even Mrs Elton can do little harm, and everyone else is comfortably settled – with the exception of poor Mrs Churchill, who had to die to clear the way for her nephew's marriage. The conditions are almost standard for romantic comedy: two love-affairs, one complicated by self-deception, the other by secrecy, both turning out well; no strong issue, no punishment.

Emma can be read so; but it has more to give, and not easily. Reginald Farrer, one of the few critics of Jane Austen who have taken the trouble to read her carefully, has observed that *Emma* 'is not an easy book to read; it should never be the beginner's primer, nor be published without a prefatory synopsis. Only when the story has been thoroughly assimilated, can the infinite delights and subtleties of its workmanship begin to be appreciated, as you realize the manifold complexity of the book's web, and find that every sentence, almost every epithet, has its definite reference to equally unemphasized points before and after in the development of the plot. Thus it is that, while twelve readings of *Pride and Prejudice* give you twelve periods of pleasure repeated, as many readings of *Emma* give you that pleasure, not repeated only, but squared and squared again with each perusal, till at every fresh reading you feel anew that you never understood anything like the widening sum of its delights.'[12]

It is this multiplicity and sureness of reference that most immediately distinguishes *Emma* from the rest of Jane Austen's work: the total confident control of all her resources, without intrusion of derivativeness or fatigue or morality. The author's vision and instrument is, of course, irony: the widening sum of delights in *Emma* is, first of all, our widening recognition of the decisive pertinence with which every word, every action, and every response of Emma's establish her nature, confirm her self-deception, and prepare for her downfall. The ironic reverberations, rather than conflicting with one another or passing out of context – as they do sometimes in *Pride and Prejudice* and often in *Northanger Abbey* – remain internal and interdependent, they reinforce one another in a structure whose apparent lightness is less remarkable only than its compact and powerful density.

When we first observe Emma's maneuverings with Harriet, it is with the consciousness of her urge to dominate. Soon, though, this urge has become inextricable from Emma's own snobbery and her vicarious snobbery for Harriet, which drive it even farther from the possibility of caution or rational direction. Why does Emma want Harriet to marry? Harriet begins to seem a kind of proxy for Emma, a means by which Emma – too reluctant, too fearful of involvement, to consider the attempt herself – may discover what marriage is like. If Harriet is a proxy for Emma, she must serve as a defense also. Emma is outraged by Mr Elton's proposal, not merely because she has not expected it (the basis of the simple irony here), but because Mr Elton dares to circumvent the buffer she has so carefully set up. Harriet is to experience for her what she refuses to commit herself to, but cannot help being curious about. Yet Harriet is a very pretty girl, and being infinitely stupid and unperceptive, may be used in other uncommitting ways. Emma's interest in Harriet is not merely mistress-and-pupil, but quite emotional and particular: for a time at least – until Harriet becomes slightly resentful of the yoke after Emma's repeated blunders – Emma is in love with her: a love unphysical and inadmissible, even perhaps undefinable in such a society; and therefore safe. And in all this web of relations, by no means exhausted here, we return always to Emma's over-powering motive: her fear of commitment.

The simple irony of Emma's flirtation with Frank Churchill rises, of course, from the fact that Churchill is in love with someone else and uses Emma as a decoy. More than this, how-ever, Churchill uses Emma so successfully only because he knows her so well. Emma is a perfect decoy for a man in love with someone else. She enjoys and invites admiration, but will draw away from any sign of serious attachment. Churchill does not use Emma merely for want of other dupes: he knows her, and exploits her with a ruthless thoroughness, not making a fool of her but revealing her as she is. 'But is it possible,' he asks Emma blandly, later, 'that you had no suspicion?' (477) He knows that she neither did nor could have had. She took part so eagerly in the flirtation because there she could be at once admired and unengaged, there she could smugly exchange scandal in the guise of wit, and be cynically and most delicately stroked into a pleasant (though wary) submissiveness by flattery without feeling, by assurances of her Olympian superiority.

The one quality which Mr Knightley may regard as Emma's

saving grace is her honesty. It is a very circumscribed honesty, it operates characteristically in the trough of failure and disaster, before the next rise of confidence and self-delusion; and it is another inextricable strand in the complex ironic web. Emma can recognize how badly her matchmaking schemes have turned out and resolve never to attempt them again – but without recognizing why she attempts them at all and keeps coming back to them. She can set her calculating nature against Harriet's simple and lachrymose one, without understanding the motives behind either, or anticipating the author's charge of sentimentality: 'It was rather too late in the day to set about being simple-minded and ignorant' (142). Most crucially, after the conventional settling of accounts, after Mr Knightley has secured his Emma and Churchill his Jane, Emma for the first time can judge herself and Churchill as they must have seemed together in their flirtation, as they have been and are now alike:

Emma could not help saying,
  'I do suspect that in the midst of your perplexities at that time, you had very great amusement in tricking us all. – I am sure you had. – I am sure it was a consolation to you.'
  'Oh! no, no, no – how can you suspect me of such a thing? – I was the most miserable wretch!'
  'Not quite so miserable as to be insensible to mirth. I am sure it was a source of high entertainment to you, to feel that you were taking us all in. – Perhaps I am the readier to suspect, because, to tell you the truth, I think it might have been some amusement to myself in the same situation. I think there is a little likeness between us.'
  He bowed.
  'If not in our dispositions,' she presently added, with a look of true sensibility, 'there is a likeness in our destiny; the destiny which bids fair to connect us with two characters so much superior to our own.'
                                                                (478)

This is honesty, and very acute. In an interlude with the man who most completely understands her, Emma recognizes and gives us the truth; and it is no mistake that Jane Austen places this clarifying exchange so close to the end of her book. Emma has finally – almost – got to know herself; but only because the knowledge is here painless and may be discarded in a little while with Mr Knightley again, where she may resume, however self-amusedly for the present, her characteristic role:

'Do you dare say this?' cried Mr Knightley. 'Do you dare to suppose me so great a blockhead, as not to know what a man is talking of? – What do you deserve?'

'Oh! I always deserve the best treatment, because I never put up with any other ...'   (474)

Emma knows that she is moving toward a happy ending. Emma and Churchill are very lucky in the irony that finds them a Mr Knightley and a Jane Fairfax to sober and direct them: this much Emma sees. So Mr Knightley, not yet accepted by Emma, speaks bitterly of Churchill:

'Frank Churchill is, indeed, the favourite of fortune. Every thing turns out for his good. – He meets with a young woman at a watering-place, gains her affection, cannot even weary her by negligent treatment – and had he and all his family sought round the world for a perfect wife for him, they could not have found her superior. – His aunt is in the way. – His aunt dies. – He has only to speak. – His friends are eager to promote his happiness. – He has used every body ill – and they are all delighted to forgive him. – He is a fortunate man indeed!'   (428)

Still, Churchill – as Mr Knightley knows – and Emma are lucky not by luck (except the luck of an invalid aunt's dying), but because in their social milieu charm conquers, even as it makes every cruel and thoughtless mistake; because, existing apart from and inevitably denying emotion and commitment, it nevertheless finds committed to it even the good and the wise, even when it is known and evaluated. The irony of *Emma* is multiple; and its ultimate aspect is that there is no happy ending, easy equilibrium, if we care to project confirmed exploiters like Emma and Churchill into the future of their marriages.

Emma's and Frank Churchill's society, which makes so much of surface, guarantees the triumph of surface. Even Mr Knightley and Jane Fairfax succumb. Jane Austen, however, does not ask us to concern ourselves beyond the happy ending: she merely presents the evidence, noncommittally.

NOTES

1. Far from thinking about it, some critics seem to drift out of it into a warm, irrelevant daydream of their own, in which they discover in the book a 'good-natured, placid, slightly dispersed and unoccupied quality . . . pleasantly reflected in the character of its heroine'. O. W. Firkins, *Jane Austen* (New York, 1920) p. 96.

2. Parenthetical references are to page numbers in the Chapman edition of *Emma* (Oxford, 1926).

3. G. Saintsbury, *The English Novel* (1919) p. 198.

4. E. Wilson, 'A Long Talk About Jane Austen', in the *New Yorker*, xx (24 June 1944) 69.

5. *Jane Austen's Letters to her sister Cassandra and others*, collected and edited by R. W. Chapman (Oxford, 1932) 1 no. 24 (27 Oct 1798).

6. Ibid. II no. 350 (14 Oct 1813).

7. Ibid. I no. 28 (17 Nov 1798).

8. Anticipating objections to Emma, Jane Austen said: 'I am going to take a heroine whom no one but myself will much like' (J. E. Austen-Leigh, *A Memoir of Jane Austen* (Oxford, 1926) p. 157); the moral finickiness of *Mansfield Park* is put decisively behind.

9. Emma 'is the type in fiction of a whole race of English ladies . . . for whom refinement is religion. Her claim to oversee and order the social things about her consisted in being refined.' G. K. Chesterton, 'The Evolution of Emma', in *Living Age*, ccxciv (25 Aug 1917) 504.

10. Mr Chapman documents 'the enormity of Jane Fairfax's deviation from right' in her particular social context (512–13).

11. R. Farrer, 'Jane Austen, *ob.* July 18, 1817', in *Quarterly Review*, ccxxviii (July 1917) 26.

12. Ibid., 23–4. The fact that great novels require frequent re-experience to produce their full effect is perhaps less insisted upon than it should be. The same fact is taken for granted with respect to lyric poetry and 'absolute' music. In a work of art, one can arrive at form only by apprehending specifically – and in a great work this is always difficult – all the individual relationships, implications, and resolutions that together make up form. In a novel, one is tempted to stop at narrative and plot, and to imagine that these – plus several lively characters – constitute all the form of which a novel is capable. *Novel* and *story* become nearly interchangeable, especially when the technique is superficially as simple and traditional as Jane Austen's.

Edgar F. Shannon Jr

EMMA: CHARACTER AND CONSTRUCTION (1956)

Emma, justly described by Lord David Cecil as 'Jane Austen's profoundest comedy',[1] has frequently been mistaken for mere 'escape literature'. It has been applauded for its 'engaging, dear, delicious, idiotic heroine', moving in 'a place of laughter and nonsense', and excoriated because 'it does not instruct . . . does not teach the modern reader . . . how to be and move in our world'. At the other extreme, it has lately provoked the sophisticated interpretation of Marvin Mudrick, who sees Emma as a disagreeable, even sinister, creature. A latent Lesbian, unwilling to commit her emotions, and devoid of tenderness, Emma, he believes, attains at the end of the novel simply 'relief and temporary awareness'. The transcendent irony of the book for Mudrick is the author's having shown an apparently reformed Emma, whereas actually she remains imperious and ruthless. Joseph M. Duffy, Jr, who describes the novel as concerned with 'the awakening of a normal, intelligent young woman to the possibilities of physical love', has produced the most apposite recent study. But knowledge of physical love is only one aspect of Emma's awakening, and even Duffy is uncertain whether she is truly regenerate.

In all her novels, Jane Austen is primarily a moral writer, striving to establish criteria of sound judgment and right conduct in human life. In *Emma* she presents her lessons so astutely and so dramatically, with such a minimum of exposition, that she places extreme demands upon the reader's perceptiveness. Yet, as the following study sets forth, analysis of Emma's enlightenment and of the rhythmic structure of the novel discloses a valid progression of the heroine from callowness to mental and emotional maturity – a development psychologically consistent and technically consonant.

For *Emma*, Jane Austen took a heroine whom, she remarked, 'no one but myself will much like'.[2] 'And', as one of her ablest critics has said, 'many a rash reader, and some who are not rash, have been shut out on the threshold of Emma's Comedy by a dislike of Emma herself.'[3] In the beginning, as every reader knows, she is spoiled and conceited. Events soon prove her to be domineering, willful, snobbish, and, at times, unfeeling. Until the end of the morning at Box Hill, which is the emotional climax of the book and the beginning of her regeneration, she has been guilty of much that is reprehensible in both thought and deed. She has induced Harriet Smith to refuse Robert Martin's proposal of marriage because of his low social status as a farmer and has directed Harriet's aspirations toward Mr Elton, the vicar. She has allowed Harriet a call of only fourteen minutes upon Martin's mother and sisters, whom Harriet had visited for six weeks the preceding summer. Emma has been ludicrously condescending toward the Coles. In her opinion of Miss Bates, expressed to Harriet, she has been brutally uncharitable (85).[4] And though she has had 'many a hint from Mr Knightley and some from her own heart', as to her dereliction in seldom calling on Miss Bates and her mother, these promptings have not been sufficient 'to counteract the persuasion of its being very disagreeable, – a waste of time–tiresome woman–and all the horror of being in danger of falling in with the second rate and third rate of Highbury' (155). She has imagined Frank Churchill to be in love with her, has coquetted with him extravagantly, and has led even Mr Knightley to believe her affections engaged. She has taken a dislike to Jane Fairfax, who should have been her natural friend and companion and, believing Jane to be the object of a married man's attentions, has repeated to Frank the slander she has concocted.

Mr Elton's unexpected proposal to herself instead of to Harriet brings Emma's first disenchantment. Her attempt to arrange a union between Harriet and Mr Elton, she realizes, 'was adventuring too far, assuming too much, making light of what ought to be serious, a trick of what ought to be simple. She was quite concerned and ashamed, and resolved to do such things no more' (137). But she has progressed towards reformation no farther than resolutions and in a few moments finds herself casting about for a successor to Mr Elton in her scheme for Harriet. She goes to bed convinced merely that she has blundered – an admission of intellectual, but not moral, error. And she abominates Mr Elton not so much for disappointing Harriet's expectations as for his presumption in aspiring to her own hand. The new day brings 'sensations of softened pain and brighter hope'; she gets up 'more disposed for comfort than she had gone to bed, more ready to see alleviations of the evil before her, and to depend on getting tolerably out of it' (138). Her complacence has been pricked, but the lesson has not been assimilated.

Nevertheless, the novelist has endowed Emma with good qualities and has provided firm basis in her character for eventual redemption. As Mr Knightley tells her when they are discussing their nieces and nephews, her nature is sound, and would lead her to clear judgments and right actions if her intelligence were not blinded by her imagination (98–9). Her self-assurance can be shaken by Mr Knightley's censure of her part in Harriet's refusal of Robert Martin (67); and she is discontented until she can re-establish herself in his good graces. Possessing both blooming health and a 'happy disposition' (1), she is also free from personal vanity (39). She is devoted to her father and dutifully ministers to the poor. With discerning verisimilitude Jane Austen does not portray these two traits as unalloyed. Emma's filial piety is tinged with a sense of security in being 'so truly beloved and important; so always first and always right' in her father's eyes (84), but her constant solicitousness toward a trying valetudinarian is distinctly a virtue – witness her arrangements for his happiness the night of the Coles's dinner (208, 213) and her staying behind at Donwell Abbey to go over 'books of engravings, drawers of medals, cameos, corals, shells', and other collections with him (362), when everyone else walks out-of-doors. And Mr Knightley speaks approvingly of 'your exertions for your father's sake' (426). Although her designs for Harriet can quickly divert her mind from philanthropy, she visits the cottages in an exemplary spirit of charity. Toward them, as toward her sister's children, she harbors none of the illusions that obscure her vision within her own set. 'Emma was very compassionate; and the distresses of the poor were as sure of relief from her personal attention and kindness, her counsel and her patience, as from her purse. She understood their ways, could allow for their ignorance and their temptations, had no romantic expectations of extraordinary virtue from those, for whom education had done so little; entered into their troubles with ready sympathy, and always gave her assistance with as much intelligence as good-will' (86).

Emma's attitude concerning Harriet's call at the Martins' furnishes an insight into her true character behind the wrong-headed façade. She knows that Harriet must respond to Elizabeth Martin's call and note of invitation (184), but she determines to manage the matter 'in a way that, if they [the Martins] had under-standing, should convince them that it was to be only a formal acquaintance. She meant to take her in the carriage, leave her at the Abbey Mill, while she drove a little farther, and call for her again so soon, as to allow no time for insidious applications or dangerous recurrences to the past, and give the most decided proof of what degree of intimacy was chosen for the future. She could think of nothing better: and though there was something in it which her own heart could not approve – something of ingratitude, merely glossed over – it must be done, or what would become of Harriet?' (185).

Thus even before the event Emma's heart, i.e. her feelings and conscience, cannot condone her plan. Its result proves un-expectedly disturbing. With Harriet back in the carriage, re-counting her conversation with the Martins, Emma, though attempting to justify her actions, perceives the misery she has caused. 'Emma could not but picture it all, and feel how justly they might resent, how naturally Harriet must suffer. It was a bad business. She would have given a great deal, or endured a great deal, to have the Martins in a higher rank of life. They were so deserving, that a *little* higher should have been enough: but as it was, how could she have done otherwise? – Impossible! – She could not repent. They must be separated; but there was a great deal of pain in the process . . .' (187).

Here, as after her instigation of Harriet's refusal of Robert Martin, Emma is not penitent – a fact that the author reiterates by using the same word, 'repent', that appears twice in the previous instance (65, 69). But Emma's reaction discloses sharp protest from her true inner self. Although not yet prepared to wish this latest deed undone and to mend her ways, she must seek at once the comforting and uncritical society of Mr and Mrs Weston: 'Her mind was quite sick of Mr Elton and the Martins. The refreshment of Randalls was absolutely necessary' (187). Her conscience is on the verge of requiring full assent to reality, and she is exasperated when the Westons' absence from home denies her the solace she requires.

Guilty of much past error, but with just instincts and growing awareness of the complexity of human relationships, Emma begins her transformation at Box Hill. After Mr Knightley's reproof of her cutting remark to Miss Bates, acknowledgment of her pride, both intellectual and social, overwhelms her. 'Never had she felt so agitated, mortified, grieved, at any circumstance in her life. She was most forcibly struck. The truth of his representation there was no denying. She felt it at her heart. How could she have been so brutal, so cruel to Miss Bates! – How could she have exposed herself to such ill opinion in any one she valued! And how suffer him to leave her without saying one word of gratitude, of concurrence, of common kindness! Time did not compose her. As she reflected more, she seemed but to feel it more. She never had been so depressed . . . and Emma felt the tears running down her cheeks all the way home, without being at any trouble to check them, extraordinary as they were' (376).

The tears, which mark the turning point of Emma's development, signify an emotional as well as a mental commitment to a new mode of conduct and to the necessity of Mr Knightley's approval. She at last recognizes that her intelligence, wealth, and social pre-eminence require kindness, rather than contempt, toward Miss Bates. She awakens to the obligations of her position. Miss Bates shall never again have cause to reproach her:

'She had been often remiss, her conscience told her so; remiss, perhaps, more in thought than fact; scornful, ungracious. But it should be so no more. In the warmth of true contrition, she would call upon her the very next morning, and it should be the beginning, on her side, of a regular, equal, kindly intercourse' (377). This time Emma acts instead of simply making resolutions soon to be forgotten; the morrow does not, as in the past, bring any alleviation of her suffering or any tendency to disparage her guilt. Not 'ashamed of the appearance of the penitence, so justly and truly hers' (377–8), she calls on Miss Bates early in the morning to make amends.

The author here explicitly tells the reader of Emma's whole-hearted change of attitude, illustrates it with action, and contrasts it with her former refusal to repent. Within the space of ten lines, the novelist refers both to Emma's 'true contrition' and to 'the penitence, so justly and truly hers'. The *NED* gives 'penitence for sin' as the meaning of 'contrition' in this sense, and 'repentance' as a synonym for 'penitence'. As Jane Austen's revered Dr Johnson declares, 'The completion and sum of repentance is a change of life'[5] – exactly what Emma has begun. Her coloring at her father's undeserved praise upon her return from Miss Bates's emphasizes this change (385), for previously she had been quite content to accept more credit for accomplishments at the piano and the easel than she knew to be her due (44). When Mr Knightley takes her hand and seems to be on the point of carrying it to his lips, she experiences 'great satisfaction' both because she is grateful for his mute commendation of her penitent act and because she is pleased by unusual gallantry from him (386). This gesture signals the beginning of tenderness between them.

The visit to Miss Bates produces further evidence of Emma's sincere alteration. 'Her heart had been long growing kinder towards Jane' (379); and after Miss Bates's account of her niece's ill health, Emma invites Jane to spend the day at Hartfield, to go for an airing in the Woodhouse carriage, and to accept, from the Hartfield stores, some fine arrowroot (389–91). When Jane refuses the invitations and returns the arrowroot, Emma learns that a few days of attention cannot compensate for several months of neglect; she understands that her former coolness merits the present rebuff (at this time Emma is, of course, unaware of Jane Fairfax's engagement to Frank Churchill and of the consequent element of jealousy in Jane's conduct). Yet she has 'the consolation of knowing that her intentions were good' (391).

Having thought and acted compassionately, Emma is ready for complete redemption, but trial and expiation are still necessary. The climax of the plot – the revelation, upon the death of Mrs Churchill, of Frank's engagement to Jane – sets the final ordeal in motion. Harriet's confession of her hopes concerning Mr Knightley explodes one of Emma's last misconceptions and impels her to recognize her own love for him. During this interview with Harriet, where, in order to spare Harriet additional pain, Emma seeks to conceal her agitation, the controlled voice and trembling frame betoken the depth of her newly discovered emotion (408–9). In the self-examination that follows, she admits her folly: 'With insufferable vanity had she believed herself in the secret of everybody's feelings; with unpardonable arrogance proposed to arrange everybody's destiny. She was proved to have been universally mistaken; and she had not quite done nothing – for she had done mischief. She had brought evil on Harriet, on herself, and she too much feared, on Mr Knightley' (412–13). She has finally absorbed the meaning of responsibility – that one must endure the consequences of one's acts; for now her own happiness is involved. It is the commencement of full awareness.

Ironically, Emma experiences the very fate that Mr Knightley, near the beginning of the novel, had cherished for her: 'I should like to see Emma in love, and in some doubt of a return' (41). She is not only in doubt of Mr Knightley's returning her love; she is virtually convinced that he loves Harriet instead. Emma, however, has progressed so far in comprehending pain and desiring to avoid giving it that, rather than hurt Mr Knightley, she is willing to submit to what she feels certain will be an announcement of his decision to marry Harriet: 'Emma could not bear to give him pain. He was wishing to confide in her – perhaps to consult her; – cost her what it would, she would listen' (429).

Appropriately, her wish to allay the distress she has caused Mr Knightley by prohibiting an explanation of why he envies Frank leads to his declaration of love for her.

Jane Austen is too serious and deft a novelist to abandon the development of Emma's character when this climax of the love story has been reached. She does not huddle her puppets back into the box and leave the rest to the reader's indulgence and credulity. Although it is clear that Emma and Mr Knightley will eventually marry, there are still for Emma three impediments to pure happiness: (1) her father's antipathy to marriage, (2) Harriet's disappointment and suffering, and (3) the necessity of concealing from Mr Knightley Harriet's hopes, which she herself had unwittingly fostered. Emma's atonement has yet to be concluded. Her care for her father's comfort brings on a melancholy, sleepless night of weeping and a belief that she cannot marry. She agonizes over Harriet and over the impossibility of being entirely ingenuous with Mr Knightley. In addition, at least three times before the end of the book, she must acknowledge and be ashamed of her calumniation of Jane Fairfax (380, 421, 477). With her own heart committed, Emma knows the pangs of love and appreciates fully the anguish Jane has endured. Although, when Emma calls, Mrs Elton's presence prevents complete expression of her sympathy in words, her 'very, very earnest' shake of Jane's hand upon arriving and her taking Jane's hand again as she departs convey the sincerity of her regard (453, 459).

No longer playing God, Emma, confused and humiliated, sees no way out of the predicament in which Mr Knightley's declaration has left her. The only scheme she allows herself – Harriet's visit to London – originates in charity and fortuitously results in Harriet's final happiness. Moreover, it is Mr Knightley's suggestion that he and Emma live at Hartfield, not, as Mudrick asserts, a condition to marriage set by Emma, which removes the obstacle of her father's comfort – 'such an alternative as this had not occurred to her' (449). Although she is relieved at the news of Harriet's engagement to Robert Martin, she gains almost as much satisfaction from the imminent end of secrecy toward Mr

Knightley as from Harriet's good fortune: 'The pain of being obliged to practise concealment towards him, was very little inferior to the pain of having made Harriet unhappy' (463).

Jane Austen's skill is patent. Emma's character develops and matures, perfectly within the credible limits of her nature as established at the outset and maintained throughout the novel. There is no sudden, unconvincing conversion, no 'flood of repentance' that may be expected soon to recede (Mudrick, p. 200). After the turning point of Emma's attitude and her genuine contrition following Box Hill, she undergoes an extended process of chastening and illumination before she attains redemption. (It is approximately four months – one third of the time span of the novel – from Box Hill to Emma's marriage at the end.) Yet the author, eschewing the temptation to overstate her theme, does not mar the portrait by converting Emma into a long-faced paragon. 'Serious she was, very serious in her thankfulness' that her past folly had not prevented both herself and Harriet from eventually attaining felicity and in 'her resolutions' of 'humility and circumspection in future' (475); but she has not lost her sense of humor. She can admit that if she had been Frank Churchill, she might have found 'some amusement' in 'taking us all in' (478) – and indeed how can anyone have failed to be entertained by Emma's deluded antics? She can give herself a 'saucy conscious smile' that she no longer feels any sense of injury to her nephew Henry as the expectant heir to Donwell Abbey, and finds 'amusement in detecting the real cause of that violent dislike of Mr Knightley's marrying Jane Fairfax, or anybody else, which at the time she had wholly imputed to the amiable solicitude of the sister and aunt' (449–50). She must laugh at Harriet's vagaries that have persuaded her she was in love with three men during the course of a few months (475).

This laugh at Harriet's expense is not a malicious one. It is a frank admission of Emma's former erroneous view of Harriet's attributes and claims to masculine attention. Yet it has been used to document Emma's supposedly unchanged, unfeeling contemptuousness (Mudrick, p. 189). True, it may be said, she is penitent, she has known pain, she has performed generous acts, she has achieved mental clarity, but after all, isn't she an un-regenerate snob?

In the other major novels, Jane Austen has portrayed her heroines as victims of snobbery. In *Emma*, she has undertaken the much more difficult task of incorporating and correcting snobbery within the character of the heroine herself. The author's abhorrence of the injustice and cruelty of snobbery in *Northanger Abbey*, *Sense and Sensibility*, *Pride and Prejudice*, *Mansfield Park*, and *Persuasion* should leave no uncertainty as to her intention in *Emma*; but muddled 'democratic' notions seem to have blinded some modern critics. Emma's entering upon 'a regular, equal, kindly intercourse' with Miss Bates heralds the purgation of her snobbish flaw; her revised attitude toward Harriet and Robert Martin evinces its completion. The judicious Mr Knightley, admired by all critics, is the yardstick against which Emma's conversion must be measured. No one accuses him of snobbery: Miss Elizabeth Jenkins declares that he is 'entirely free from it'; Miss G. B. Stern goes so far as to say that he 'has no class-consciousness whatsoever'.[6] But of Emma's assertion that it would be 'a degradation' for Harriet to marry Robert Martin, he exclaims, 'A degradation to illegitimacy and ignorance, to be married to a respectable, intelligent gentleman-farmer' (62) and warns Emma:

'You will puff her up with such ideas of her own beauty, and of what she has a claim to, that, in a little while, nobody within her reach will be good enough for her. Vanity working on a weak head, produces every sort of mischief. Nothing so easy as for a young lady to raise her expectations too high. Miss Harriet Smith may not find offers of marriage flow in so fast, though she is a very pretty girl. Men of sense, whatever you may chuse to say, do not want silly wives. Men of family would not be very fond of connecting themselves with a girl of such obscurity – and most prudent men would be afraid of the inconvenience and disgrace they might be involved in, when the mystery of her parentage came to be revealed.' (64)

Although Mr Knightley alters his opinion of Harriet somewhat, conceding that he finds her more intelligent and 'conversable' than he had at first supposed (331), his appraisal of her expectations represents the judgment of common sense, as Emma later confesses to herself. When she thinks she has encouraged Harriet's hopes toward Frank Churchill (though actually toward Mr Knightley), she realizes, 'Common sense would have directed her to tell Harriet, that she must not allow herself to think of him, and that there were five hundred chances to one against his ever caring for her. – "But with common sense," she added, "I have had little to do" ' (402). When Harriet turns out to be the offspring of neither family nor fortune, the last exposure of Emma's fantasy has occurred. 'Such was the blood of gentility which Emma had formerly been so ready to vouch for! – It was likely to be as untainted, perhaps, as the blood of many a gentleman; but what a connexion she had been preparing for Mr Knightley, or for the Churchills – or even for Mr Elton! The stain of illegitimacy, unbleached by nobility or wealth, would have been a stain indeed' (482). Taken by itself this quotation (which has several ironic implications) might conceivably be cited as evidence of Emma's (and Jane Austen's) residual snobbery, but in the context of the novel it reveals an acceptance of Mr Knightley's rational estimate. Nobility and wealth in Harriet's lineage represent figments of Emma's imagination proved false by sober fact. The statement is not a supercilious aspersion upon Harriet but Emma's final perception of the truth – that neither a Mr Knightley, a Frank Churchill, nor a Mr Elton (of any century) would, as she had fondly supposed, be inclined to marry an illegitimate girl of simple mind and unpropitious heritage.

Emma's opinion of Robert Martin sustains a similar, though opposite, reversal. Whereas formerly she held him as beneath her notice (29), 'a very inferior creature' (33), 'a completely gross, vulgar farmer' (33), by the close of the book, she can see he is an 'unexceptionable young man' (413). Now she assures Mr Knightley that in her previous objections to Martin, she 'was a fool' (474); now, 'It would be a great pleasure to know Robert Martin' (475). And when he is introduced at Hartfield 'she fully acknowledged in him all the appearance of sense and worth which could bid fairest for her little friend. She had no doubt of

Harriet's happiness with any good tempered man; but with him, and in the home he offered, there would be the hope of more, of security, stability, and improvement. She would be placed in the midst of those who loved her, and who had better sense than herself; retired enough for safety, and occupied enough for cheerfulness. She would be never led into temptation, nor left for it to find her out. She would be respectable and happy . . .' (482).

Through generosity toward Harriet and out of mistaken deference to what he believes to be Emma's wish, Mr Knightley says of Robert Martin, 'His rank in society I would alter if I could' (472). In a rigidly stratified society such a change is, of course, impossible. Still, by bringing Harriet into equilibrium with Robert Martin, Jane Austen has not been betrayed by the beliefs of her own time. In any age, differences of background, education, intelligence, force of character, and occupation create varying degrees of familiarity among people. Increasingly drawn as Harriet is by her engagement and marriage into a different circle from Emma's, the intimacy between them, unfortunate for both, as Mr Knightley foresaw, because it hindered Harriet's natural inclinations and nourished Emma's vanity, consequently subsides; but Emma has none of her prior illusions about ceasing to be acquainted with the wife of Robert Martin. There is now no disdain, no self-importance, no artificial barrier. Like Mr Knightley, sensibly aware of limitations in Harriet and Robert, but gladly avowing their estimable traits, Emma respects them for what they are. False values have been succeeded by genuine 'goodwill' (482).

Rhythm in a novel has been defined as 'repetition plus variation',[7] and Jane Austen unfolds the reorientation of Emma's character, just traced, by means of a rhythmic structure of situation and incident. Perhaps taking a cue from the accepted three-volume form of the novel of her time, her repetitions appear in sequence of three (an anagogic number) or a multiple of it. There are, for instance, six major social events, each of which is extremely important to the plot or to the steps in Emma's education – the Christmas party at Randalls, the dinner at the Coles's and

Emma's own dinner party, the ball at the Crown Inn, the day at Donwell Abbey, and the morning at Box Hill. The first occurs in volume one, the second two in volume two, and the last three in volume three, thus making a progression that sustains Duffy's reference to Emma's movement from the relative seclusion of Hartfield to an extensive involvement in society. The framework of the novel, however, does not actually depend upon such mechanical correspondence of repetition to the external divisions. As Duffy points out, Emma's three experiences with mutations of love – vicarious and unwanted with Mr Elton, flirtatious with Frank Churchill, and true with Mr Knightley – provide the basic tripartite structure. The business with Mr Elton culminates within volume one; but the flirtation with Frank Churchill, though Emma realizes in volume two that she is not in love with him, carries over well into volume three; and the avowed love of Mr Knightley occupies only a short portion of the last volume. The three climaxes, already alluded to, of emotion, plot, and story, in close sequence but expertly separated (chapters 7, 10, 13), take place in volume three. Hence the formal, superimposed upon the actual, structure of the novel creates a kind of counterpoint.

Three proposal scenes punctuate and symbolically enrich the significance of each of Emma's experiences with love. The novelist parallels increasing social activity with the advancing seasons conducive to it in a rural community; and when she employs the midsummer heat at Donwell Abbey and Box Hill in conjunction with the heightening emotional tension that reaches the breaking point in Emma's tears and the breach between Jane Fairfax and Frank Churchill, it is not fanciful to read overtones into the background of these proposals. On the evening of his declaration Mr Elton is described as 'spruce, black, and smiling' (114). Black appropriately describes his clerical attire, but the color seems to have an ominous connotation as well and to prepare for Emma's subsequent aversion. His insincere, fruitless proposal vents itself not only in the confined dark of the carriage but on a bleak, snowy December night. Darkness, coldness, and confinement reflect the unpropitiousness and, for Emma, the distastefulness of the incident. Frank Churchill's proposal, prevented only, as Emma thinks, by the arrival of his father (259–261), happens indoors in February, still the barren season; and its purely imaginary nature – not a proposal at all but the prelude to a confession of his engagement to Jane Fairfax – symbolizes the sterility of Emma's relationship with Frank. In manifest contrast to these two, and especially to Mr Elton's wine-bolstered plea, Mr Knightley discloses his love among the shrubbery of Hartfield in the slanting sunlight of a July evening.[8] Light, warmth, and spaciousness replace darkness, coldness, and confinement. The wind had 'changed into a softer quarter' (424) and the clouds had disappeared. Emma and Mr Knightley enjoy 'the exquisite sight, smell, sensation of nature, tranquil, warm, and brilliant after a storm' (424) – it is the understated equivalent of the fructifying natural surroundings that impel Tess and Angel Clare in Froom Vale. Mr Knightley's confession of deep love comes at the height of fertile summer, and the marriage is solemnized in October, the harvest time of year. (Three couples married in three successive months, August, September, and October, continue the triple pattern.) Emma's previous brief moments of physical contact with a man intensify the pitch of feeling during the promenade with Mr Knightley. When Mr Elton seized her hand in the carriage, she had been shocked and repelled; she had dwelt with pleasure upon Mr Knightley's taking her hand and almost raising it to his lips after her visit to Miss Bates. The author need not comment in the third instance to express Emma's sensation when she finds her arm drawn through Mr Knightley's and more than once pressed against his heart.

As to the meaning of the entire novel, the most telling use of repetition with variation involves Mr Knightley's proposal of marriage in another way. The evening of the day after Emma discovers Harriet's aspirations toward Mr Knightley

was very long, and melancholy at Hartfield. The weather added what it could of gloom. A cold stormy rain set in, and nothing of July appeared but in the trees and shrubs, which the wind was despoiling, and the length of the day, which only made such cruel sights the longer visible.

The weather affected Mr Woodhouse, and he could only be kept tolerably comfortable by almost ceaseless attention on his daughter's side, and by exertions which had never cost her half so much before. It reminded her of their first forlorn tête-à-tête, on the evening of Mrs Weston's wedding day; but Mr Knightley had walked in then, soon after tea, and dissipated every melancholy fancy. Alas! such delightful proofs of Hartfield's attraction, as those sort of visits conveyed, might shortly be over. (421–2)

The novelist specifically calls to mind the opening chapter of the book and invites comparison of Emma's present, though not absolute, awareness with her former state of illusion. Then she anticipated matchmaking with delight; now she sees bitterly the evils of her designs, 'and the only source whence any thing like consolation or composure could be drawn, was in the resolution of her own better conduct, and the hope that, however inferior in spirit and gaiety might be the following and every future winter of her life to the past, it would yet find her more rational, more acquainted with herself, and leave her less to regret when it were gone' (423). As on the former occasion, Mr Knightley, having just returned from London and having walked over from Donwell with direct news of Isabella's family in Brunswick Square, arrives to dispel the gloom, not, however, until the following evening and not as a friend but as a lover. When he and Emma join Mr Woodhouse indoors, their happiness is secure. 'They sat down to tea – the same party round the same table – how often it had been collected! – and how often had her eyes fallen on the same shrubs in the lawn, and observed the same beautiful effect of the western sun! – But never in such a state of spirits, never in anything like it . . .' (434). Besides the rhythm explicit in the passage itself, the western sun of the summer evening contrasts with the autumn moonlight night of the first chapter; and Emma, instead of being engrossed with her plans for others, can think of nothing but her own joy.

The third recurrence of this tableau – Mr Woodhouse, Emma, and Mr Knightley sitting together at Hartfield – after Emma has achieved full awareness, is only implied; but inevitably the three must gather at the tea table on an evening during the first week in November, when the Knightleys have returned from their two weeks' wedding journey. The author avoids the ineptness of depicting this scene at the end of the book – as much as to say, 'Look, here we are again, back where we started from, but with what a change in Emma!' Yet she provides for the thoughtful reader such a resolution of her work. In the three months since the evenings in July, Emma has completed her ordeal and penance. A marriage has recently taken place, but for Mr Woodhouse as well as for Emma such an event is no longer the melancholy one it was exactly a year before. And Emma's having declared then that she would never accept a husband ironically emphasizes the transformation she has undergone. Mr Knightley, who brings comfort to Mr Woodhouse and wisdom and contentment to his daughter is, as twice formerly, present; but this time he will not have to leave them at the end of the evening. Tranquillity has replaced the stress created by Emma's misguided opinions and willful behavior. It is an artistically satisfying and realistically acceptable conclusion.

Yet some critics dissent, protesting against Emma's and Mr Knightley's living with her father. Miss Stern, for example, exclaims, 'Oh, Miss Austen, it was *not* a good solution; it was a bad solution, an unhappy ending could we see beyond the last pages of the book' (p. 239). Jane Austen's retort is to put this very objection in the mouth of the egregious Mrs Elton, 'Shocking plan, living together. It would never do. She knew a family near Maple Grove who had tried it, and been obliged to separate before the end of the first quarter' (469). Pundits, who may not relish being classed with Mrs Elton, might have spared themselves embarrassment if they had recollected that the author foresaw the death of Mr Woodhouse in two years.[9] But no matter how long he lived, they could never have erred if they had fully understood *Emma*. There is nothing 'lightly satiric' about Jane Austen's assurance of the 'perfect happiness of the union' (484) between Emma and Mr Knightley. Not merely a 'prediction', it is an unequivocal statement of fact, to which a close reading of the novel compels assent (Duffy, p. 53).

Emma, as Reginald Farrer says, 'is *the* novel of character, and of character alone, and of one dominating character in particular'.[10] And it is imperative that we read that character aright. The book is Jane Austen's masterpiece because she has accomplished the hazardous feat of portraying and resolving disharmony deriving entirely from within the heroine herself. She has done so with such economy, with such consummate artistry, that the surface brilliance has obscured for many the emotional depth and moral significance of the novel. Hers is no world of nonsense, but a real world of intricate human relationships. Irony is the bright instrument with which she delights, stimulates, and enlightens the reader, but with which she has practised no ultimate deception. Far from having nothing worthwhile to say to modern men and women, through the discrepancy between appearance and reality she reminds us of human fallibility and the need for modesty, unselfishness, and compassion. She requires charity and forbearance toward the less gifted and fortunate than we. She shows the advisability of openness and sincerity, the evil of slander and of hastening to derogatory conclusions, the cruelty of inflicting mental pain, the falseness of snobbery. She demonstrates that we cannot escape the consequences of our acts, that love is not an emotion to be tampered with, and that marriage is not a game. Such truths she inculcates objectively through Emma's progress from self-deception and vanity to perception and humility.

NOTES

1. *Jane Austen* (Cambridge, 1935) p. 39. Subsequent quotations in the paragraph are from Sheila Kaye-Smith and G. B. Stern, *Speaking of Jane Austen* (New York and London, 1944) p. 263; E. N. Hayes, ' "Emma": A Dissenting Opinion', in *Nineteenth-century Fiction*, IV (June 1949) 20; Marvin Mudrick, *Jane Austen: Irony as Defense and Discovery* (Princeton, 1952) p. 200; and Duffy, 'Emma: The Awakening from Innocence', in *Journal of English Literary History*, XXI (March 1954) 40.

2. James Edward Austen-Leigh, *A Memoir of Jane Austen*, ed. R. W. Chapman (Oxford, 1926) p. 157.

3. Reginald Farrer, 'Jane Austen, *ob.* July 18, 1817', in *Quarterly Review*, CCXXVIII (July 1917) 24.

4. Parenthetical page references are to *Emma* in *The Novels of Jane Austen*, ed. R. W. Chapman, 3rd ed. (1948).

5. *Rambler*, no. 110.

6. *Jane Austen: A Biography* (1938) p. 254; *Speaking of Jane Austen*, p. 242.

7. E. M. Forster, *Aspects of the Novel* (1927) p. 240. For an expanded treatment, see E. K. Brown, *Rhythm in the Novel* (Toronto, 1950).

8. Duffy notes a 'no doubt coincidental' contrast between the black night of Mr Elton's proposal and the pleasant day of Mr Knightley's.

9. William and Richard Arthur Austen-Leigh, *Jane Austen: Her Life and Letters: A Family Record* (1913), p. 307.

10. *Quarterly Review*, CCXXVIII 24.

Lionel Trilling

EMMA AND THE LEGEND
OF JANE AUSTEN (1957)

I

IT is possible to say of Jane Austen, as perhaps we can say of no other writer, that the opinions which are held of her work are almost as interesting, and almost as important to think about, as the work itself. This statement, even with the qualifying 'almost', ought to be, on its face, an illegitimate one. We all know that the reader should come to the writer with no preconceptions, taking no account of any previous opinion. But this, of course, he cannot do. Every established writer exists in the aura of his legend – the accumulated opinion that we cannot help being aware of, the image of his personality that has been derived, correctly or incorrectly, from what he has written. In the case of Jane Austen, the legend is of an unusually compelling kind. Her very name is a charged one. The homely quaintness of the Christian name, the cool elegance of the surname, seem inevitably to force upon us the awareness of her sex, her celibacy, and her social class. 'Charlotte Brontë' rumbles like thunder and drowns out any such special considerations. But 'Jane Austen' can by now scarcely fail to imply femininity, and, at that, femininity of a particular kind and in a particular social setting. It dismays many new readers that certain of her admirers call her Jane, others Miss Austen. Either appellation suggests an unusual, and questionable, relation with this writer, a relation that does not consort with the literary emotions we respect. The new reader perceives from the first that he is not to be permitted to proceed in simple literary innocence. Jane Austen is to be for him not only a writer but an issue. There are those who love her; there are those – no doubt they are fewer but they are no less passionate – who detest her; and the new reader understands that he is being solicited to a fierce partisanship, that he is required to make no mere literary judgment but a decision about his own character and personality, and about his relation to society and all of life.

And indeed the nature of the partisanship is most intensely personal and social. The matter at issue is: What kind of people like Jane Austen? What kind of people dislike her? Sooner or later the characterization is made or implied by one side or the other, and with extreme invidiousness. It was inevitable that there should arise a third body of opinion, which holds that it is not Jane Austen herself who is to be held responsible for the faults that are attributed to her by her detractors, but rather the people who admire her for the wrong reasons and in the wrong language and thus create a false image of her. As far back as 1905 Henry James was repelled by what a more recent critic, Professor Marvin Mudrick, calls 'gentle-Janeism' and he spoke of it with great acerbity. James admired Jane Austen; his artistic affinity with her is clear, and he may be thought to have shared her social preferences and preoccupations. Yet James could say of her reputation that it had risen higher than her intrinsic interest warranted: the responsibility for this, he said, lay with 'the body of publishers, editors, illustrators, producers of magazines, which have found their "dear", our dear, everybody's dear Jane so infinitely to their material purpose'.[1] In our own day, Dr Leavis's admiration for Jane Austen is matched in intensity by his impatience with her admirers. Mr D. W. Harding in a well-known essay[2] has told us how the accepted form of admiration of Jane Austen kept him for a long time from reading her novels, and how he was able to be at ease with them only when he discovered that they were charged with scorn of the very people who set the common tone of admiration. And Professor Mudrick, in the preface to his book on Jane Austen,[3] speaks of the bulk of the criticism of her work as being 'a mere mass of cozy family adulation, self-glorif[ication] ... and nostalgic latterday enshrinements of the gentle-hearted chronicler of Regency order'. It is the intention of Professor Mudrick's book to rescue Jane Austen from coziness and nostalgia by representing her as a writer who may be admired for her literary achievement, but who is not to be loved, and of whom it is to be said that certain deficiencies of temperament account for certain deficiencies of her literary practice.

The impatience with the common admiring view of Jane Austen is not hard to understand and sympathize with, the less so because (as Mr Harding and Professor Mudrick say) admiration seems to stimulate self-congratulation in those who give it, and to carry a reproof of the deficient sensitivity, reasonableness, and even courtesy, of those who withhold their praise. One may refuse to like almost any author and incur no other blame from his admirers than that of being wanting in taste in that one respect. But not to like Jane Austen is to put oneself under suspicion of a general personal inadequacy and even – let us face it – of a want of breeding.

This is absurd and distasteful. And yet we cannot deal with this unusual – this extravagantly personal – response to a writer simply in the way of condemnation. No doubt every myth of a literary person obscures something of the truth. But it may also express some part of the truth as well. If Jane Austen is carried outside the proper confines of literature, if she has been loved in a fashion that some temperaments must find objectionable and that a strict criticism must call illicit, the reason is perhaps to be found not only in the human weakness of her admirers, in their impulse to self-flattery, or in whatever other fault produces their deplorable tone. Perhaps a reason is also to be found in the work itself, in some unusual promise that it seems to make, in some hope that it holds out.

II

Of Jane Austen's six great novels *Emma* is surely the one that is most fully representative of its author. *Pride and Prejudice* is of course more popular. It is the one novel in the canon that 'everybody' reads, the one that is most often reprinted. *Pride and Prejudice* deserves its popularity, but it is not a mere snobbery, an affected aversion from the general suffrage, that makes thoughtful readers of Jane Austen judge *Emma* to be the greater book – not the more delightful but the greater. It cannot boast the brilliant, unimpeded energy of *Pride and Prejudice*, but that is because the energy which it does indeed have is committed to dealing with a more resistant matter. In this it is characteristic of all three novels of Jane Austen's mature period, of which it is the second. *Persuasion*, the third and last, has a charm that is traditionally, and accurately, called 'autumnal', and it is beyond question a beautiful book. But *Persuasion*, which was published posthumously and which may not have been revised to meet the author's full intention, does not have the richness and substantiality of *Emma*. As for *Mansfield Park*, the first work of the mature period, it quite matches *Emma* in point of substantiality but it makes a special and disturbing case. Greatly admired in its own day – far more than *Emma* – *Mansfield Park* is now disliked by many readers who like everything else that Jane Austen wrote. They are repelled by its heroine and by all that she seems to imply of the author's moral and religious preferences at this moment of her life, for Fanny Price consciously devotes herself to virtue and piety, which she achieves by a willing submissiveness that goes against the modern grain. What is more, the author seems to be speaking out against wit and spiritedness (while not abating her ability to represent these qualities), and virtually in praise of dullness and acquiescence, and thus to be condemning her own peculiar talents. *Mansfield Park* is an extraordinary novel, and only Jane Austen could have achieved its profound and curious interest, but its moral tone is antipathetic to contemporary taste, and no essay I have ever written has met with so much resistance as the one in which I tried to say that it was not really a perverse and wicked book. But *Emma*, as richly complex as *Mansfield Park*, arouses no such antagonism, and the opinion that holds it to be the greatest of all Jane Austen's novels is, I believe, correct.

Professor Mudrick says that everyone has misunderstood *Emma*, and he may well be right, for *Emma* is a very difficult novel. We in our time are used to difficult books and like them. But *Emma* is more difficult than any of the hard books we admire. The difficulty of Proust arises from the sheer amount and complexity of his thought, the difficulty of Joyce from the

brilliantly contrived devices of representation, the difficulty of
Kafka from a combination of doctrine and mode of communication. With all, the difficulty is largely literal; it lessens in the
degree that we attend closely to what the books say; after each
sympathetic reading we are the less puzzled. But the difficulty of
Emma is never overcome. We never know where to have it. If
we finish it at night and think we know what it is up to, we wake
the next morning to believe it is up to something quite else; it
has become a different book. Reginald Farrer speaks at length
of the difficulty of *Emma* and then goes on to compare its effect
with that of *Pride and Prejudice*. 'While twelve readings of *Pride
and Prejudice* give you twelve periods of pleasure repeated, as
many readings of *Emma* give you that pleasure, not repeated
only, but squared and squared again with each perusal, till at
every fresh reading you feel anew that you never understood
anything like the widening sum of its delights.'[4] This is so, and
for the reason that none of the twelve readings permits us to
flatter ourselves that we have fully understood what the novel is
doing. The effect is extraordinary, perhaps unique. The book is
like a person – not to be comprehended fully and finally by any
other person. It is perhaps to the point that it is the only one of
Jane Austen's novels that has for its title a person's name.

For most people who recognize the difficulty of the book, the
trouble begins with Emma herself. Jane Austen was surely aware
of what a complexity she was creating in Emma, and no doubt
that is why she spoke of her as 'a heroine whom no one but
myself will much like'. Yet this puts it in a minimal way – the
question of whether we will like or not like Emma does not en-
compass the actuality of the challenge her character offers. John
Henry Newman stated the matter more accurately, and very
charmingly, in a letter of 1837. He says that Emma is the most
interesting of Jane Austen's heroines, and that he likes her. But
what is striking in his remark is this sentence: 'I feel kind to her
whenever I think of her.' This does indeed suggest the real
question about Emma, whether or not we will find it in our hearts
to be kind to her.

Inevitably we are attracted to her, we are drawn by her energy and style, and by the intelligence they generate. Here are some samples of her characteristic tone:

'Never mind, Harriet, I shall not be a poor old maid; it is poverty only which makes celibacy contemptible to a generous public!'

Emma was sorry; to have to pay civilities to a person she did not like through three long months! – to be always doing more than she wished and less than she ought!

'I do not know whether it ought to be so, but certainly silly things do cease to be silly if they are done by sensible people in an impudent way. Wickedness is always wickedness, but folly is not always folly.'

'Oh! I always deserve the best treatment, because I never put up with any other. . . .'

[On an occasion when Mr Knightley comes to a dinner party in his carriage, as Emma thinks he should, and not on foot:] '. . . There is always a look of consciousness or bustle when people come in a way which they know to be beneath them. You think you carry it off very well, I dare say, but with you it is a sort of bravado, an air of affected unconcern; I always observe it whenever I meet you under these circumstances. *Now* you have nothing to try for. You are not afraid of being supposed ashamed. You are not striving to look taller than any body else. *Now* I shall really be happy to walk into the same room with you.'

We cannot be slow to see what is the basis of this energy and style and intelligence. It is self-love. There is a great power of charm in self-love, although, to be sure, the charm is an ambiguous one. We resent it and resist it, yet we are drawn by it, if only it goes with a little grace or creative power. Nothing is easier to pardon than the mistakes and excesses of self-love: if we are quick to condemn them, we take pleasure in forgiving them. And with good reason, for they are the extravagance of the first of virtues, the most basic and biological of the virtues, that of self-preservation.

But we distinguish between our response to the self-love of men and the self-love of women. No woman could have won the forgiveness that has been so willingly given (after due condemnation) to the self-regard of, say, Yeats and Shaw. We understand self-love to be part of the moral life of all men; in men of genius we expect it to appear in unusual intensity and we take it to be an essential element of their power. The extraordinary thing about Emma is that she has a moral life as a man has a moral life. And she doesn't have it as a special instance, as an example of a new kind of woman, which is the way George Eliot's Dorothea Brooke has her moral life, but quite as a matter of course, as a given quality of her nature.

And perhaps that is what Jane Austen meant when she said that no one would like her heroine – and what Newman meant when he said that he felt kind to Emma whenever he thought of her. She needs kindness if she is to be accepted in all her exceptional actuality. Women in fiction only rarely have the peculiar reality of the moral life that self-love bestows. Most commonly they exist in a moonlike way, shining by the reflected moral light of men. They are 'convincing' or 'real' and sometimes 'delightful', but they seldom exist as men exist – as genuine moral destinies. We do not take note of this; we are so used to the reflected quality that we do not observe it. It is only on the rare occasions when a female character like Emma confronts us that the difference makes us aware of the usual practice. Nor can we say that novels are deficient in realism when they present women as they do: it is the presumption of our society that women's moral life is not as men's. No change in the modern theory of the sexes, no advance in status that women have made, has yet contradicted this. The self-love that we do countenance in women is of a limited and passive kind, and we are troubled if it is as assertive as the self-love of men is permitted, and expected, to be. Not men alone, but women as well, insist on this limitation, imposing the requirement the more effectually because they are not conscious of it.

But there is Emma, given over to self-love, wholly aware of it and quite cherishing it. Mr Knightley rebukes her for heedless conduct and says, 'I leave you to your own reflections.' And Emma wonderfully replies: 'Can you trust me with such flatterers? Does my vain spirit ever tell me I am wrong?' She is

'Emma, never loth to be first', loving pre-eminence and praise, loving power and frank to say so.

Inevitably we are drawn to Emma. But inevitably we hold her to be deeply at fault. Her self-love leads her to be a self-deceiver. She can be unkind. She is a dreadful snob.

Her snobbery is of the first importance in her character, and it is of a special sort. The worst instance of it is very carefully chosen to put her thoroughly in the wrong. We are on her side when she mocks Mrs Elton's vulgarity, even though we feel that so young a woman (Emma is twenty) ought not set so much store by manners and tone – Mrs Elton, with her everlasting barouche-landau and her '*caro sposo*' and her talk of her spiritual 'resources', is herself a snob in the old sense of the word, which meant a vulgar person aspiring to an inappropriate social standing. But when Emma presumes to look down on the young farmer, Robert Martin, and undertakes to keep little Harriet Smith from marrying him, she makes a truly serious mistake, a mistake of nothing less than national import.

Here it is to be observed that *Emma* is a novel that is touched – lightly but indubitably – by national feeling. Perhaps this is the result of the Prince Regent's having expressed his admiration for *Mansfield Park* and his willingness to have the author dedicate her next book to him:[5] it is a circumstance which allows us to suppose that Jane Austen thought of herself, at this point in her career, as having, by reason of the success of her art, a relation to the national ethic. At any rate, there appears in *Emma* a tendency to conceive of a specifically English ideal of life. Knightley speaks of Frank Churchill as falling short of the demands of this ideal: 'No, Emma, your amiable young man can be amiable only in French, not in English. He may be very "aimable", have very good manners, and be very agreeable; but he can have no English delicacy towards the feelings of other people: nothing really amiable about him.' Again, in a curiously impressive moment in the book, we are given a detailed description of the countryside as seen by the party at Donwell Abbey, and this comment follows: 'It was a sweet view – sweet to the eye and the mind. English verdure, English culture [agriculture, of course, is meant], English comfort, seen under a sun bright without being oppressive.' This is a larger consideration than the occasion would appear to require; there seems no reason to expect this vision of 'England's green and pleasant land'. Or none until we note that the description of the view closes thus: '. . . and at the bottom of this bank, favourably placed and sheltered, rose the Abbey-Mill Farm, with meadows in front, and the river making a close and handsome curve around it'. Abbey-Mill Farm is the property of young Robert Martin, for whom Emma has expressed a principled social contempt, and the little burst of strong feeling has the effect, among others, of pointing up the extremity of Emma's mistake.

It is often said, sometimes by way of reproach, that Jane Austen took no account in her novels of the great political events of her lifetime, nor of the great social changes that were going on in England. 'In Jane Austen's novels', says Arnold Hauser in his *Social History of Art*, 'social reality was the soil in which characters were rooted but in no sense a problem which the novelist made any attempt to solve or interpret.' The statement, true in some degree, goes too far. There is in *some* sense an interpretation of social problems in Jane Austen's contrivance of the situation of Emma and Robert Martin. The yeoman class had always held a strong position in English class feeling, and, at this time especially, only stupid or ignorant people felt privileged to look down upon it. Mr Knightley, whose social position is one of the certainties of the book, as is his freedom from any trace of snobbery, speaks of young Martin, who is his friend, as a 'gentleman farmer', and it is clear that he is on his way to being a gentleman pure and simple. And nothing was of greater importance to the English system at the time of the French Revolution than the relatively easy recruitment to the class of gentlemen. It made England unique among European nations. Here is Tocqueville's view of the matter as set forth in the course of his explanation of why England was not susceptible to revolution as France was:

It was not merely parliamentary government, freedom of speech, and the jury system that made England so different from the rest of contemporary Europe. There was something still more distinctive and more far-reaching in its effects. England was the only country in which the caste system had been totally abolished, not merely modified. Nobility and commoners joined forces in business enterprises, entered the same professions, and – what is still more significant – intermarried. The daughter of the greatest lord in the land could marry a 'new' man without the least compunction. . . .

Though this curious revolution (for such in fact it was) is hidden in the mists of time, we can detect traces of it in the English language. For several centuries the word 'gentleman' has had in England a quite different application from what it had when it originated. . . . A study of the connection between the history of language and history proper would certainly be revealing. Thus if we follow the mutation in time and place of the English word 'gentleman' (a derivative of our *gentilhomme*), we find its connotation being steadily widened in England as the classes draw nearer to each other and intermingle. In each successive century we find it being applied to men a little lower in the social scale. Next, with the English, it crosses to America. And now in America, it is applicable to all male citizens, indiscriminately. Thus its history is the history of democracy itself.[6]

Emma's snobbery, then, is nothing less than a contravention of the best – and safest – tendency of English social life. And to make matters worse, it is a principled snobbery. 'A young farmer . . . is the very last sort of person to raise my curiosity. The yeomanry are precisely the order of people with whom I feel that I can have nothing to do. A degree or two lower, and a creditable appearance might interest me; I might hope to be useful to their families in some way or other. But a farmer can need none of my help, and is therefore in one sense as much above my notice as in every other he is below it.' This is carefully contrived by the author to seem as dreadful as possible; it quite staggers us, and some readers will even feel that the author goes too far in permitting Emma to make this speech.

Snobbery is the grossest fault that arises from Emma's self-love, but it is not the only fault. We must also take account of her capacity for unkindness. This can be impulsive and brutal, as in the witticism directed to Miss Bates at the picnic, which makes one of the most memorable scenes in the whole range of English fiction; or extended and systematic, as in her conspiracy with Frank Churchill to quiz Jane Fairfax. Then we know her to be a gossip, at least when she is tempted by Frank Churchill. She finds pleasure in dominating and has no compunctions about taking over the rule of Harriet Smith's life. She has been accused, on the ground of her own estimate of herself, of a want of tenderness, and she has even been said to be without sexual responsiveness.

Why, then, should anyone be kind to Emma? There are several reasons, of which one is that we come into an unusual intimacy with her. We see her in all the elaborateness of her mistakes, in all the details of her wrong conduct. The narrative technique of the novel brings us very close to her and makes us aware of each misstep she will make. The relation that develops between ourselves and her becomes a strange one – it is the relation that exists between our ideal self and our ordinary fallible self. We become Emma's helpless conscience, her un-availing guide. Her fault is the classic one of *hubris*, excessive pride, and it yields the classic result of blindness, of an inability to interpret experience to the end of perceiving reality, and we are aware of each false step, each wrong conclusion, that she will make. Our hand goes out to hold her back and set her straight, and we are distressed that it cannot reach her.

There is an intimacy anterior to this. We come close to Emma because, in a strange way, she permits us to – even invites us to – by being close to herself. When we have said that her fault is *hubris* or self-love, we must make an immediate modification, for her self-love, though it involves her in self-deception, does not lead her to the ultimate self-deception – she believes she is clever, she insists she is right, but she never says she is good. A con-sciousness is always at work in her, a sense of what she ought to be and do. It is not an infallible sense, anything but that, yet she does not need us, or the author, or Mr Knightley, to tell her, for example, that she is jealous of Jane Fairfax and acts badly to her; indeed, 'she never saw [Jane Fairfax] without feeling that she had injured her'. She is never offended – she never takes the high self-defensive line – when once her bad conduct is made apparent to her. Her sense of her superiority leads her to the 'insufferable vanity' of believing 'herself in the secret of everybody's feelings' and to the 'unpardonable arrogance' of 'proposing to arrange everybody's destiny', yet it is an innocent vanity and an innocent arrogance which, when frustrated and exposed, do not make her bitter, but only ashamed. That is why, bad as her behavior may be, we are willing to be implicated in it. It has been thought that in the portrait of Emma there is 'an air of confession', that Jane Austen was taking account of 'something offensive' that she and others had observed in her own earlier manner and conduct, and whether or not this is so, it suggests the quality of intimacy which the author contrives that we shall feel with the heroine.

Then, when we try to explain our feeling of kindness to Emma, we ought to remember that many of her wrong judgments and actions are directed to a very engaging end, a very right purpose. She believes in her own distinction and vividness and she wants all around her to be distinguished and vivid. It is indeed unpardonable arrogance, as she comes to see, that she should undertake to arrange Harriet Smith's destiny, that she plans to 'form' Harriet, making her, as it were, the mere material or stuff of a creative act. Yet the destiny is not meanly conceived, the act is meant to be truly creative – she wants Harriet to be a distinguished and not a commonplace person, she wants nothing to be commonplace, she requires of life that it be well shaped and impressive, and alive. It is out of her insistence that the members of the picnic shall cease being dull and begin to be witty that there comes her famous insult to Miss Bates. Her requirement that life be vivid is too often expressed in terms of social deportment – she sometimes talks like a governess or a dowager – but it is, in its essence, a poet's demand.

She herself says that she lacks tenderness, although she makes the self-accusation in her odd belief that Harriet possesses this quality; Harriet is soft and 'feminine', but she is not tender. Professor Mudrick associates the deficiency with Emma's being not susceptible to men. This is perhaps so; but if it is, there may be found in her apparent sexual coolness something that is impressive and right. She makes great play about the feelings and about the fineness of the feelings that one ought to have; she sets great store by literature (although she does not read the books she prescribes for herself) and makes it a condemnation of Robert Martin that he does not read novels. Yet although, like Don Quixote and Emma Bovary, her mind is shaped and deceived by fiction, she is remarkable for the actuality and truth of her sexual feelings. Inevitably she expects that Frank Churchill will fall in love with her and she with him, but others are more deceived in the outcome of this expectation than she is – it takes but little time for her to see that she does not really respond to Churchill, that her feeling for him is no more than the lively notice that an attractive and vivacious girl takes of an attractive vivacious young man. Sentimental sexuality is not part of her nature, however much she feels it ought to be part of Harriet Smith's nature. When the right time comes, she chooses her husband wisely and seriously and eagerly.

There is, then, sufficient reason to be kind to Emma, and perhaps for nothing so much as the hope she expresses when she begins to understand her mistakes, that she will become 'more acquainted with herself'. And, indeed, all through the novel she has sought better acquaintance with herself, not wisely, not adequately, but assiduously. How modern a quest it is, and how thoroughly it confirms Dr Leavis's judgment that Jane Austen is the first truly modern novelist of England. 'In art,' a critic has said, 'the decision to be revolutionary usually counts for very little. The most radical changes have come from personalities who were conservative and even conventional . . .'[7] Jane Austen, conservative and even conventional as she was, perceived the nature of the deep psychological change which accompanied the establishment of democratic society – she was aware of the increase of the psychological burden of the individual, she understood the new necessity of conscious self-definition and self-criticism, the need to make private judgments of reality.[8] And there is no reality about which the modern person is more uncertain and more anxious than the reality of himself.

III

But the character of Emma is not the only reason for the difficulty of the novel. We must also take into account the particular genre to which the novel in some degree belongs – the pastoral idyll. It is an archaic genre which has the effect of emphasizing by contrast the brilliant modernity of Emma, and its nature may be understood through the characters of Mr Woodhouse and Miss Bates.

These two people proved a stumbling-block to one of Jane Austen's most distinguished and devoted admirers, Sir Walter Scott. In his review of *Emma* in the *Quarterly Review*, Scott said that 'characters of folly and simplicity, such as old Woodhouse and Miss Bates' are 'apt to become tiresome in fiction as in real society'. But Scott is wrong. Mr Woodhouse and Miss Bates are remarkably interesting, even though they have been created on a system of character portrayal that is no longer supposed to have validity – they exist by reason of a single trait which they display whenever they appear. Miss Bates is possessed of continuous speech and of a perfectly free association of ideas which is quite beyond her control; once launched into utterance, it is impossible for her to stop. Mr Woodhouse, Emma's father, has no other purpose in life than to preserve his health and equanimity, and no other subject of conversation than the means of doing so. The commonest circumstances of life present themselves to him as dangerous – to walk or to drive is to incur unwarrantable risk, to eat an egg not coddled in the prescribed way is to invite misery; nothing must ever change in his familial situation; he is appalled by the propensity of young people to marry, and to marry *strangers* at that.

Of the two 'characters of folly and simplicity', Mr Woodhouse is the more remarkable because he so entirely, so extravagantly, embodies a principle – of perfect stasis, of entire inertia. Almost in the degree that Jane Austen was interested in the ideal of personal energy, she was amused and attracted by persons

F

capable of extreme inertness. She does not judge them harshly, as we incline to do – we who scarcely recall how important a part in Christian feeling the dream of *rest* once had. Mr Woodhouse is a more extreme representation of inertness than Lady Bertram of *Mansfield Park*. To say that he represents a denial of life would not be correct. Indeed, by his fear and his movelessness, he affirms life and announces his naked unadorned wish to avoid death and harm. To life, to mere life, he sacrifices almost everything.

But if Mr Woodhouse has a more speculative interest than Miss Bates, there is not much to choose between their achieved actuality as fictional characters. They are, as I have said, created on a system of character portrayal that we regard as primitive, but the reality of existence which fictional characters may claim does not depend only upon what they do, but also upon what others do to or about them, upon the way they are regarded and responded to. And in the community of Highbury, Miss Bates and Mr Woodhouse are sacred. They are fools, to be sure, as everyone knows. But they are fools of a special and transcendent kind. They are innocents – of such is the kingdom of heaven. They are children, who have learned nothing of the guile of the world. And their mode of existence is the key to the nature of the world of Highbury, which is the world of the pastoral idyll. London is but sixteen miles away – Frank Churchill can ride there and back for a haircut – but the proximity of the life of London serves but to emphasize the spiritual geography of Highbury. The weather plays a great part in *Emma*; in no other novel of Jane Austen's is the succession of the seasons, and cold and heat, of such consequence, as if to make the point which the pastoral idyll characteristically makes, that the only hardships that man ought to have to endure are meteorological. In the Forest of Arden we suffer only 'the penalty of Adam, / The seasons' difference', and Amiens' song echoes the Duke's words:

> Here shall he see
> No enemy
> But winter and rough weather.

Some explicit thought of the pastoral idyll is in Jane Austen's mind, and with all the ambivalence that marks the attitude of *As You Like It* toward the dream of man's life in nature and simplicity. Mrs Elton wants to make the strawberry party at Donwell Abbey into a *fête champêtre*: 'It is to be a morning scheme, you know, Knightley; quite a simple thing. I shall wear a large bonnet, and bring one of my little baskets hanging on my arm. Here, – probably this basket with pink ribbon. Nothing can be more simple, you see. And Jane will have such another. There is to be no form or parade – a sort of gipsy party. – We are to walk about your gardens, and gather the strawberries ourselves, and sit under trees; – and whatever else you may like to provide, it is to be all out of doors – a table spread in the shade, you know. Every thing as natural and simple as possible. Is not that your idea?' To which Knightley replies: 'Not quite. My idea of the simple and natural will be to have the table spread in the dining-room. The nature and the simplicity of gentlemen and ladies, with their servants and furniture, I think is best observed by meals within doors. When you are tired of eating strawberries in the garden, there will be cold meat in the house.'

That the pastoral idyll should be mocked as a sentimentality by its association with Mrs Elton, whose vulgarity in large part consists in flaunting the cheapened version of high and delicate ideals, and that Knightley should answer her as he does – this is quite in accordance with our expectation of Jane Austen's judgment. Yet it is only a few pages later that the members of the party walk out to see the view and we get that curious passage about the sweetness of the view, 'sweet to the eye and to the mind'. And we cannot help feeling that 'English verdure, English culture, English comfort, seen under a sun bright without being oppressive' make an England seen – if but for the moment – as an idyll.

The idyll is not a genre which nowadays we are likely to understand. Or at least not in fiction, the art which we believe must always address itself to actuality. The imagination of felicity is difficult for us to exercise. We feel that it is a betrayal of our awareness of our world of pain, that it is politically inappropriate.

And yet one considerable critic of literature thought otherwise. Schiller is not exactly of our time, yet he is remarkably close to us in many ways and he inhabited a world scarcely less painful than ours, and he thought that the genre of the idyll had an important bearing upon social and political ideas. As Schiller defines it, the idyll is the literary genre that 'presents the idea and description of an innocent and happy humanity'.[9] This implies remoteness from the 'artificial refinements of fashionable society'; and to achieve this remoteness poets have commonly set their idylls in actually pastoral surroundings and in the infancy of humanity. But the limitation is merely accidental – these circumstances 'do not form the object of the idyll, but are only to be regarded as the most natural means to attain this end. The end is essentially to portray man in a state of innocence, which means a state of harmony and peace with himself and the external world.' And Schiller goes on to assert the political importance of the genre: 'A state such as this is not merely met with before the dawn of civilization; it is also the state to which civilization aspires, as to its last end, if only it obeys a determined tendency in its progress. The idea of a similar state, and the belief in the possible reality of this state, is the only thing that can reconcile man with all the evils to which he is exposed in the path of civilization. . . .'

It is the poet's function – Schiller makes it virtually the poet's political duty – to represent the idea of innocence in a 'sensuous' way, that is, to make it seem real. This he does by gathering up the elements of actual life that do partake of innocence, and that the predominant pain of life leads us to forget, and forming them into a coherent representation of the ideal.[10]

But the idyll as traditionally conceived has an aesthetic deficiency of which Schiller is quite aware. Works in this genre, he says, appeal to the heart but not to the mind. 'We can only seek them and love them in moments in which we need calm, and not when our faculties aspire after movement and exercise. A morbid mind will find its *cure* in them, a sound soul will not find its *food* in them. They cannot vivify, they can only soften.' For the idyll excludes the idea of activity, which alone can satisfy the mind – or at least the idyll as it has been traditionally conceived makes this exclusion, but Schiller goes on to imagine a transmutation of the genre in which the characteristic calm of the idyll shall be 'the calm that follows accomplishment, not the calm of indolence – the calm that comes from the equilibrium re-established between the faculties and not from the suspending of their exercise.'

It is strange that Schiller, as he projects this new and as yet unrealized idea, does not recur to what he has previously said about comedy. To the soul of the writer of tragedy he assigns the adjective 'sublime', which for him implies reaching greatness by intense effort and strength of will; to the soul of the writer of comedy he assigns the adjective 'beautiful', which implies the achievement of freedom by an activity which is easy and natural. 'The noble task of comedy', he says, 'is to produce and keep up in us this freedom of mind.' Comedy and the idyll, then, would seem to have a natural affinity with each other. Schiller does not observe this, but Shakespeare knew it – the curious power and charm of *As You Like It* consists of bringing the idyll and comedy together, of making the idyll the subject of comedy, even of satire, yet without negating it. The mind teases the heart, but does not mock it. The unconditioned freedom that the idyll hypothecates is shown to be impossible, yet in the demonstration a measure of freedom is gained.

So in *Emma* Jane Austen contrives an idyllic world, or the closest approximation of an idyllic world that the genre of the novel will permit, and brings into contrast with it the actualities of the social world, of the modern self. In the precincts of Highbury there are no bad people, and no adverse judgments to be made. Only a modern critic, Professor Mudrick, would think to call Mr Woodhouse an idiot and an old woman: in the novel he is called 'the kindhearted, polite old gentleman'. Only Emma, with her modern consciousness, comes out with it that Miss Bates is a bore, and only Emma can give herself to the thought that Mr Weston is *too* simple and openhearted, that he would be a 'higher character' if he were not quite so friendly with everyone. It is from outside Highbury that the peculiarly modern traits of insincerity and vulgarity come, in the person of Frank Churchill

and Mrs Elton. With the exception of Emma herself, every person
in Highbury lives in harmony and peace – even Mr Elton would
have been all right if Emma had let him alone! – and not merely
because they are simple and undeveloped: Mr Knightley and
Mrs Weston are no less innocent than Mr Woodhouse and Miss
Bates. If they please us and do not bore us by a perfection of
manner and feeling which is at once lofty and homely, it is
because we accept the assumptions of the idyllic world which
they inhabit – we have been led to believe that man may actually
live 'in harmony and peace with himself and the external world'.

The quiet of Highbury, the unperturbed spirits of Mr Woodhouse and Miss Bates, the instructive perfection of Mr Knightley
and Mrs Weston, constitute much of the charm of *Emma*. Yet
the idyllic stillness of the scene and the loving celebration of
what, for better or worse, is fully formed and changeless, is of
course not what is decisive in the success of the novel. On the
contrary, indeed: it is the idea of activity and development that is
decisive. No one has put better and more eloquently what part
this idea plays in Jane Austen's work than an anonymous critic
writing in the *North British Review* in 1870:[11]

Even as a unit, man is only known to [Jane Austen] in the process
of his formation by social influences. She broods over his history,
not over his individual soul and its secret workings, nor over the
analysis of its faculties and organs. She sees him, not as a solitary
being completed in himself, but only as completed in society.
Again, she contemplates virtues, not as fixed quantities, or as
definable qualities, but as continual struggles and conquests, as
progressive states of mind, advancing by repulsing their con-
traries, or losing ground by being overcome. Hence again the
individual mind can only be represented by her as a battle-field
where contending hosts are marshalled, and where victory
inclines now to one side and now to another. A character therefore unfolded itself to her, not in statuesque repose, not as a
model without motion, but as a dramatic sketch, a living history,
a composite force, which could only exhibit what it was by
exhibiting what it did. Her favourite poet Cowper taught her,

'By ceaseless action all that is subsists.'

The mind as a battlefield: it does not consort with some of the views of Jane Austen that are commonly held. Yet this is indeed how she understood the mind. And her representation of battle is the truer because she could imagine the possibility of victory – she did not shrink from the idea of victory – and because she could represent harmony and peace.

The anonymous critic of the *North British Review* goes on to say a strange and startling thing – he says that the mind of Jane Austen was 'saturated' with a 'Platonic idea'. In speaking of her ideal of 'intelligent love' – the phrase is perfect – he says that it is based on the 'Platonic idea that the giving and receiving of knowledge, the active formation of another's character, or the more passive growth under another's guidance, is the truest and strongest foundation of love'.[12] It is an ideal that not all of us will think possible of realization and that some of us will not want to give even a theoretical assent to. Yet most of us will consent to think of it as one of the most attractive of the idyllic elements of the novel. It proposes to us the hope of victory in the battle that the mind must wage, and it speaks of the expectation of allies in the fight, of the possibility of community – not in actuality, not now, but perhaps again in the future, for do we not believe, or almost believe, that there was community in the past?

The impulse to believe that the world of Jane Austen really did exist leads to notable error. 'Jane Austen's England' is the thoughtless phrase which is often made to stand for the England of the years in which our author lived, although any serious history will make it sufficiently clear that the England of her novels was not the real England, except as it gave her the license to imagine the England which we call hers. This England, especially as it is represented in *Emma*, is an idyll. The error of identifying it with the actual England ought always to be remarked. Yet the same sense of actuality that corrects the error should not fail to recognize the remarkable force of the ideal that leads many to make the error. To represent the possibility of controlling the personal life, of becoming acquainted with ourselves, of creating a community of 'intelligent love' – this is indeed to make an extraordinary promise and to hold out a rare hope. We ought not be shocked and repelled if some among us think there really was a time when such promises and hopes were realized. Nor ought we be entirely surprised if, when they speak of the person who makes such promises and holds out such hopes, they represent her as not merely a novelist, if they find it natural to deal with her as a figure of legend and myth.

NOTES

1. *The Question of Our Speech; The Lesson of Balzac: Two Lectures* (Boston, New York and London, 1905).

2. 'Regulated Hatred: An Aspect of the Work of Jane Austen', *Scrutiny* VIII (March 1940); [reprinted in part in this volume, pp. 69–74].

3. *Jane Austen: Irony as Defense and Discovery* (Princeton, 1952).

4. 'Jane Austen', in *Quarterly Review*, CCXXVIII (July 1917).

5. [Editor's Note. This is doubtful, as Jane Austen finished *Emma* on 29 March 1815, and did not learn of the Regent's interest in her work until the autumn of that year. See R. W. Chapman, *Facts and Problems* (Oxford, 1948) pp. 81 and 138.]

6. Alexis de Tocqueville, *The Old Régime and the French Revolution* (Anchor ed. 1955) pp. 82–3. Tocqueville should not be understood as saying that there was no class system in England but only that there was no caste system, caste differing from class in its far greater rigidity. In his sense of the great advantage that England enjoyed, as compared with France, in having no caste system, Tocqueville inclines to represent the class feelings of the English as being considerably more lenient than in fact they were. Still, the difference between caste and class and the social and political importance of the 'gentleman' are as great as Tocqueville says.

7. Harold Rosenberg, 'Revolution and the Idea of Beauty', in *Encounter*, Dec 1953.

8. See Abram Kardiner, *The Psychological Frontiers of Society* (New York and London, 1945) p. 410. In commenting on the relatively simple society which is described in James West's *Plainville, U.S.A.*, Dr Kardiner touches on a matter which is dear, and all too dear, to Emma's heart – speaking of social mobility in a democratic, but not classless, society, he says that the most important criterion of class is 'manners', that 'knowing how to behave' is the surest means of rising in the class hierarchy. Nothing is more indicative of Jane Austen's accurate awareness of the mobility of her society than her concern not so much with manners themselves as with her characters' concern with manners.

9. 'On Simple and Sentimental Poetry', in *Essays Aesthetical and Philosophical* (1875).

10. Schiller, in speaking of the effectiveness that the idyll should have, does not refer to the pastoral-idyllic element of Christianity which represents Christ as an actual shepherd.

11. Vol. XXCII (April) 129–52. I am grateful to Professor Joseph Duffy for having told me of this admirable study. [Editor's note. The anonymous critic has been identified as Richard Simpson. Extracts from his article are given on p. 52–7.]

12. Emma's attempt to form the character of Harriet is thus a perversion of the relation of Mrs Weston and Mr Knightley to herself – it is a perversion, says the *North British* critic, adducing Dante's '*amoroso uso de sapienza*', because it is without love.

Mark Schorer

THE HUMILIATION
OF EMMA WOODHOUSE (1959)

JANE AUSTEN'S *Emma*, 1816, stands at the head of her achievements, and, even though she herself spoke of Emma as 'a heroine
whom no one but myself will much like', discriminating readers
have thought the novel her greatest. Her powers here are at their
fullest, her control at its most certain. As with most of her novels,
it has a double theme, but in no other has the structure been
raised so skillfully upon it. The novel might have been called
Pride and Perception, or *Perception and Self-Deception*, for the
comedy is concerned with a heroine who must be educated out of
a condition of self-deception brought on by the shutters of pride
into a condition of perception when that pride had been humbled
through the exposure of the errors of judgment into which it has
led her. No novel shows more clearly Jane Austen's power to
take the moral measurement of the society with which she was
concerned through the range of her characters.

Morality in the novel lies not in spread but in scale, in the
discrimination of values on scale and the proportion that is held
between values within scale. In *Emma*, the word *scale* has a
special meaning, for its subject is a fixed social scale in need of
measurement by moral scale. As the social scale is represented by
the scene as a whole, by all the characters, so the chief characters
establish, in addition, the moral scale. The story is the progress
of the heroine on this second scale toward her position on
the first. *Emma* gives us the picture of an externally balanced
society which the novel itself readjusts, or puts in perspective,
through the internal balance that is the root of moral, not social,
judgment.

Can we permit the notion that Jane Austen is capable of making moral judgment on that social world which she herself accepts

and from which her novels emerge? I have argued elsewhere that our surest way of knowing the values out of which a novel comes lies in an examination of style, more particularly, of metaphor. Jane Austen's style is, of course, remarkably nonmetaphorical, if we are thinking of explicit metaphor, the stated analogy, but it is no less remarkable in the persistency with which the buried or dead metaphors in her prose imply one consistent set of values. These are the values of commerce and property, of the counting house and the inherited estate. I will divide this set of values rather arbitrarily into five categories. First of all, of *scale* itself, all that metaphor of high and low, sink and rise, advance and decline, superior and inferior, rank and fortune, power and command; as 'held below the level', 'raise her expectations too high', 'materially cast down', 'the intimacy between her and Emma must sink'. Second, of *money*: credit, value, interest, rate, reserve, secure, change and exchange, alloy, resources, gain, want, collect (for 'assume'), reckon, render, account, claim, profit, loss, accrue, tax, due, pay, lose, spend, waste, fluctuate, dispense, 'precious deposit', appropriate, commission, safety. Third, of *business and property*: inherit, certify, procure, solicit, entitle, business, venture, scheme, arrangement, insure, cut off, trust, charge, stock. Fourth, of *number and measure*: add, divide, multiply, calculate, how much and how little, more and less. And fifth, of *matter*: incumbrance, weight, substance, material (as, material change, or material alteration), comfort.

These terms are constantly appearing, both singly and in clusters. One or two illustrations must suffice:

She listened, and found it well *worth* listening to. That very *dear* part of Emma, her fancy, *received* an amusing *supply* . . . it became henceforth her *prime object of interest*; and during the ten days of their stay at Hartfield it was not to be expected – she did not herself expect – that anything beyond occasional fortuitous assistance could be *afforded by her* to the lovers. They *might advance* rapidly if they would, however; they *must advance* somehow or other, whether they would or no. She hardly wished to have more leisure for them. They are people, who *the more you do* for them, *the less they will do* for themselves. Mr and Mrs John

Knightley . . . were exciting, of course, rather *more than the usual interest*. Till this year, every long vacation since their marriage had been *divided* between Hartfield and Donwell Abbey.

This language, as a functioning element in the novel, begins to call attention to itself when we discover it in clusters where moral and material values are either juxtaposed or equated: 'no material injury *accrued* either to body or mind'; 'glad to have *purchased* the mortification of having loved'; 'except in a moral light, as a penance, a lesson, a source of *profitable humiliation* to her own mind, she would have been thankful to be *assured* of never seeing him again . . . his welfare twenty miles off would *administer* most satisfaction'.

It would seem that we are in a world of peculiarly *material* value, a world of almost instinctive material interests in its basic, intuitive response to experience. The style has created a texture, the 'special feel' of that world. At the same time, on the surface of the action, this is usually a world of refined sensibility, of concern with moral propriety, and in Emma's case, presumably at least, of intelligent clarity of evaluation. A large portion of Jane Austen's comedy arises from the discrepancy that we see here, from the tension between these two kinds of value, these different *scales*, material and moral, which the characters, like the metaphors, are all the time juxtaposing and equating. But when we say that, we have moved from considerations of language alone, into the function of the language in the whole.

How do we transfer ourselves from one to the other? Notice, first of all, that in some very impressive details, the implicit stylistic values erupt every now and then into explicit evaluation in the action, explicit of evaluations that are, of course, ironical illuminations of the characters in their special situations. 'You were very popular before you came, because you were Mr Weston's son; but lay out half a guinea at Ford's, and your popularity will stand upon your own virtues.'

'No – I cannot call them gifts; but they are things that I have valued very much.'

She held the parcel towards her, and Emma read the words *Most Precious treasures* on the top.

Emma's charity: 'Emma was very compassionate; and the distress of the poor were as sure of relief from her personal attention and kindness, her counsel and her patience, as from her purse.'

Emma's judgment of Mr Martin:

'. . . He will be a completely gross, vulgar farmer, totally inattentive to appearances, and thinking of nothing but profit and loss.'

'Will he, indeed? That will be very bad.'

'How much his business engrosses him already, is very plain from the circumstance of his forgetting to inquire for the book you recommended. He was a great deal too full of the market to think of anything else – which is just as it should be, for a thriving man. What has he to do with books? And I have no doubt that he *will* thrive, and be a very rich man in time; and his being illiterate and coarse need not disturb *us*.'

Most impressive, because most central to the theme of the book, this passage:

Emma perceived that her taste was not the only taste on which Mr Weston depended, and felt that to be the favourite and intimate of a man who had so many intimates and confidantes, was not *the very first distinction in the scale of vanity*. She liked his open manners, but a little less of openheartedness would have made him a higher character.

We may summarize this much as follows:

(1) The language itself defines for us, and defines most clearly, that area of available experience and value from which this novel takes its rise, and on which the novel itself must place the seal of its value. The texture of the style itself announces, therefore, the subject, and warns us, suggesting that we not be deceived by the fine sentiments and the moral scruples of the surface; that this is a material world where property and rank are major and probably as important as 'characters'. More specifically, that this is not simply a novel of courtship and marriage, but a novel about the economic and social significance of courtship and marriage. (The basic situation in all the novels arises from the economics of marriage.) There is other evidence that Jane Austen knew mar-

riage, in her world, to be a market; in her *Letters*, she wrote, 'Single women have a dreadful propensity for being poor — which is one very strong argument in favor of matrimony.'

(2) The implicit textural values created by language become explicit thematic statements in important key phrases such as 'the scale of vanity' and 'their intimacy must sink'. In such phrases we detect the novel's themes (what it has to say about its subject) and its tone, too (how Jane Austen feels about it). We are led now, from language merely, to structure, to observe the particularized dramatic expression, the actualization, of this general narrative material, this 'world'.

Let us consider structure from the two points of view of architectural and thematic development. The two are of course interdependent, but we may see the novel more clearly, finally, if we make the separation.

From an architectural point of view, *Emma* seems to consist of four movements, or of four intermeshing blocks, each larger than the preceding. Emma is always the focus for us, but her own stature is altered as one block gives way to the next — that is, she bulks less large in the whole action of each as one follows upon another. The first block is the 'Harriet Smith' block, and here Emma's dimensions are nearly coextensive with the block itself; this gives way to the Eltons' block (and that includes, of course, others); that, in turn, gives way to the Frank Churchill–Jane Fairfax block; and that, finally, to the Knightley block, where Emma is completely absorbed. John Knightley observes at one point, 'Your neighborhood is increasing and you mix more with it.' That is, of course, precisely what happens in the structure: an 'increasing neighborhood' diminishes Emma. This development is perhaps best represented by the Coles' dinner party, where she finds herself in danger of exclusion and is herself alarmed, and it is completely dramatized in Frank Churchill's casual readiness to use — to abuse — her for his own purposes. Thus, as the plot becomes more intricate, and even as we view it through Emma's eyes, she actually plays a less and less central or relevant part in it.

Now on these blocks of increasing size we must imagine another figure, a cone, to represent Knightley. Its point would lie somewhere near the end of the first – the Harriet – block, and through each of the following blocks it would widen, until, in the final block, it would be nearly coextensive with the limits of the block itself. It is important to see that the movement from block to block is accomplished not only by new elements in the action (the arrival of Mrs Elton; of Jane Fairfax; the death of Mrs Churchill) but by scenes between Emma and Mr Knightley himself, scenes in which he usually upbraids her for an error of judgment and scenes out of which she emerges with an altered awareness, a dim alteration in the first, a slightly clearer alteration in the second and third, and at last, in the fourth, as full an awareness as she is capable of. The first of these is in chapter 8, and the subject is Harriet; the second, chapter 18, and the subject is Frank Churchill; the third, chapter 33, the subject Jane Fairfax; and the last, chapter 43, the subject Miss Bates. These scenes are debates between moral obstinacy and moral wisdom, and the first is slowly brought up to the proportion of the second. In the last scene, when Knightley takes Emma to task for her cruelty to Miss Bates, she fully recognizes and bitterly repents her fault. She *alters* at last: 'could he *even* have seen into her heart', she thinks, 'he would not, on this occasion, have found anything to reprove'. Only then is she prepared to know that it is only Knightley that she can love, and with that the movement of awareness swells: 'Every other part of her mind was disgusting.' And then, before his declaration, the movement comes to rest:

When it came to such a pitch as this, she was not able to refrain from a start, or a heavy sigh, or even from walking about the room for a few seconds; and the only source whence anything like consolation or composure could be drawn, was in the resolution of her own better conduct, and the hope that, however inferior in spirit and gaiety might be the following and every future winter of her life to the past, it would yet find her more rational, more acquainted with herself, and leave her less to regret when it were gone.

Thus we have a double movement in the architecture – the diminution of Emma in the social scene, her reduction to her proper place in the whole scale of value (which is her expiation), and the growth of Emma in the moral scheme (which is her enlargement). It is very beautiful.

Now most of this we are never told, and of Emma's diminution, not at all. We are made to experience this double development through the movement of the plot itself. This fact calls attention to Jane Austen's method, and makes us ask what her reasons were for developing it. The method consists of an alteration of narration conducted almost always through the heroine's eyes, with dramatic scenes illustrative of the narrative material. There is almost no direct statement of the significance of the material, and there is a minimum of reported action. The significance of the material comes to us through two chief sources: the dramatized scene itself, and the play of irony through the narration. Of Jane Austen's skill in making scene speak, I will say nothing, except to point out our awareness of the significance of Emma's silence – she says not a word – in the scene in chapter 12 where her sister is praising Jane Fairfax and explaining why Jane and Emma had always seemed to everyone to be perfectly suited for an equal friendship; and that later scene, in chapter 21, where we are made so acutely aware of the presence of the others and their several emotions, as Miss Bates blunders along on the matter of how some people had mistakenly felt that Mr Elton might have married a certain person – well, clearly, it is Miss Woodhouse herself, who is there, again stonily silent. Now just as the dramatic values of scene are left to speak for themselves, so the moral values are left, implicit *in* the scenes, not discussed through them.

Such a method, intermingling as it does dramatic scene with narrative observations of the heroine, requires from the author a constant irony that at all times transcends the ironic habit of mind of the heroine herself. Sometimes Jane Austen achieves this simply by seeming to accept the scene as the characters pretend that it was; as, for example, following on Emma's silence when Isabella praises Jane, the narrative proceeds: 'This topic was discussed very happily, and others succeeded of similar moment, and passed away with similar harmony.' Sometimes she achieves it through an unobtrusive verbal pointing, as: 'Poor Mr Woodhouse was silent from consternation; but everybody else had something to say; everybody was either surprised, or not surprised, and had some question to ask, or some comfort to offer.' Could the triviality of the situation find a more effective underlining? On still other occasions, Jane Austen achieves this necessary irony simply by shifting her point of view a fraction away from the person who presumably holds it. This is shown nowhere more effectively than in the passage I have already cited, in which we begin with Emma's observation, then shift to that phrase, 'the scale of vanity', which cannot possibly be hers, and then return at once to her.

Emma perceived that her taste was not the only taste on which Mr Weston depended, and felt that to be the favourite and intimate of a man who had so many intimates and confidantes, was not the very first distinction in the scale of vanity. She liked his open manners, but a little less of open-heartedness would have made him a higher character. General benevolence, but not general friendship, made a man what he ought to be. She could fancy such a man.

I am pressing this matter of the method of scene and the method of irony not only because it is through this method that the significance of the architectural structure of the work is brought home to us, that double movement I have described, but because it reveals an important fact about Jane Austen's relation to her audience, then and now, and because, unless we understand this relation, we cannot see as much as we should see in that thematic structure to which I will presently turn, or see at all that relationship of social and moral scale that is the heart of the book. Jane Austen was in an ambiguous situation in relation to her readers, a situation in which she was committed simultaneously to cherish and abominate her world. Within the framework of what is presumably a happy story, where everyone gets married off properly in the end, she must still make her comment, from her deepest moral evaluations, on the misery of this happiness. The texture of her style already has suggested that the world she pictures is hardly founded on the highest values. But that is not enough. She must besides develop a technique which could both reveal and conceal, that would give only as much as the reader wished to take. (That is why she can still be read in both the most frivolous and the most serious spirit.) Her problem – and perhaps this is the problem of every novelist of manners, at least if he is a satirist, who criticizes the society within which he yet wishes to remain and, indeed, whose best values are his own – her problem was to develop a novelistic technique that would at once conceal and reveal her strongest feelings, her basic observation of her heroine and her heroine's world, and that would express with sufficient clarity, if one looks at that technique closely, the ultimate values here involved.

For those who do not read while they run, the range of Jane Austen's irony, from the gentlest to the most corrosive, will suggest that she was perfectly able to see with absolute clarity the defects of the world she used. I will not trouble with the mild examples, but only with the gradation at the extreme: 'It was a delightful visit – perfect, in being much too short.' And she leaned back in the corner to indulge her murmurs, or to reason them away; probably a little of both – such being the commonest process of a not ill-disposed mind.'

Surely a mind that throws out observations such as these is not an entirely well-disposed one. But to go on – 'I am persuaded that you can be as insincere as your neighbours, when it is necessary.' Still further: Emma on Miss Bates: 'and nobody is afraid of her – that is a great charm'.

Consider next the bitter violence of the verb, in that comment on boarding schools, where young women are '*screwed* out of health and into vanity'. And come last to the extreme, an amazing irruption into this bland social surface of what has been called her 'regulated hatred' – 'Miss Bates stood in the very worst predicament in the world for having much of the public favour; and she had no intellectual superiority to make atonement to herself, or *frighten those who might hate her into outward respect.*' Surely there is no failure here to judge the values of the social scale. We, in turn, are enabled to recognize these values, to judge the material, in other words, to place our evaluation upon it, not only by these oblique uses of irony, but by two other means: first, the dramatization of Emma's diminution in the community as we see more and more of it; second, by judging the real significance of her end.

The first, the dramatization of value, or moral scale, is achieved through what I have been calling 'thematic structure', a structure that supports and unifies the architectural structure, the thematic integration of characters. Thematic structure exists, first of all, in the selection and disposal of characters around the heroine, and the relationship in moral traits which we are meant to observe between the heroine and the others. Emma is in many ways a charming heroine, bright and attractive and energetic, but Jane Austen never lets us forget that if she is superior to the Eltons, for example, the author (or, if you wish, Knightley) is superior to her. Emma's vanity is of no trivial kind. She is not 'personally vain', Knightley tells us; 'her vanity lies another way'. It lies, for example, in her very charity. 'Harriet would be loved as one to whom she could be useful. For Mrs Weston there was nothing to be done; for Harriet everything.' It is the vanity of giving, and brings to mind E. M. Forster's remark that, for many people indeed, it is better to receive than to give. It is the vanity, next, of power, for through the exercise of her charity, she succeeds in the imposition of her will. It is the vanity of abstract intellect. That Emma is capable of sound judgment is evident in her recognition of the real Elton even as she is urging him upon Harriet; it is evident again in her analysis of the real relation that probably pertains between Frank Churchill and his step-mother, even as she is herself about to fall in love with him. It is evident again in some of her self-studies, when, for example, after the Elton–Harriet fiasco, she resolves, in tears, that, since it is too late to be 'simpleminded and ignorant', like Harriet, she will be at least 'humble and discreet'. In the next chapter she reveals herself incapable of acting on her own self-judgment, and Mr Knightley again points up the discrepancy for us.

[Emma] 'He may have as strong a sense of what would be right as you can have, without being so equal, under particular circumstances, to act up to it.'

[Knightley] 'Then it would not be so strong a sense. If it failed to produce equal exertion, it could not be an equal conviction.'

Emma's intellectual judgments do not relate sufficiently to her conduct; in short, she is immoral. And we are not to be surprised when, rather early in the novel, she announces her own values: 'those pleasantest feelings of our nature – eager curiosity and warm prepossession'. The novel shows us the disastrous moral consequences of such insufficient standards.

This is Emma in her vanity. Let us observe, now, the kind of symbolic relationships in which her vanity is placed: First, of contrast, the contrast being with Miss Bates, and none in the novel more explicit: 'Emma Woodhouse, handsome, clever and rich, with a comfortable home and happy disposition seemed to unite some of the best blessings of existence; and had lived nearly twenty-one years in the world with very little to distress or vex her.' Ten pages later: 'Miss Bates . . . a woman neither young, handsome, rich, nor married. Miss Bates stood in the very worst predicament in the world for having much of the public favour . . . and yet she was a happy woman.' That Emma unites with 'some of the best blessings of existence', some of the worst possibilities of human society, is all too soon quite evident, but nowhere more evident than when she says of Miss Bates, 'so silly, so satisfied, so smiling'.

The second kind of symbolic relationship is not contrasting but comparative, and is evident in Harriet and Mrs Elton. Of Harriet we need only point out that she is a silly but harmless girl educated by Emma into exactly the same sort of miscalculations, only to be abused by Emma for her folly. The comparison with Mrs Elton is more fully developed: Emma's judgment on the Coles, who are struggling to rise above the stigma of trade, is exactly duplicated by Mrs Elton's judgment on a family living near Maple Grove, called Tupman: 'very lately settled there, and encumbered with many low connections, but giving themselves immense airs, and expecting to be on a footing with the old established families. . . . They came from Birmingham. . . . One has not great hopes for Birmingham.' The analogy with Emma is detailed: Mrs Elton, like Emma, has an almost aggressive determination to 'do' for other people, and to ride over their wishes; on the 'scale of vanity', she is precisely where we begin with Emma: 'a vain woman, extremely well satisfied with herself, and thinking much of her own importance; that she meant to shine and be very superior; but with manners which had been formed in a bad school; pert and familiar; that all her notions were drawn from one set of people, and one style of living; that, if not foolish, she was ignorant'. And Emma makes this analysis: Emma, who herself is 'amused by such a picture of another set of beings' – the Martins; who broods on the inferior society of Highbury; who makes one test only, the class test, except when she judges creations of her own, like Harriet, and even Harriet's high-born antecedents, as Emma fancies them, are apparent in her face; Emma, whose manners at one point, at any rate, are not merely pert and familiar, but coldly cruel, which even Mrs Elton never is.

The third kind of symbolic relationship is the contrasting-comparative kind that is evident in Jane Fairfax. This is a crucial relationship in the thematic structure. We are told that they are alike in many ways – age, station, accomplishments. They are alike, furthermore, in that Emma *thinks* of Jane as complacent and reserved, whereas we *know* Emma to be both. Her reserve with Jane Fairfax is complete from the beginning, and stoney. Her complacency is nearly admitted: she 'could not quarrel with herself'; 'I cannot really change for the better'. What a contrast, then, in actuality. Jane, whom we see through Emma's eyes as complacent, cold, tiresome, and in some ways rather disgusting, is, really, as much an antithesis to Emma as Miss Bates, and a much more difficult antithesis for Emma ever to deal with, to really admit. She is a woman capable of rash and improper behavior, a genuine commitment to passion, a woman torn by feeling, and feeling directed at an object not entirely worthy. She is hardly prudent. In short, she is quite different from what Emma sees, and quite different from what Emma is – all too complacent and perhaps really cold – and she stands in the novel as a kind of symbolic rebuke to Emma's emotional deficiencies, just as

Knightley stands as a rebuke to her moral deficiencies. That Emma has emotional deficiencies is perhaps sufficiently apparent in her attachment to her father, and in her use of that attachment. Jane Fairfax is the blurred threat to Emma's complacency, the threat that Emma herself has never brought into focus in her own life and character, and at the end of the novel still has not, and so still has not achieved it for herself, or any radical reform of her qualities. They have merely moved on the scale.

So much for the heroine and the female characters. If we look now at the men, we can consider them as variations, or gradations, on the two traits, egotism and sociability, or 'Candor', which is the positive virtue sought by Mr Knightley. These characters run from Mr Elton, the vain social snob, all egotism; through Frank Churchill, the man whose candor conceals a treacherous egotism; through Mr Weston, so thoroughly amiable as to be nearly without judgment, and yet an egotist himself, the egotism of parenthood; to Mr Knightley, who is the pivot, the middleman, moderate and sound, balanced and human, neither an egotist nor a gadabout. From him, we shade off into his brother, the dour social egotist, to Mr Woodhouse, the destructive (though comic, of course) malingering egotist.

Emma's relationships to them are revealing: she patronizes and then scorns Elton, of course; she 'loves' Frank Churchill; she is fond of Weston; toward Knightley she holds a friendly animosity; she has tolerance for John; she adores her father. These relationships or emotional responses are Jane Austen's way of dramatizing Emma, of showing us her value. We see her through them, even as we are seeing them through her. It is a process of reciprocal illumination. And so in both the men and women, we come to see her above and beyond her presentation of herself, and at the same time, of course, we come to see the community at large through them – they represent Jane Austen's social 'analysis', her breakdown of a community into its major traits, its two poles. If we study the bulking up at one end or the other of the scale, we can hardly conclude that the analysis is entirely friendly.

Thus we begin to see the real accomplishment of this objective technique, how deep it can go, how much subtle work it can do, how it defines its interpretations and analysis of the material, how it separates the material (which is trivial) and the effect (which is grave). Most remarkable, perhaps, how it holds together, makes one, the almost bland, comic tone, appropriate to the kind of society, too brittle for a severer tone, and a really bitter, sometimes acrid theme.

To define the theme completely we have to look closely at the real history of Emma. For all her superiority, Emma's values are really the values of the society she patronizes, and although she partially resolves her personal dilemma (hers really is a 'profitable humiliation'), she *retains* those qualities: complacency, a kind of social cruelty, snobbery (Harriet must sink), and even greed (little Henry, who must inherit Donwell). Emma's self-study has always been partially mistaken; will it always be correct henceforth? Except for her final moment of awareness, her others have always exempted herself from judgment; can we believe that that is never to happen again? Does the final comment not come from Knightley, when Emma says, 'Poor child! . . . what will become of her?' and he replies, 'Nothing very bad. The fate of thousands. She will be disagreeable in infancy, and correct herself as she grows older. I am losing all my bitterness against spoilt children, my dearest Emma.' The modification is minor. Does Jane Austen say less? Near the end she tells us:

Seldom, very seldom does complete truth belong to any human disclosure; seldom can it happen that something is not a little disguised, or a little mistaken; but where, as in this case, though the conduct is mistaken, the feelings are not, it may not be very material. Mr Knightley could not impute to Emma a more relenting heart than she possessed or a heart more disposed to accept of his.

How severely does Jane Austen 'chasten' Emma? 'Do not physic them,' says Isabella of her children; are we not left to 'physic' Emma, to chasten her and her world together, with all necessary guidance from the style and the basic motives that analysis reveals in the work itself?

When we say that Emma is diminished at the end, as her

world is, in a way, for us – the bright, easy society put in a real shade – we are really saying that she has been absorbed into that world, and has become inseparable from it. This observation suggests that we look again at the end of the novel. There is something apparently aimless and long-winded about it. Of *Pride and Prejudice* the author said, 'The work is rather too light, bright, and sparkling; it wants shade; it wants to be stretched out here and there, with a long chapter of sense, if it could be had.' In *Pride and Prejudice* and *Sense and Sensibility*, Jane Austen's heroines were superior to their world. Then, in *Mansfield Park*, her dull Fanny was completely submissive to the conventional pieties of this same world, somewhat white-washed. In *Emma*, Jane Austen seems to do what the remark about *Pride and Prejudice* aims at. Emma is finally nearly at the top of the moral scale, with Knightley, but the moral scale still has its relation to the social scale. The entire end of *Emma* is such a 'shade' (even as it busily gets its characters happily married off, it is creating the shade, the moral shade, in which they will live) and the only justification for that long ending, once the Emma–Knightley arrangements have been made, is that it is needed there, as a kind of decrescendo into the social twilight that lies at the heart of the book. And so the end remains 'open' – a question, in a way. It is Emma who at one point near the end exclaims, 'I like everything decided and open'; everything here is at once decided and, in another sense, open.

How completely resolved are these strains of feeling? Emma and Jane, for example? Emma and Frank? How much 'candor' is there? And how 'happy' is this marriage, with Knightley having to move into old Mr Woodhouse's establishment? Isn't it all, perhaps, a little superficial – not the writing but the self-avowals of the characters? A little perfunctory, as comedy may be, telling us thereby that this *is* comedy? One is reminded of the end of *Mansfield Park*:

I purposefully abstain from dates on this occasion, that everyone may be at liberty to fix their own, aware that the cure of un-conquerable passions, and the transfer of unchanging attach-ments, must vary as to time in different people. I only entreat everybody to believe that exactly at the time when it was quite natural that it should be so, and not a week earlier, Edmund did cease to care about Miss Crawford, and became as anxious to marry Fanny as Fanny herself could desire.

Emma, then, is a complex study of self-importance and egotism and malice, as these are absorbed from a society whose morality and values are derived from the economics of class; and a study, further, in the mitigation of these traits, as the heroine comes into partial self-recognition, and at the same time sinks more completely into that society. Just as with Elizabeth Bennet, her individual being, as she has discovered it, will make that society better, but it will not make it different. This is moral realism, and it shows nowhere more clearly than in the very end, when the pilfering of a poultry house is given us as the qualification of 'the perfect happiness of the union'. The irresolution of the book gives it its richness, and its tautness and precision of structure and style give it its clarity. The two together make it great.

We have not said enough about Knightley, and if we are to see Jane Austen's values as they positively underlie her drama, we must look at him. Only a little pompous, he is the humanely civilized man; it is he whose judgments move beyond class; only he seems to breathe deeply; only he, certainly, ventures out impervious to that 'weather' that is always keeping the others in a state of alarm and inside their littleness; it is he who wants complete candor and no mystery; it is he who makes Jane Austen's demand that awareness and conduct be brought into the relationship which is morality. In the only unclear speech in the novel (a haunting speech, in chapter 33) he observes the separation: 'her own comparative littleness in action, if not in consciousness'. This is likewise Jane Austen's demand, although she lets Emma speak it: 'faith engaged ... and manners so *very* disengaged'. But if there were a complete congruity between profession and conduct, there would be no comedy in the world; and Jane Austen wants comedy.

That comedy was sufficient for her purposes she certainly knew, just as she knew the size of the world her comedy measures. John Knightley says, 'Business, you know, may bring money, but friendship hardly does.' Frank Churchill says, 'I would have given worlds – all the worlds one ever has to give – for another half-hour.' And chiefly that phrase 'a crowd in a little room', varied four times in a dozen lines:

Emma demurred. 'It would be a crowd – a sad crowd; and what could be worse than dancing without space to turn in? . . . Nothing can be further from pleasure than to be dancing in a crowd – and a crowd in a little room.'
'There is no denying it,' he replied. 'I agree with you exactly. A crowd in a little room – Miss Woodhouse, you have the art of giving pictures in a few words.'

Miss Woodhouse has, in fact, given us a picture of Jane Austen's art. And it suggests that a narrow scene, like a good plot, is the occasion of pressure on the characters, to squeeze out their moral essence.

Their being fixed, so absolutely fixed, in the same place, was bad for each, for all three. Not one of them had the power of removal, or of effecting any material change of society. They must encounter each other, and make the best of it.

And again:

When she considered how peculiarly unlucky poor Mr Elton was in being in the same room at once with the woman he had just married, the woman he had wanted to marry, and the woman whom he had been expected to marry, she must allow him to have the right to look as little wise . . . as could be.

The weather, so much a part of this book as of the others, is a double device for Jane Austen: it keeps these characters on the narrow social stage where they enact their moral drama; and it underlines, for us, the fact of their enclosure, their narrowness. It is only in Christmas weather, in the season of love, we are told, that everyone ventures boldly out. In Highbury, as elsewhere, it comes, alas, only once a year. We may conclude then, that the scene may be narrow, the action trivial, the feelings (from the point of view of other kinds of novels) thin – but the condition is the human condition, and the problem is nothing less than original sin – the dry destructiveness of egotism. And so the novel, if one is pressed to say so, is really about the narrowness of a wholly 'secularized' life – in Eliot's meaning – no prevailing spiritual awareness, no prevailing emotional fullness, no prevailing gravity except in the author's construction, in the character she allows to speak for her, in her own oblique comment. We are reminded of all this in one of the few metaphorical outbursts of the novel. Jane Fairfax, resigning herself to the life of a schoolteacher, is thrown into the posture of religious renunciation:

With the fortitude of a devoted novitiate, she had resolved at one-and-twenty to complete the sacrifice, and retire from all the pleasures of life, of rational intercourse, equal society, peace and hope, to penance and mortification for ever.

And her motive? The deplorable absence of a fortune!

R. E. Hughes

THE EDUCATION
OF EMMA WOODHOUSE (1961)

THERE are two different, but complementary, views to be taken of Jane Austen's novels. The first is the microscopic, which assumes the exquisite but limited sensibility of Jane Austen. When this view receives critical expression, that criticism assumes a particular focus: its orientation is either biographical or autotelic; it examines, and usually justifies, the internal architecture of the novels; it emphasizes the irony of Jane Austen, but sees the irony as verbal, part of the mechanism of character-creation; and concludes by acclaiming the *précieuse* quality of Jane Austen's vision.[1]

The second view is the microcosmic, which assumes the analogical disposition of the author. The critical focus of this view is explicative and comparative: it is concerned not only with the narrative value of Jane Austen's detail, but considers much of the detail to be indicative of the larger society which lies outside the limits of the novels; it also emphasizes the irony of Jane Austen, but it sees the irony as dramatic as well as verbal, relying on the reader's discovery of an equivalence between the data of the novel and the data of his own world; and concludes by indicating the novels themselves as the applied half of a massive metaphor with the world beyond the novels acting as the unexpressed literal half of the metaphor.[2]

It has been the fault of much otherwise penetrating criticism of Jane Austen that these two views have been accepted as self-supporting, and their complementary nature overlooked. In examining *Emma*, two of the more recent critics have applied the microscopic approach with admirable success: Joseph M. Duffy, Jr, added a dimension to Emma by pointing out that her development within the novel was both moral and sexual,[3] and Edgar F.

Shannon, Jr, demonstrated the role played by the novel's structure in symbolizing Emma's growth to maturity.[4] Both Duffy and Shannon, however, saw the formative elements of Emma as lying entirely within the novel. On the other side, Leonard Woolf[5] argued that we must keep in mind the social milieu in which Jane Austen wrote, since the novel must inevitably bear the imprint of that milieu. But if Duffy and Shannon erred in ignoring the social macrocosm, Woolf erred in ignoring the novel: for he concludes only that Jane Austen's 'social and economic standards ... we associate with a capitalist bourgeoisie': a classic case of a hobby-horse galloping away with the critical faculties.

The underlying theme of this novel is the education of Emma Woodhouse; and the recurrent irony is that Emma, who must become pupil, insists on acting as teacher. Her mismanagement of the affairs of Harriet, and the consequent difficulties to Harriet, herself, Elton, Knightley (indeed, to nearly every character in the novel) all come out of Emma's confusion of two roles. The question is, in what must Emma be educated? Obviously, she is incredibly naïve in matters of passion and sex. Her awareness of how much is involved in the act of loving is a theme capable of development totally within the novel's framework. But she is just as naïve in her notions of society, and as soon as love and a particular definition of society are brought face to face, we are invited to move outside the novel's framework. The spirit of society is liquid, shifting: and much as Mr Woodhouse and his daughter would prefer to ignore it, the state of society beyond Highbury and Randalls is not the same as it once was: no society ever is. Emma must also be educated in this respect; and her awareness of the new spirit of society cannot be developed totally within the novel for the simple reason that the spirit lies outside the novel, that is to say, beyond Highbury and in the whole transitional state of English society in the early 1800s. Emma's education is not single, but double: first, she must recognize love as it is defined outside of her own cloistered fancies; second, she must recognize society as it is defined outside the cloister of the world of the novel. Only when she recognizes that there is something outside is Emma redeemed; the invasion by the outside of the inside becomes a dominant theme of the novel; and it is the crossing and recrossing of the two outsides (real love, real society) which establishes the meaning and the pattern of the novel.

First, there is the education in love. Thanks to her own inexperience and her father's myopic influence, Emma has a fairyland notion of love, which is compounded of a nonsexual concern for comfortable establishment and Arcadian romance. It never occurs to her that Mr Elton and Harriet might wish to spend their time in any other way but assembling and interpreting charades. She begins her matchmaking in the face of a significant warning from Knightley: 'Depend upon it, Elton will not do. Elton is a very good sort of man, and a very respectable vicar of Highbury, but not at all likely to make an imprudent match. He knows the value of a good income as well as anybody.'[6]

That such a prosaic concern as money should have any relevance to love is ridiculed by Emma: her ephemeral notions will not accept such ballast. But here is the first sign of her second education: when Frank Churchill heaves into sight, she will begin to learn her lesson in love; with Elton she must learn her lesson in economics as a factor in society. Highbury society could have given her no such idea: in this small world, society is still generally thought of in terms of yeoman, gentry, and aristocrat – a world picture already challenged outside the novel.

The compound education begins when Emma's composure is given its first bad shock: Mr Elton's proposal to her on the way home from the Weston household (ch. 15). Knightley's warning comes back to her, and Emma's amorphous notions begin to harden. About love, she had been completely wrong; she must redefine. She begins her redefinition by overreacting. Unwise to begin with, Emma examines this first phase of her education and decides that she must now keep the economic factor uppermost in her mind. At this point in the novel, Emma's vocabulary runs along new lines: in reconsidering her mistake with Elton, she estimates the value of her inheritance and decides he was impertinent; on hearing of Jane Fairfax's intended visit to Highbury, she speculates on her economic status; she compliments the gift of a piano to Jane, which she assumes to be from Colonel Campbell, as showing wealth and liberality (not kindness or affection); she dismisses rumors of a match between Jane and Mr Knightley on economically prudential grounds; she toys with the idea of a Frank Churchill–Harriet match for the material advantages that would accrue to Harriet; she is concerned over what she interprets to be Knightley's plans to marry, since it might affect the disposition of his estate. Emma's whole conceptualism has shifted: from a completely unrealistic attitude toward love, she has swung over to a completely mercantile attitude. Once this reversal has been established in the novel, Jane Austen introduces Augusta Hawkins, the new Mrs Elton: she comes from the outside world, away from Highbury, and is an incarnation of the lesson Emma has learned. A deliberately flat character, Mrs Elton is a walking emblem of an acquisitive society: 'the glory of Miss Hawkins', as Jane Austen summarizes it, is her connection with £10,000, a prosperous mercantile family (for a moment, Emma, still Highbury-bred, hesitates to accept this message from the outer world): 'Miss Hawkins was the youngest of the two daughters of a Bristol – merchant, of course, he must be called' (p. 873), and being sister-in-law to a gentleman who kept two carriages. Mrs Elton's evaluation of all that goes on around her depends on 'what Selina would say', Selina being, of course, more than her sister: she functions in the novel as the spirit of the world outside the novel, a spirit of acquisition, moneyed success, and economic prosperity. Mrs Elton, coming into the novel at the point she does, becomes a projection of Emma's new attitude as well as a type of the new social spirit.

Having begun most amorphously, Emma has now reached a stasis. From her experience with Elton she has assembled a philosophy of love, and she proceeds to put this philosophy to work. Just as her first vagueness had unfortunate results, so now does this rigidity. Still underexposed to a larger world, Emma is confused by being faced with a new set of defining terms.

Once again, the definers come from the outside. As Mrs Elton brings into the novel-world the unadulterated notion of love-money, now Frank Churchill and Jane Fairfax bring in the unadulterated notion of love-mature affection. Like Mrs Elton, both characters are from beyond Highbury. With her new set of values, Emma is as unprepared to cope with this new triangle (herself–Frank–Jane) as she was to cope with the first (herself–Elton–Harriet). This time, she is the victim exactly as Harriet was in the previous débâcle. Unable to accept a romance between Frank and Jane (for Jane, as a mere ward, can claim no affluence either from the Bateses or from the Campbells; *ergo*, there can be no thought of love) or between Frank and Harriet (the fantasy of Harriet as an unclaimed daughter of a hypothetical nobleman notwithstanding, Harriet at the moment has no dowry; *ergo*, no possibility of love), Emma sets up the only equation her new knowledge can support: between herself and Frank. The folly of all this breaks through with the same purgative effect as Emma's first disillusionment. She must learn that there are factors at work of which she had no notion, in this case the possibility of a passion not to be dictated to by economic details. This is so patently contradictory of what Emma has so recently learned that she is not prepared for what happens next. As there had been the erection of a symbol for the first phase of Emma's education (Mrs Elton – mercantilism), so now there is a symbol erected for the second phase: the scene at Box Hill, the humiliation of Miss Bates, the result of Emma's disregarding the claims of compassion and the feelings (ch. 43).

Once this point in the novel has been reached, we can see the structure which is being assembled. Both Emma and Highbury are being invaded: an unreal and inexperienced attitude toward society and love is challenged. The challenge comes from two directions: from a frankly pragmatic admission that money is a factor in society, and from a frankly passionate admission that the emotions are not to be ignored. Each challenge comes from the outside, each is concretized in an appropriate symbol, and each demands that the inside readjust. The two sets of outside values are brought into conflict in the person of Emma and within the environs of her little world. Her mistakes are accountable to her first inability to discover a synthesis resolving the conflict.

But the synthesis does, eventually, take place. (To describe the novel's structure as Hegelian is a temptation.) It occurs most efficiently in and through Mr Knightley, who is eminently well qualified as arbiter, as representative of both elements, and as an emblem of enlightened Highburyism. In his outlook, he combines the opposing sets of values: in finally disposing of Harriet, he remarks that the Harriet Smith–Robert Martin marriage is valid in both terms, compassionately and economically. In his own position, he combines both terms: the proprietor of Donwell Abbey, he yet is capable of romantic affection; a resident landowner, he yet has made excursions into the world beyond Emma's. Reminiscent of *Pride and Prejudice*, the entire prism of love-economics is resolved in the several marriages of the novel: The Weston–Taylor, Churchill–Fairfax marriages which give affection the ascendency; the Elton–Hawkins marriage which gives economics the ascendency; and the Smith–Martin, Woodhouse–Knightley marriages which satisfy both elements, showing the synthesis to be effective in widely differing economic spheres.

Emma's education has finally been completed. What she has had to learn is to admit the outside into her experience, and the outside lies beyond the confined geographical boundaries of her existence (not to mention their lying beyond the confined chronological boundaries of the entire novel: the education of Becky Sharp, which involves the same tensions as Emma's, but in more violent terms, is soon to begin). Emma's small world, bordered by Highbury, Randalls, and Donwell, is brushed by the larger world which is introduced by Knightley's sporadic trips to and returns from London, by Augusta Hawkins, by Frank Churchill; and her redemption from foolishness depends on her absorbing what the reader recognizes as a conflict not to be circumscribed.

The deduction which can be made from this is that the regularity of Jane Austen's structure (thesis, antithesis, synthesis) and the enclosed setting connote precision and conservatism; this conservatism does not exclude an awareness of a larger world, but rather subordinates that larger world to itself; that the conflicts of the macrocosm are seen to be solvable in terms of the microcosm, but that the microcosm itself must be resilient enough to adopt new attitudes. What Ruskin had to say of himself – that he was a Tory of the old school, which is to say Sir Walter Scott's school, and Homer's – is more than applicable to Jane Austen. She deserves to be called a philosophic Tory, and her argument is that of the future Victorian Toryism: what Carlyle, Ruskin, and Arnold will see as the crucial debate of their age, and clash of values in the nineteenth century, is already resolved in terms of a conservative compromise, for which Highbury and all its inhabitants are apt symbols.

NOTES

1. A good example of this 'in-stressed' approach is James Gregory Murray's 'Measure and Balance in Jane Austen's *Emma*', in *College English*, XVI (Dec 1954) 160–6. Murray demonstrates how the 'classical' ideals of measure and balance determine organization, characterization, and tone of the novel.

2. Mark Schorer's 'Fiction and the "Analogical Matrix"', in *Critiques and Essays on Modern Fiction*, ed. John W. Aldridge (New York, 1952) pp. 83–98, points out how the language of *Pride and Prejudice* constantly forces the reader to an awareness of a world which none of the characters is willing to admit even exists. An interesting comparative inference can be made here: whereas Henry James's characters often are destroyed by their unwillingness to admit a world beyond themselves (e.g. *Washington Square*, *Daisy Miller*). Jane Austen's Emma is reclaimed by her final acceptance and mastery of a world beyond her own.

3. '*Emma*: The Awakening from Innocence', in *Journal of English Literary History*, XXI (March 1954) 39–53.

4. '*Emma*: Character and Construction', in *PMLA* LXXI (Sept 1956) 637–50; [reprinted in this volume, pp. 130–47.]

5. 'Jane Austen's Economic Determinism', in *New Statesman*, 18 July 1942.

6. Jane Austen, *Emma. The Complete Novels of Jane Austen* (Modern Library edition) p. 801.

Wayne Booth

CONTROL OF DISTANCE
IN JANE AUSTEN'S *EMMA* (1961)

Sympathy and judgment in Emma

HENRY JAMES once described Jane Austen as an instinctive novelist whose effects, some of which are admittedly fine, can best be explained as 'part of her unconsciousness'. It is as if she 'fell-a-musing' over her work-basket, he said, lapsed into 'wool-gathering', and afterward picked up 'her dropped stitches' as 'little master-strokes of imagination'.[1] The amiable accusation has been repeated in various forms, most recently as a claim that Jane Austen creates characters towards whom we cannot react as she consciously intends.[2]

Although we cannot hope to decide whether Jane Austen was entirely conscious of her own artistry, a careful look at the technique of any of her novels reveals a rather different picture from that of the unconscious spinster with her knitting needles. In *Emma* especially, where the chances for technical failure are great indeed, we find at work one of the unquestionable masters of the rhetoric of narration.

At the beginning of *Emma*, the young heroine has every requirement for deserved happiness but one. She has intelligence, wit, beauty, wealth, and position, and she has the love of those around her. Indeed, she thinks herself completely happy. The only threat to her happiness, a threat of which she is unaware, is herself: charming as she is, she can neither see her own excessive pride honestly nor resist imposing herself on the lives of others. She is deficient both in generosity and in self-knowledge. She discovers and corrects her faults only after she has almost ruined herself and her closest friends. But with the reform in her character, she is ready for marriage with the man she loves, the man who throughout the book has stood in the reader's mind for what she lacks.

It is clear that with a general plot of this kind Jane Austen gave herself difficulties of a high order. Though Emma's faults are comic, they constantly threaten to produce serious harm. Yet she must remain sympathetic or the reader will not wish for and delight sufficiently in her reform.

Obviously, the problem with a plot like this is to find some way to allow the reader to laugh at the mistakes committed by the heroine and at her punishment, without reducing the desire to see her reform and thus earn happiness. In *Tom Jones* this double attitude is achieved, as we have seen, partly through the invention of episodes producing sympathy and relieving any serious anxiety we might have, and partly through the direct and sympathetic commentary. In *Emma*, since most of the episodes must illustrate the heroine's faults and thus increase either our emotional distance or our anxiety, a different method is required. If we fail to see Emma's faults as revealed in the ironic texture from line to line, we cannot savor to the full the comedy as it is prepared for us. On the other hand, if we fail to love her, as Jane Austen herself predicted we would[3] – if we fail to love her more and more as the book progresses – we can neither hope for the conclusion, a happy and deserved marriage with Knightley following upon her reform, nor accept it as an honest one when it comes.[4] Any attempt to solve the problem by reducing either the love or the clear view of her faults would have been fatal.

Sympathy through control of inside views

The solution to the problem of maintaining sympathy despite almost crippling faults was primarily to use the heroine herself as a kind of narrator, though in third person, reporting on her own experience. So far as we know, Jane Austen never formulated any theory to cover her own practice; she invented no term like James's 'central intelligence' or 'lucid reflector' to describe her method of viewing the world of the book primarily through Emma's own eyes. We can thus never know for sure to what extent James's accusation of 'unconsciousness' was right. But whether she was inclined to speculate about her method scarcely matters; her solution was clearly a brilliant one. By showing most of the story through Emma's eyes, the author insures that we shall travel with Emma rather than stand against her. It is not simply that Emma provides, in the unimpeachable evidence of her own conscience, proof that she has many redeeming qualities that do not appear on the surface; such evidence could be given with authorial commentary, though perhaps not with such force and conviction. Much more important, the sustained inside view leads the reader to hope for good fortune for the character with whom he travels, quite independently of the qualities revealed.

Seen from the outside, Emma would be an unpleasant person, unless, like Mr Woodhouse and Knightley, we knew her well enough to infer her true worth. Though we might easily be led to laugh at her, we could never be made to laugh sympathetically. While the final unmasking of her faults and her humiliation would make artistic sense to an unsympathetic reader, her marriage with Knightley would become irrelevant if not meaningless. Unless we desire Emma's happiness and her reform, which alone can make that happiness possible, a good third of this book will seem irredeemably dull.

Yet sympathetic laughter is never easily achieved. It is much easier to set up a separate fool for comic effects and to preserve your heroine for finer things. Sympathetic laughter is especially difficult with characters whose faults do not spring from sympathetic virtues. The grasping but witty Volpone can keep us on his side so long as his victims are more grasping and less witty than he, but as soon as the innocent victims, Celia and Bonario, come on stage, the quality of the humor changes; we no longer delight unambiguously in his triumphs. In contrast to this, the great sympathetic comic heroes often are comic largely because their faults, like Uncle Toby's sentimentality, spring from an excess of some virtue. Don Quixote's madness is partly caused by an excess of idealism, an excess of loving concern for the unfortunate. Every crazy gesture he makes gives further reason for loving the well-meaning old fool, and we can thus laugh at him in somewhat the same spirit in which we laugh at our own faults – in a benign, forgiving spirit. We may be contemptible for doing so; to persons without a sense of humor such laughter often seems a wicked escape. But self-love being what it is, we laugh at ourselves in a thoroughly forgiving way, and we laugh in the same way at Don Quixote: we are convinced that his heart, like ours, is in the right place.

Nothing in Emma's comic misunderstandings can serve for the same effect. Her faults are not excesses of virtue. She attempts to manipulate Harriet not from an excess of kindness but from a desire for power and admiration. She flirts with Frank Churchill out of vanity and irresponsibility. She mistreats Jane Fairfax because of Jane's *good* qualities. She abuses Miss Bates because of her own essential lack of 'tenderness' and 'good will'.

We have only to think of what Emma's story would be if seen through Jane Fairfax' or Mrs Elton's or Robert Martin's eyes to recognize how little our sympathy springs from any natural view, and to see how inescapable is the decision to use Emma's mind as a reflector of events – however beclouded her vision must be. To Jane Fairfax, who embodies throughout the book most of the values which Emma discovers only at the end, the early Emma is intolerable.

But Jane Austen never lets us forget that Emma is not what she might appear to be. For every section devoted to her misdeeds – and even they are seen for the most part through her own eyes – there is a section devoted to her self-reproach. We see her rudeness to poor foolish Miss Bates, and we see it vividly. But her remorse and act of penance in visiting Miss Bates after Knightley's rebuke are experienced even more vividly. We see her successive attempts to mislead Harriet, but we see at great length and in high color her self-castigation (chs. 16, 17, 48). We see her boasting proudly that she does not need marriage, boasting almost as blatantly of her 'resources' as does Mrs Elton (ch. 10). But we know her too intimately to take her conscious thoughts at face value. And we see her, thirty-eight chapters later, chastened to an admission of what we have known all along to be her true human need for love. 'If all took place that might take place among the circle of her friends, Hartfield must be comparatively deserted; and she left to cheer her father with the spirits only of ruined happiness. The child to be born at Randalls must be a tie there even dearer than herself; and Mrs Weston's heart and time would be occupied by it. . . . All that were good would be withdrawn' (ch. 48).

Perhaps the most delightful effects from our sustained inside view of a very confused and very charming young woman come from her frequent thoughts about Knightley. She is basically right all along about his pre-eminent wisdom and virtue, and she is our chief authority for taking *his* authority so seriously. And yet in every thought about him she is misled. Knightley rebukes her; the reader knows that Knightley is in the right. But Emma?

Emma made no answer, and tried to look cheerfully unconcerned, but was really feeling uncomfortable, and wanting him very much to be gone. She did not repent what she had done; she still thought herself a better judge of such a point of female right and refinement than he could be; but yet she had a sort of habitual respect for his judgment in general, which made her dislike having it so loudly against her; and to have him sitting just opposite to her in angry state, was very disagreeable.   (ch. 8)

Even more striking is the lack of self-knowledge shown when Mrs Weston suggests that Knightley might marry Jane Fairfax.

Her objections to Mr Knightley's marrying did not in the least subside. She could see nothing but evil in it. It would be a great disappointment to Mr John Knightley [Knightley's brother]; consequently to Isabella. A real injury to the children – a most mortifying change, and material loss to them all; – a very great deduction from her father's daily comfort – and, as to herself, she could not at all endure the idea of Jane Fairfax at Donwell Abbey. A Mrs Knightley for them all to give way to! – No, Mr Knightley must never marry. Little Henry must remain the heir of Donwell.
                                                                        (ch. 26)

Self-deception could hardly be carried further, at least in a person of high intelligence and sensitivity.

Yet the effect of all this is what our tolerance for our own faults produces in our own lives. While only immature readers ever really identify with any character, losing all sense of distance and hence all chance of an artistic experience, our emotional reaction to every event concerning Emma tends to become like her own. When she feels anxiety or shame, we feel analogous emotions. Our modern awareness that such 'feelings' are not identical with those we feel in our own lives in similar circumstances has tended to blind us to the fact that aesthetic form can be built out of patterned emotions as well as out of other materials. It is absurd to pretend that because our emotions and desires in responding to fiction are in a very real sense disinterested, they do not or should not exist. Jane Austen, in developing the sustained use of a sympathetic inside view, has mastered one of the most successful of all devices for inducing a parallel emotional response between the deficient heroine and the reader.

Sympathy for Emma can be heightened by withholding inside views of others as well as by granting them of her. The author knew, for example, that it would be fatal to grant any extended inside view of Jane Fairfax. The inadequacies of impressionistic criticism are nowhere revealed more clearly than in the suggestion often made about such minor characters that their authors would have liked to make them vivid but didn't know how.[5] Jane Austen knew perfectly well how to make such a character vivid; Anne in *Persuasion* is a kind of Jane Fairfax turned into heroine. But in *Emma*, Emma must shine supreme. It is not only that the slightest glance inside Jane's mind would be fatal to all of the author's plans for mystification about Frank Churchill, though this is important. The major problem is that any extended view of her would reveal her as a more sympathetic person than Emma herself. Jane is superior to Emma in most respects except the stroke of good fortune that made Emma the heroine of the book. In matters of taste and ability, of head and of heart, she is Emma's superior, and Jane Austen, always in danger of losing our sympathy for Emma, cannot risk any degree of distraction. Jane could, it is true, be granted fewer virtues, and *then* made more vivid. But to do so would greatly weaken the force of Emma's mistakes of heart and head in her treatment of the almost faultless Jane.

Control of judgment

But the very effectiveness of the rhetoric designed to produce sympathy might in itself lead to a serious misreading of the book. In reducing the emotional distance, the natural tendency is to reduce – willy-nilly – moral and intellectual distance as well. In reacting to Emma's faults from the inside out, as if they were our own, we may very well not only forgive them but overlook them.

There is, of course, no danger that readers who persist to the end will overlook Emma's serious mistakes; since she sees and reports those mistakes herself, everything becomes crystal clear at the end. The real danger inherent in the experiment is that readers will overlook the mistakes as they are committed and thus miss much of the comedy that depends on Emma's distorted view from page to page. If readers who dislike Emma cannot enjoy the preparation for the marriage to Knightley, readers who do not recognize her faults with absolute precision cannot enjoy the details of the preparation for the comic abasement which must precede that marriage.

It might be argued that there is no real problem, since the conventions of her time allowed for reliable commentary whenever it was needed to place Emma's faults precisely. But Jane Austen is not operating according to the conventions, most of which she had long since parodied and outgrown; her technique is determined by the needs of the novel she is writing. We can see this clearly by contrasting the manner of *Emma* with that of *Persuasion*, the next, and last-completed, work. In *Emma* there are many breaks in the point of view, because Emma's beclouded mind cannot do the whole job. In *Persuasion*, where the heroine's viewpoint is faulty only in her ignorance of Captain Wentworth's love, there are very few. Anne Elliot's consciousness is sufficient, as Emma's is not, for most of the needs of the novel which she dominates. We can never rely completely on Emma. It is hardly surprising that Jane Austen has provided many correctives to insure our placing her errors with precision.

The chief corrective is Knightley. His commentary on Emma's errors is a natural expression of his love; he can tell the reader and Emma at the same time precisely how she is mistaken. Thus, nothing Knightley says can be beside the point. Each affirmation of a value, each accusation of error is in itself an action in the plot. When he rebukes Emma for manipulating Harriet, when he attacks her for superficiality and false pride, when he condemns her for gossiping and flirting with Frank Churchill, and finally when he attacks her for being 'insolent' and 'unfeeling' in her treatment of Miss Bates, we have Jane Austen's judgment on Emma, rendered dramatically. But it has come from someone who is essentially sympathetic toward Emma, so that his judgments against her are presumed to be temporary. His sympathy reinforces ours even as he criticizes, and her respect for his opinion, shown in her self-abasement after he has criticized, is one of our main reasons for expecting her to reform.

If Henry James had tried to write a novel about Emma, and had cogitated at length on the problem of getting her story told dramatically, he could not have done better than this. It is possible, of course, to think of *Emma* without Knightley as *raisonneur*, just as it is possible to think of *The Golden Bowl*, say, without the Assinghams as *ficelles* to reflect something not seen by the Prince or Princess. But Knightley, though he receives less independent space than the Assinghams and is almost never seen in an inside view, is clearly more useful for Jane Austen's purposes than any realistically limited *ficelle* could possibly be. By combining the role of commentator with the role of hero, Jane Austen has worked more economically than James, and though economy is as dangerous as any other criterion when applied universally, even James might have profited from a closer study of the economies that a character like Knightley can be made to achieve. It is as if James had dared to make one of the four main characters, say the Prince, into a thoroughly good, wise, perceptive man, a thoroughly clear rather than a partly confused 'reflector'.

Since Knightley is established early as completely reliable, we need no views of his secret thoughts. He has no secret thoughts, except for the unacknowledged depths of his love for Emma and his jealousy of Frank Churchill. The other main characters have more to hide, and Jane Austen moves in and out of minds with great freedom, choosing for her own purposes what to reveal and what to withhold. Always the seeming violation of consistency is in the consistent service of the particular needs of Emma's story. Sometimes a shift is made simply to direct our suspense, as when Mrs Weston suggests a possible union of Emma and Frank Churchill, at the end of her conversation with Knightley about the harmful effects of Emma's friendship with Harriet (ch. 5). 'Part of her meaning was to conceal some favourite thoughts of her own and Mr Weston's on the subject, as much as possible. There were wishes at Randalls respecting Emma's destiny, but it was not desirable to have them suspected.'

One objection to this selective dipping into whatever mind best serves our immediate purposes is that it suggests mere trickery and inevitably spoils the illusion of reality. If Jane Austen can tell us what Mrs Weston is thinking, why not what Frank Churchill and Jane Fairfax are thinking? Obviously, because she chooses to build a mystery, and to do so she must refuse, arbitrarily and obtrusively, to grant the privilege of an inside view to characters whose minds would reveal too much. But is not the mystery purchased at the price of shaking the reader's faith in Jane Austen's integrity? If she simply withholds until later what she might as well relate now – if her procedure is not dictated by the very nature of her materials – why should we take her seriously?

If a natural surface were required in all fiction, then this objection would hold. But if we want to read *Emma* in its own terms, the real question about these shifts cannot be answered by an easy appeal to general principles. Every author withholds until later what he 'might as well' relate now. The question is always one of desired effects, and the choice of any one effect always bans innumerable other effects. There is, indeed, a question to be raised about the use of mystery in *Emma*, but the conflict is not between an abstract end that Jane Austen never worried about and a shoddy mystification that she allowed to betray her. The conflict is between two effects, both of which she cares about a good deal. On the one hand she cares about maintaining some sense of mystery as long as she can. On the other, she works at all points to heighten the reader's sense of dramatic irony, usually in the form of a contrast between what Emma knows and what the reader knows.

As in most novels, whatever steps are taken to mystify inevitably decrease the dramatic irony, and, whenever dramatic irony is increased by telling the reader secrets the characters have not yet suspected, mystery is inevitably destroyed. The longer we are in doubt about Frank Churchill, the weaker our sense of ironic contrast between Emma's views and the truth. The sooner we see through Frank Churchill's secret plot, the greater our pleasure in observing Emma's innumerable misreadings of his behavior and the less interest we have in the mere mystery of the situation. And we all find that on second reading we discover new intensities of dramatic irony resulting from the complete loss of mystery; knowing what abysses of error Emma is preparing for herself, even those of us who may on first reading have deciphered nearly all the details of the Churchill mystery find additional ironies.

But it is obvious that these ironies could have been offered even on a first reading, if Jane Austen had been willing to sacrifice her mystery. A single phrase in her own name – 'his secret engagement to Jane Fairfax' – or a short inside view of either of the lovers could have made us aware of every ironic touch.

The author must, then, choose whether to purchase mystery at the expense of irony. For many of us Jane Austen's choice here is perhaps the weakest aspect of this novel. It is a commonplace of our criticism that significant literature arouses suspense not about the 'what' but about the 'how'. Mere mystification has been mastered by so many second-rate writers that her efforts at mystification seem second-rate.

But again we must ask whether criticism can be conducted effectively by balancing one abstract quality against another. Is there a norm of dramatic irony for all works, or even for all works of a given kind? Has anyone ever formulated a 'law of first and second readings' that will tell us just how many of our pleasures on page one should depend on our knowledge of what happens on page the last? We quite properly ask that the books we call great be able to stand up under repeated reading, but we need not ask that they yield identical pleasures on each reading. The modern works whose authors pride themselves on the fact that they can never be read but only re-read may be very good indeed, but they are not *made* good by the fact that their secret pleasures can only be wrested from them by repeated readings.

In any case, even if one accepted the criticism of Jane Austen's efforts at mystification, the larger service of the inside views is clear: the crosslights thrown by other minds prevent our being blinded by Emma's radiance.

The reliable narrator and the norms of Emma

If mere intellectual clarity about Emma were the goal in this work, we should be forced to say that the manipulation of inside views and the extensive commentary of the reliable Knightley are more than is necessary. But for maximum intensity of the comedy and romance, even these are not enough. The 'author herself' – not necessarily the real Jane Austen but an implied author, represented in this book by a reliable narrator – heightens the effects by directing our intellectual, moral, and emotional progress. She performs, of course, most of the functions described in chapter 7. But her most important role is to reinforce both aspects of the double vision that operates throughout the book: our inside view of Emma's worth and our objective view of her great faults.

The narrator opens *Emma* with a masterful simultaneous presentation of Emma and of the values against which she must be judged: 'Emma Woodhouse, handsome, clever, and rich, with a comfortable home and happy disposition, seemed to unite some of the best blessings of existence, and had lived nearly twenty-one years in the world with very little to distress or vex her.' This 'seemed' is immediately reinforced by more directly stated reservations. 'The real evils of Emma's situation were the power of having rather too much her own way, and a disposition to think a little too well of herself; these were the disadvantages which threatened alloy to her many enjoyments. The danger, however, was at present so unperceived, that they did not by any means rank as misfortunes with her.'

None of this could have been said by Emma, and if shown through her consciousness, it could not be accepted, as it must be, without question. Like most of the first three chapters, it is non-dramatic summary, building up, through the ostensible business of getting the characters introduced, to Emma's initial blunder with Harriet and Mr Elton. Throughout these chapters we learn much of what we must know from the narrator, but she turns over more and more of the job of summary to Emma as she feels more and more sure of our seeing precisely to what degree Emma is to be trusted. Whenever we leave the 'real evils' we have been warned against in Emma, the narrator's and Emma's views coincide: we cannot tell which of them, for example, offers the judgment on Mr Woodhouse that 'his talents could not have recommended him at any time', or the judgment on Mr Knightley that he is 'a sensible man', 'always welcome' at Hartfield, or even that 'Mr Knightley, in fact, was one of the few people who could see faults in Emma Woodhouse, and the only one who ever told her of them'.

But there are times when Emma and her author are far apart, and the author's direct guidance aids the reader in his own break with Emma. The beautiful irony of the first description of Harriet, given through Emma's eyes (ch. 3) could no doubt be grasped intellectually by many readers without all of the preliminary commentary. But even for the most perceptive its effect is heightened, surely, by the sense of standing with the author and observing with her precisely how Emma's judgment is going astray. Perhaps more important, we ordinary, less perceptive readers have by now been raised to a level suited to grasp the ironies. Certainly, most readers would overlook some of the barbs directed against Emma if the novel began, as a serious modern novelist might well begin it, with this description:

[Emma] was not struck by any thing remarkably clever in Miss Smith's conversation, but she found her altogether very engaging – not inconveniently shy, not unwilling to talk – and yet so far from pushing, shewing so proper and becoming a deference, seeming so pleasantly grateful for being admitted to Hartfield, and so artlessly impressed by the appearance of every thing in so superior a style to what she had been used to, that she must have good sense and deserve encouragement. Encouragement should be given. Those soft blue eyes . . . should not be wasted on the inferior society of Highbury. . . .

And so Emma goes on, giving herself away with every word, pouring out her sense of her own beneficence and general value Harriet's past friends, 'though very good sort of people, must be doing her harm'. Without knowing them, Emma knows that they 'must be coarse and unpolished, and very unfit to be the intimates of a girl who wanted only a little more knowledge and elegance to be quite perfect'. And she concludes with a beautiful burst of egotism: '*She* would notice her; she would improve her; she would detach her from her bad acquaintance, and introduce her into good society; she would form her opinions and her manners. It would be an interesting, and certainly a very kind undertaking; highly becoming her own situation in life, her leisure, and powers.' Even the most skilful reader might not easily plot an absolutely true course through these ironies without the prior direct assistance we have been given. Emma's views are not so outlandish that they could never have been held by a female novelist writing in her time. They cannot serve effectively as signs of *her* character unless they are clearly disavowed as signs of Jane Austen's views. Emma's unconscious catalogue of her egotistical uses for Harriet, given under the pretense of listing the services *she* will perform, is thus given its full force by being framed explicitly in a world of values which Emma herself cannot discover until the conclusion of the book.

The full importance of the author's direct imposition of an elaborate scale of norms can be seen by considering that conclusion. The sequence of events is a simple one: Emma's faults and mistakes are brought home to her in a rapid and humiliating chain of rebukes from Knightley and blows from hard fact. These blows to her self-esteem produce at last a genuine reform (for example, she brings herself to apologize to Miss Bates, something she could never have done earlier in the novel). The change in her character removes the only obstacle in the way of Knightley's proposal, and the marriage follows. 'The wishes, the hopes, the confidence, the predictions of the small band of true friends who witnessed the ceremony, were fully answered in the perfect happiness of the union.'

It may be that if we look at Emma and Knightley as real people, this ending will seem false. G. B. Stern laments, in *Speaking of Jane Austen*, 'Oh, Miss Austen, it was *not* a good solution; it was a bad solution, an unhappy ending, could we see beyond the last pages of the book.' Edmund Wilson predicts that Emma will find a new protégé like Harriet, since she has not been cured of her inclination to 'infatuations with women'. Marvin Mudrick even more emphatically rejects Jane Austen's explicit rhetoric; he believes that Emma is still a 'confirmed exploiter', and for him the ending must be read as ironic.[6]

But it is precisely because this ending is neither life itself nor a simple bit of literary irony that it can serve so well to heighten our sense of a complete and indeed perfect resolution to all that has gone before. If we look at the values that have been realized in this marriage and compare them with those realized in conventional marriage plots, we see that Jane Austen means what she says: this will be a happy marriage because there is simply nothing left to make it anything less than perfectly happy. It fulfils every value embodied in the world of the book— with the possible exception that Emma may never learn to apply herself as she ought to her reading and her piano! It is a union of intelligence: of 'reason', of 'sense', of 'judgment'. It is a union of virtue: of 'good will', of generosity, of unselfishness. It is a union of feeling: of 'taste', 'tenderness', 'love', 'beauty'.[7]

In a general way, then, this plot offers us an experience super-ficially like that offered by most tragicomedy as well as by much of the cheapest popular art: we are made to desire certain good things for certain good characters, and then our desires are gratified. If we depended on general criteria derived from our justified boredom with such works, we should reject this one. But the critical difference lies in the precise quality of the values appealed to and the precise quality of the characters who violate or realize them. All of the cheap marriage plots in the world should not lead us to be embarrassed about our pleasure in Emma and Knightley's marriage. It is more than just the marriage: it is the *rightness* of *this* marriage, as a conclusion to all of the comic wrongness that has gone before. The good for Emma includes both her necessary reform and the resulting marriage. Marriage to an intelligent, amiable, good, and attractive man is the best thing that can happen to this heroine, and the readers who do not experience it as such are, I am convinced, far from knowing what Jane Austen is about – whatever they may say about the 'bitter spinster's' attitude towards marriage.

Our modern sensibilities are likely to be rasped by any such formulation. We do not ordinarily like to encounter perfect endings in our novels – even in the sense of 'perfectedness' or completion, the sense obviously intended by Jane Austen. We refuse to accept it when we see it: witness the many attempts to deny Dostoevski's success with Alyosha and Father Zossima in *The Brothers Karamazov*. Many of us find it embarrassing to talk of emotions based on moral judgment at all, particularly when the emotions have any kind of affirmative cast. Emma herself is something of a 'modern' in this regard throughout most of the book. Her self-deception about marriage is as great as about most other important matters. Emma boasts to Harriet of her indifference to marriage, at the same time unconsciously betraying her totally inadequate view of the sources of human happiness.

'If I know myself, Harriet, mine is an active, busy mind, with a great many independent resources; and I do not perceive why I should be more in want of employment at forty or fifty than one-and-twenty. Woman's usual occupations of eye and hand and mind will be as open to me then, as they are now; or with no important variation. If I draw less, I shall read more; if I give up music, I shall take to carpet-work.'

Emma at carpet-work! If she knows herself indeed.

'And as for objects of interest, objects for the affections, which is, in truth, the great point of inferiority, the want of which is really the great evil to be avoided in *not* marrying [a magnificent concession, this] I shall be very well off, with all the children of a sister I love so much, to care about. There will be enough of them, in all probability, to supply every sort of sensation that declining life can need. There will be enough for every hope and every fear; and though my attachment to none can equal that of a parent, it suits my ideas of comfort better than what is warmer and blinder. My nephews and nieces! – I shall often have a niece with me.'   (ch. 10)

Without growing solemn about it – it is wonderfully comic – we can recognize that the humor springs here from very deep sources indeed. It can be fully enjoyed, in fact, only by the reader who has attained to a vision of human felicity far more profound than Emma's 'comfort' and 'want' and 'need'. It is a vision that includes not simply marriage, but a kind of loving converse not based, as is Emma's here, on whether the 'loved' person will serve one's irreducible needs.

The comic effect of this repudiation of marriage is considerably increased by the fact that Emma always thinks of marriage for others as *their* highest good, and in fact unconsciously encourages her friend Harriet to fall in love with the very man she herself loves without knowing it. The delightful denouement is thus what we want not only because it is a supremely good thing for Emma, but because it is a supremely comic outcome of Emma's profound misunderstanding of herself and of the human condition. In the schematic language of chapter 5, it satisfies both our practical desire for Emma's well-being and our appetite for the qualities proper to these artistic materials. It is thus a more resounding resolution than either of these elements separately could provide. The other major resolution of the work – Harriet's marriage with her farmer – reinforces this interpretation. Emma's sin against Harriet has been something far worse than the mere meddling of a busybody. To destroy Harriet's chances for happiness – chances that depend entirely on her marriage – is as close to viciousness as any author could dare to take a heroine designed to be loved. We can laugh with Emma at this mistake (ch. 54) only because Harriet's chance for happiness is restored.

Other values, like money, blood, and 'consequence', are real enough in *Emma*, but only as they contribute to or are mastered by good taste, good judgment, and good morality. Money alone can make a Mrs Churchill, but a man or woman 'is silly to marry without it'. Consequence untouched by sense can make a very inconsequential Mr Woodhouse; untouched by sense or virtue it can make the much more contemptible Mr and Miss Elliot of *Persuasion*. But it is a pleasant thing to have, and it does no harm unless, like the early Emma, one takes it too seriously. Charm and elegance without sufficient moral force can make a Frank Churchill; unschooled by morality it can lead to the baseness of Henry Crawford in *Mansfield Park* or of Wickham in *Pride and Prejudice*. Even the supreme virtues are inadequate in isolation: good will alone will make a comic Miss Bates or a Mr Weston, judgment with insufficient good will a comic Mr John Knightley, and so on.

I am willing to risk the commonplace in such a listing because it is only thus that the full force of Jane Austen's comprehensive view can be seen. There is clearly at work here a much more detailed ordering of values than any conventional public philosophy of her time could provide. Obviously, few readers in her own time, and far fewer in our own, have ever approached this novel in full and detailed agreement with the author's norms. But they were led to join her as they read, and so are we.

Explicit judgments on Emma Woodhouse

We have said in passing almost enough of the other side of the coin – the judgment of particular actions as they relate to the general norms. But something must be said of the detailed 'placing' of Emma, by direct commentary, in the hierarchy of values established by the novel. I must be convinced, for example, not only that tenderness for other people's feelings is an important trait but also that Emma's particular behavior violates the true standards of tenderness, if I am to savor to the full the episode of Emma's insult to Miss Bates and Knightley's reproach which follows. If I refuse to blame Emma, I may discover a kind of intellectual enjoyment in the episode, and I will probably think that any critic who talks of 'belief' in tenderness as operating in such a context is taking things too seriously. But I can never enjoy the episode in its full intensity or grasp its formal coherence. Similarly, I must agree not only that to be dreadfully boring is a minor fault compared with the major virtue of 'good will', but also that Miss Bates's exemplification of this fault and of this virtue entitle her to the respect which Emma denies. If I do not – while yet being able to laugh at Miss Bates – I can hardly understand, let alone enjoy, Emma's mistreatment of her.

But these negative judgments must be counteracted by a larger approval, and, as we would expect, the novel is full of direct apologies for Emma. Her chief fault, lack of good will or tenderness, must be read not only in relationship to the code of values provided by the book as a whole – a code which judges her as seriously deficient; it must also be judged in relationship to the harsh facts of the world around her, a world made up of human beings ranging in degree of selfishness and egotism from Knightley, who lapses from perfection when he tries to judge Frank Churchill, his rival, down to Mrs Elton, who has most of Emma's faults and none of her virtues. In such a setting, Emma is easily forgiven. When she insults Miss Bates, for example, we remember that Miss Bates lives in a world where many others are insensitive and cruel. 'Miss Bates, neither young, handsome, rich, nor married, stood in the very worst predicament in the world for having much of the public favour; and she had no intellectual superiority to make atonement to herself, or frighten those who might hate her, into outward respect.' While it would be a mistake to see only this 'regulated hatred' in Jane Austen's world, overlooking the tenderness and generosity, the hatred of viciousness is there, and there is enough vice in evidence to make Emma almost shine by comparison.

Often, Jane Austen makes this apology-by-comparison explicit. When Emma lies to Knightley about Harriet, very close to the end of the book, she is excused with a generalization about human nature: 'Seldom, very seldom, does complete truth belong to any human disclosure; seldom can it happen that something is not a little disguised, or a little mistaken; but where, as in this case, though the conduct is mistaken, the feelings are not, it may not be very material. – Mr Knightley could not impute to Emma a more relenting heart than she possessed, or a heart more disposed to accept of his.'

The implied author as friend and guide

With all of this said about the masterful use of the narrator in *Emma*, there remain some 'intrusions' unaccounted for by strict service to the story itself. 'What did she say?' the narrator asks, at the crucial moment in the major love scene. 'Just what she ought, of course. A lady always does. – She said enough to show there need not be despair – and to invite him to say more himself.' To some readers this has seemed to demonstrate the author's inability to write a love scene, since it sacrifices 'the illusion of reality'.[8] But who has ever read this far in *Emma* under the delusion that he is reading a realistic portrayal which is suddenly shattered by the unnatural appearance of the narrator? If the narrator's superabundant wit is destructive of the kind of illusion proper to this work, the novel has been ruined long before.

But we should now be in a position to see precisely why the narrator's wit is not in the least out of place at the emotional climax of the novel. We have seen how the inside views of the characters and the author's commentary have been used from the beginning to get the values straight and to keep them straight and to help direct our reactions to Emma. But we also see here a beautiful case of the dramatized author as friend and guide. 'Jane Austen', like 'Henry Fielding', is a paragon of wit, wisdom, and virtue. She does not talk about her qualities; unlike Fielding she does not in *Emma* call direct attention to her artistic skill. But we are seldom allowed to forget about her for all that. When we read this novel we accept her as representing everything we admire most. She is as generous and wise as Knightley; in fact, she is a shade more penetrating in her judgment. She is as subtle and witty as Emma would like to think herself. Without being sentimental she is in favor of tenderness. She is able to put an adequate but not excessive value on wealth and rank. She recognizes a fool when she sees one, but unlike Emma she knows that it is both immoral and foolish to be rude to fools. She is, in short, a perfect human being, within the concept of perfection established by the book she writes; she even recognizes that human perfection of the kind *she* exemplifies is not quite attainable in real life. The process of her domination is of course circular; her character establishes the values for us according to which her character is then found to be perfect. But this circularity does not affect the success of her endeavor; in fact it insures it.

Her 'omniscience' is thus a much more remarkable thing than is ordinarily implied by the term. All good novelists know all about their characters – all that they need to know. And the question of how their narrators are to find out all that *they* need to know, the question of 'authority', is a relatively simple one. The real choice is much more profound than this would imply. It is a choice of the moral, not merely the technical, angle of vision from which the story is to be told.

Unlike the central intelligences of James and his successors, 'Jane Austen' has learned nothing at the end of the novel that she did not know at the beginning. She needed to learn nothing. She knew everything of importance already. We have been privileged to watch with her as she observes her favorite character climb from a considerably lower platform to join the exalted company of Knightley, 'Jane Austen', and those of us readers who are wise enough, good enough, and perceptive enough to belong up there too. As Katherine Mansfield says, 'the truth is that every true admirer of the novels cherishes the happy thought that he alone – reading between the lines – has become the secret friend of their author'.[9] Those who love 'gentle Jane' as a secret friend may undervalue the irony and wit; those who see her in effect as the greatest of Shaw's heroines, flashing about her with the weapons of irony, may undervalue the emphasis on tenderness and good will. But only a very few can resist her.

The dramatic illusion of her presence as a character is thus fully as important as any other element in the story. When she intrudes, the illusion is not shattered. The only illusion we care about, the illusion of traveling intimately with a hardy little band of readers whose heads are screwed on tight and whose hearts are in the right place, is actually strengthened when we are refused the romantic love scene. Like the author herself, we don't care about the love scene. We can find love scenes in almost any novelist's works, but only here can we find a mind and heart that can give us clarity without oversimplification, sympathy and romance without sentimentality, and biting irony without cynicism.

NOTES

1. 'The Lesson of Balzac', in *The Question of Our Speech* (Cambridge, 1905) p. 63.

2. See, for example, Mudrick, *Jane Austen: Irony as Defense and Discovery* (Princeton, 1952) pp. 91, 165; Frank O'Connor, *The Mirror in the Roadway* (1957) p. 30.

3. 'A heroine whom no one but myself will much like'; see James Edward Austen-Leigh, *Memoir of His Aunt* (London, 1870; Oxford, 1926) p. 157.

4. What is probably the best discussion of this double-edged problem is buried in Reginald Farrer's essay on 'Jane Austen', in *Quarterly Review*, CCXXVIII (July 1917) 1–30. For one critic the book fails because the problem was never recognized by Jane Austen herself: Mr E. N. Hayes, in what may well be the least sympathetic discussion of *Emma* yet written, explains the whole book as the *author's* failure to see Emma's faults. 'Evidently Jane Austen wished to protect Emma.' 'The author is therefore in the ambiguous position of both loving and scorning the heroine' – see '*Emma*: A Dissenting Opinion', in *Nineteenth-century Fiction*, IV (June 1949) 18, 19. [Extracts from these articles are reprinted in this volume, pp. 64–9 and 74–8.]

5. A. C. Bradley, for example, once argued that Jane Austen intended Jane Fairfax to be as interesting throughout as she becomes at the end, but 'the moralist in Jane Austen stood for once in her way. The secret engagement is, for her, so serious an offence, that she is afraid to win our hearts for Jane until it has led to great unhappiness.' 'Jane Austen', in *Essays and Studies, by Members of the English Association*, II (Oxford, 1911) 23.

6. The first two quotations are from Wilson's 'A Long Talk about Jane Austen', in *A Literary Chronicle: 1920–1950* (New York, 1952). The third is from *Jane Austen* (Princeton, 1952) p. 206.

7. It has lately been fashionable to underplay the value of tenderness and good will in Jane Austen, in reaction to an earlier generation that overdid the picture of 'gentle Jane'. The trend seems to have begun in earnest with D. W. Harding's 'Regulated Hatred: An Aspect of the Work of Jane Austen', in *Scrutiny*, VIII (March 1940) 346–62 [reprinted in this volume, pp. 69–74.] While I do not feel as strongly aroused against this school of readers as does R. W. Chapman – (see his *A Critical Bibliography* (Oxford, 1953) p. 52, and his review of Mudrick's work in the *Times Literary Supplement* (19 Sept 1952)) – it seems to me that another swing of the pendulum is called for: when Jane Austen praises the 'relenting heart', she means that praise, though she is the same author who can lash the unrelenting heart with 'regulated hatred'.

8. Edd Winfield Parks, 'Exegesis in Austen's Novels', in *South Atlantic Quarterly*, LI (Jan 1952) 117.

9. *Novels and Novelists*, ed. J. Middleton Murry (1930) p. 304.

Malcolm Bradbury

JANE AUSTEN'S *EMMA* (1962)

'JANE AUSTEN', said Henry James in one of his few great misjudgments, 'was instinctive and charming. . . . For signal examples of what composition, distribution, arrangement can do, of how they intensify the life of a work of art, we have to go elsewhere.' We do not, of course; and my purpose here is to suggest something of the complexity of the structure that Jane Austen creates to express the elaborate pattern of values contained in *Emma*. 'I am going to take a heroine whom no-one but myself will much like', said Jane Austen of the novel; and one might set the remark against her comment that Anne Elliot, the heroine of *Persuasion* (surely Jane Austen's best novel) was almost too good for her. It is presumably a moral objection she fears will be brought against Emma; and it is to be by resolving this situation – by fitting Emma into the moral expectations which she projects outwards into the audience, as it were – that the book must work. The self-willed quality of Emma, in which her attractiveness for reader and for novelist resides, must be contained and adapted, adapted to a norm which is neither social (though it is a norm which *lives* in society) nor doctrinaire (though it is a norm pragmatic simply in the sense that it re-establishes by proof of value the best traditional decencies).

Jane Austen is concerned with two kinds of world – the social world and the moral world – and their interaction, an interaction that is intimate, but also complex. It is often complained of her that she measured life from the conventional social standards of the upper middle class about which she writes and to which she belongs, and that this limits her wider relevance and 'excludes' her from the modern novel, one of the attributes of which is a greater range in its treatment of character and value. Leavis disposes of one aspect of this idea in *The Great Tradition*, and it is worth stressing here the degree to which she dissipates and tests her own predilections, and is capable of having predilections that seem to violate the rigidities we associate with her. Of course it is true that class attitudes are of the greatest importance; but it is in the evaluation of these attitudes, and the building up of a scale of them for the proper conduct of the moral life, that she excels. She is nothing if not stringent. The whole structure of her inventions is recurrently that of a kind of moral assault course, an extended interview in which candidates give their qualifications, undergo a succession of tests, and are finally rewarded by the one prize that is possible and appropriate in their social context – marriage, a marriage which is aesthetically right, morally and humanly balanced, financially sound. (Lawrence in some of his novels uses a similar structure, the tests here being emotional and sexual, the final reward genital.)

What Jane Austen has to do, then, in *Emma* is to establish side by side a social world and a moral world, the latter setting up a higher level of action and judgment than the former. The social world is carefully and precisely given; it is elaborate in range, though not in class. The action takes place in Highbury, a 'large and prosperous village, almost amounting to a town', sixteen miles out of London; its life is the life of the time of writing (*Emma* was published in 1816). The landscape of Highbury is a landscape of property; there is Hartfield, the home of the Woodhouses, who are 'the first in consequence in Highbury'; there is Randalls, home of Mr Weston, 'a little estate'; there is Donwell Abbey 'in the parish adjoining, the seat of Mr Knightley'. Emma's sister lives in London, in Brunswick Square, only relatively accessible; Highbury is a more or less self-contained social unit, and it certainly contains most of the action. Further, the upper-middle-class level of Highbury life includes most of the significant characters; and this is the level we see from. There are persons of higher rank, but they are *felt* to be high – in particular, the Churchills, the great Yorkshire family, are presented as rather 'above' the novel. There are, too, characters clearly 'below' the novel, like the tenant-farmer Robert Martin and the former Miss Taylor and Mrs Goddard and Miss Bates, who come from the depressed 'professional' middle class. And then there are the socially indeterminate characters, who serve so importantly in the action – Miss Harriet Smith, illegitimate, of obscure origins, unfixed by kinship or duty; Frank Churchill, split between families; and Jane Fairfax. These figures, coming from outside the locale and existing in uncertain relation to it, are the disturbing forces; and their presence promotes most of the action. In particular Miss Harriet Smith is an anarchic force and, especially, a test of people's observations of innate quality, because she can fit in at any of a number of possible class levels; indeed, she can claim her class by her own merits, and so is in the singular position of being mobile in a largely stable society. And the novel, by concentrating on the period prior to marriage in these people, is able to show them at their most mobile; they exist in a state of uncertainty, finished by marriage, which 'fixes' them at a deserved level in the class system.

Now the central characters of the fiction are landowners with tenant farmers, persons of private income, or persons dependent on the professions or trade; they are small in number in the novel, and are concentrated in houses and families, with few points of reference outside Highbury; they live in a controlled and stable world. Most of the characters know one another before the action of the novel begins and enlarge existing relationships in the course of it; they are related by kinship or common social duties; they live most of their lives in the place where they are born. The limits of the world of the novel are, indeed, determined from the centre – all the characters exist in some kind of established relationship to the heroine or her immediate friends. In picaresque novels the relationships with the hero are usually those of casual encounter, a structure that is consonant with a pragmatic and open view of the universe; but here we have a homogeneous world, taking its standards of life from within itself, and communicating outside only rarely. The characters are inhibited by a strong sense of rank and social duty, and no real violation of rank is within the novel's probabilities. The Highbury equals are capable of intimate relationships with one another; but, as rank changes, the relation to the Woodhouses grows more distant (the vicar is not close, the schoolmistress is received, the poor are visited), while characters in mobile situations create most of the tensions – like the rising Coles: 'The Coles were very respectable in their way, but they ought to be taught that it was not for them to arrange the terms on which superior families would visit them.' (But this is by no means the *final* standard of judgment; the thought is Emma's, and the reader is invited soon to wonder, when he meets the Coles and finds their pleasantness stressed, what constitutes 'superiority'.) The constraints of a fixed society are firmly felt, and Jane Austen never tests the values that arise within this world outside the area in which they are possible (in industrial cities or in lower social brackets); there is no need to; in this agrarian and hierarchical world, subscribing by assent to a stylized system of properties and duties, she finds a context in which they can yield their full resources.

The society in which the moral action takes place is then a local, limited, stylized world, with its own operative values and its own occasions. Its social intercourse is unelaborate. When people meet they do so over dinner or at balls or in Ford's shop; encounters occur by formal arrangement; there are few accidental meetings, and so precise are the circumstances of this life that when these occur (as when Harriet meets Robert Martin in the shop) they are deeply disturbing. Persons stand out large, while the formalities make for a controlled universe, in which our own sense of propriety as readers is engaged to the degree that, when Jane Fairfax and Frank Churchill are, by a conjunction of accidents, left alone with the sleeping Miss Bates and this 'breach' goes unobserved, we alone are called on to observe it and reflect on its significance. The degree of social stability, the preciseness of social expectations, the limitations on eccentric behaviour or concealments or violent action, reinforce and make significant the moral order. They enable a concentration on the quality of the individual life. They create a high degree of consensus about behaviour – about what constitutes decent action. They provide a relatively closed and rounded world in which, once a level of adequate living has been acquired, it can be reinforced from without, for the future will be reasonably like the present.

Within these limits, though, the society throws up a broad range of values, out of which the tensions of the novel arise. The characters think about similar things, but they think differently about them. They think differently about the importance of rank, about the relative value of taste or courtesy or honour, and about the importance of reason or emotion in conduct. Certain things are commonly approved or frowned upon – frivolity is disliked and goodwill valued – while on other matters different characters take different stands. And this is the way in which we are coerced, by the novelist, into perceiving and adopting a measure, for, either through direct authorial intervention or more commonly by the relative elevation and demotion of various characters, this latter done by a complex strategy and tone, we perceive a pattern. The public values are placed according to a private and, as I've said, an interestingly pragmatic view. People define themselves by their actions, and as they act we perceive that there are in the novel superior and inferior people in moral as well as social terms. The social order yields to the moral. The morally inferior people tend in fact to be socially high, to considerable dramatic effect; Emma herself, at the beginning, is one of them and Frank Churchill another, while people of lower rank, like the Martins and the Coles, elevate themselves by their actions. In this fashion certain values emerge as positive – particularly values having to do with care and respect for others, the decent discharge of one's duties, and the scrupulous improvement of oneself. They are values associated with, but by no means intrinsic to, an upper-middle-class social position. So frivolity may be despised, but accomplishments count high, since they evidence self-discipline and self-enlargement and please others – the fact that Mr Martin reads is highly in his favour in this emergent scale, while Harriet Smith's taking a long time to choose materials at Ford's is not in hers. A friendly and social disposition is valued, but not *too* highly, since Emma's criticism of Jane Fairfax's reserve comes to tell more against Emma than it does against Jane and, what is more, it blinds her to some of the excellence of Mr Knightley. Goodwill and a contented temper are valued, but have their associated failures – Mr Weston is too easy-going for reasonable living, and Emma at once too indulgent over moral matters and not indulgent enough over social ones. To be 'open, straight-forward and well judging', like Martin, is important, but not as important as the rewarding side of Mr Knightley's more closed and critical temper. All this is the central area of the action, for it is what is at issue between Knightley and Emma; and yet we do come to value Emma's warmth and openness, only wanting it placed and ordered.

Birth and good manners are important, but only when there is something behind them. Elegance is admired, highly by Emma, less so by others. Mr Elton is 'self-important, presuming, familiar, ignorant and ill-bred'; the observations are Emma's, and have to be mediated by us carefully, for they show up Mr Elton *and* Emma. This picking up of tone is most important for the book, and we are helped by alternative views – for instance, Jane Fairfax is more tolerant of Mr Elton. Mr Weston is a little too open-hearted for Emma – 'General benevolence, and not general friendship, make a man what he ought to be. She could fancy such a man.' To Harriet she commends 'the habit of self-com-mand', but responds to Harriet's 'tenderness of heart' – 'There is nothing to be compared to it. Warmth and tenderness of heart, with an affectionate, open manner, will beat all clearness of head in the world for attraction.' But Mr Knightley, in one of the debates in which the education of Emma – and to a lesser extent of Knightley himself – is conducted and in which a permissible range of *difference* of value is reconciled, offers a more rational and mature view; he states the case for a plan of life strictly adhered to, a sense of duty and of courtesy, and a right realization of what one owes to one's social situation and therefore one's function. This competition of values between Knightley and Emma, which is one of our main guides to the direction of the book, touches on other issues and other people, of course – an interesting example of its method being the way in which Knightley reappraises Emma's description of Churchill as 'amiable':

'No, Emma; your amiable young man can be amiable only in French, not in English. He may be very 'aimable', have very good manners, and be very agreeable; but he can have no English delicacy towards the feelings of other people – nothing really amiable about him.'

Other issues come into these debates, to add to the dense moral atmosphere. Thus Churchill is criticized early for being above his connections, later for being too exuberant; while he himself criticizes 'civil falsehoods', but employs them. Emma admires elegance highly; she has a practical, advantage-seeking view of attractive qualities in people; she criticizes Mr Knightley for inventing lines of conduct that are not practical. Mr Knightley reverses this case, condemns Emma's fancy and whim, and recommends 'judging by nature'. In consequence, the moral life is in the front of the character's minds throughout; it is *linked* with class – as in the description of the estate at Donwell Abbey as belonging to 'a family of such true gentility, untainted in blood *and understanding*' – but understanding is insistently prior to blood as the notion of gentility begins to take a kind of ideal shape.

And so from the very first page of the book we are conscious of a disparity between the moral and the social scale. Emma's situation is, from the start, shown to be happy –

Emma Woodhouse, handsome, clever, and rich, with a comfortable home and happy disposition, seemed to unite some of the best blessings of existence; and had lived nearly twenty-one years in the world with little to distress or vex her.

But the complexities of the handling are already present. There is the hint, offered through nuances of diction, that the 'best blessings of existence' only *seem* to be hers; there is the point, further taken up and insisted on, that she has not been vexed but rather over-indulged. Her father is 'affectionate, indulgent'; her governess has 'a mildness of temper' that 'had hardly allowed her to impose any restraint', and presently by an explicit statement Jane Austen converts the hints into a direct moral observation – 'The real evils, indeed, of Emma's situation were the power of having rather too much of her own way, and a disposition to think a little too well of herself.'

A distinction is to be made between social and moral 'success', then; and this is reinforced when we are told, for instance, of the history of Mr Weston's previous marriage into a family of high rank, which

was an unsuitable connection, and did not produce much happiness. Mrs Weston ought to have found more in it, for she had a husband whose warm heart and sweet temper made him think everything due to her in return for the great goodness of being in love with him; but though she had one sort of spirit, she had not the best. She had resolution enough to pursue her own will in spite of her brother, but not enough to refrain from unreasonable regrets ...

The moral scale is centred rather particularly, throughout, upon what is reasonable and desirable in a social life whose basic unit is the family, what makes for good and open dealing between people, prospers and opens their relationships and makes them dutiful and considerate in all their public actions. Jane Austen's novels are domestic novels, novels centred on marriage; most of the commentary and moral discussion is in fact directed toward defining the conditions for a good marriage, and preparing the one good marriage which contrasts with all others in the novel and so dominates it. But marriage is a social pact and so must answer to the public dimension. The general expectations of this book are that people will make the marriages they deserve, and that the climax will be Emma's marriage, made when she has answered to her faults and resolved her dilemmas.

Whom, then, will Emma marry? This is the question on which the plot turns. This plot, simply summarised, is concerned with a girl of many fine qualities, but of certain considerable errors deriving from the misuse of her own powers, who realises these errors, perceives that they have made her make false attributions of worth to the people in her circle and, repenting, marries the man who can instruct her in an accurate reaction to the world. The first part of the plot, the Aristotelian 'beginning', takes us to chapter 17. In this section Emma is a detached agent in someone else's destiny; this is that part of the novel concerned with Emma's attempt to intervene in the life of Harriet Smith by marrying her to Mr Elton, and its function is to demonstrate the nature of Emma's mistakes about the world, and the dangers of detached and desultory action. By the time we reach chapters 16 and 17, where we are presented with Emma's regrets, we have all we need in the way of moral direction for the rest of the book. Mr Knightley's interpretation of character and event has been shown to be better than Emma's, and we have a clear sense of Emma's tendency to misread what is before her, as well as of the faults, particularly snobbery and whimsy, which make her do this. The use of Harriet Smith as a device to expose the two different versions of the world espoused by Emma and Mr Knightley is singularly skilful. For Harriet's illegitimacy means that she can be judged very differently by different people; and each of them associate her with a rank that indicates the nature of their judgment. The uncertainty about Harriet's background thus becomes a dramatic delaying device, and much depends on the discovery of her true station, for then we shall see who is correct about her. The point is, as I have indicated, that her statement of herself, unlike that of any other characters in the book, depends entirely upon her *own* attributes; she is not reinforced by any class position. And so the question that arises is – is it Emma who is snobbish about Mr Martin, and damaging to Harriet in seeking to link her with Mr Elton; or is it Mr Knightley who is snobbish in his assumption that she deserves no better than Mr Martin, and that she is harmful company for Emma? The matter goes further – for to Emma Harriet has the virtues which commend a woman to men (beauty and good nature) and with these she has all she needs to win affection. But Mr Knightley sees the marriage connection as involving larger issues –'Men of sense, whatever you may choose to say, do not want silly wives. Men of family would not be very fond of connecting themselves with a girl of such obscurity . . .'.

The beautifully managed scene where Knightley puts this to Emma, and dissipates any feeling we may have of *his* snobbery by talking of Robert Martin's 'sense, sincerity and good humour' and his 'true gentility' of mind, is quickly supported by his being proved right about Mr Elton – 'Depend upon it. Elton will not do ... Elton may talk sentimentally, but he will act rationally. He is as well acquainted with his own claims as you can be with Harriet's.' Indeed, Knightley's criticism of Emma's behaviour has a precise moral tenor; he points to a specific fault – 'If you were as much guided by nature in your estimate of men and women, and as little under the power of fancy and whim in your dealings with them as you are where these children are concerned, we might always think alike.' That Emma *is* guided by fancy and whim we begin to see the more when, after a succession of delightfully handled comic scenes founded on the ambiguity of Mr Elton's supposed wooing of Harriet, Mr John Knightley points out to Emma that Mr Elton seems to have an interest in her. Emma's response is clearly self-deluding:

She walked on, amusing herself in the consideration of the blunders which often arise from a partial knowledge of circumstances, of the mistakes which people of high pretensions to judgment are for ever falling into; and not very well pleased with her brother for imagining her blind and ignorant, and in want of counsel.

The irony is turned directly against her; and her ignorance on the matter, her failure to perceive that it is *she* who is being courted by Mr Elton, takes on a dimension beyond the comic – takes on the status of a moral fault.

The second part of the novel, the 'middle', is that concerned with Emma's mistakes about the nature of Frank Churchill's and Jane's characters, and her inability to infer the truth here because of her pre-judgments. The situations are now more complicated, but Emma repeats her errors without real improvement, inventing a romance before she has even met her between Jane and Mr Dixon, and another between Churchill and herself. Here the purpose of the action is to show how she behaves in events which increasingly come to involve not a protégé's but her own destiny, to show how she is capable of misusing herself. This part of the plot ends with a significant and crucial discovery. Emma's discovery that she is in love.

The 'end' of the book beautifully enforces the weight and meaning of the book; the waters clear, and all the significances are laid bare in a simple delaying action which enables Jane Austen to make clear all the inadequacies of her characters and the moral lesson to be learned from them. Repentance in Emma is delayed to the last and therefore most effective moment, and it comes after a train of thought in which we see Emma affected, involved, pressed into realisation of her follies. On top of understanding comes marriage, a right resolution to the plot in that it enforces the significance of true understanding. The preparation is over and by extending the novel indefinitely by a closing sentence referring to 'the perfect happiness of the union' Jane Austen assures us that it is an effective understanding that Emma has come to.

These final effects are so precisely controlled and placed that it is evident that we *do* have a plot in which 'composition, distribution and arrangement' are handled with the greatest finesse. It is reached through such indirect methods that one can't but wonder at the vast number of threads that need to be woven into the resolution. The most complex strategy of the novel is the device of filtering it through the eyes of a character of whom Jane Austen doesn't wholly approve, yet with whom she is strongly in sympathy. There is no unsureness about the moments of understanding and improvement that must (despite her position as heroine) come to her. The device is handled particularly by the use of Mr Knightley as a 'corrective'; but that is by no means the whole of the effect, for Mr Knightley is not always right either. Another force exists to handle this; it resides in the values that emerge when we have taken away the irony from the treatment of events seen through Emma's eyes. For we must be careful to see that Emma is right sometimes; we must know, however, precisely when she is wrong. How well this is managed! Emma judges excessively by elegance; but though her criticism of Mrs Elton is that she lacks elegance, she perceives most of her faults. Indeed Emma is by no means consistently in error; she is clever enough to be right on nearly all the occasions where she is not giving rein to her snobbery and her prejudice – or pre-judgment.

It is Mrs Elton's snobbery that makes Emma's seem mild; and we need the scene where the two talk together to place Emma in that good light. The point then is that if Emma were judged by Jane Austen from 'outside', she would be unlikeable and highly criticized. In fact she is a violator of Jane Austen's moral scale to such a degree that it is hard at first to understand how she could have been made a heroine by her. And the fact that she *is* the heroine is the most remarkable thing about her – *Emma* is Jane Austen's *Tom Jones* in which the most devout expectation roused in the reader is the expectation that she will in some way come to grief; but we demand that her grief, like Tom Jones', will not be too painful, that repentance will occur, redemption be won and all the blessings of the prodigal son be given to her. This is what happens. The artistic problem of the book is then to make us care for Emma in such a way that we care about her fate, and like her, but that we in no way subdue our moral feelings about her faults.

And here another aspect of the tone is involved. For *Emma* is a comic novel, a novel concerned with comedy of manners in such a way as to make this the comedy of morals. There is comedy in various veins. There is the straightforward humorous treatment of Mr Woodhouse and Miss Bates as 'comic characters'. This, of course, does function in the moral dimension of the book – Mr Woodhouse's affectations are based on an indulgence to himself and it is an indulgence of the same order that has harmed Emma, while Miss Bates's absurdities make her a kind of test-case for Emma's power of responding to other people. But the significant action of the comedy in the management of the plot is to be found, for example, in the comic flavour of the scenes at the beginning where Emma, Harriet and Mr Elton are playing at picture-making and with riddles. These scenes are treated lightly, and they are designedly about trivial events; but they are organized to show us one thing above all, that Emma is capable of misreading radically the significance of these situations. What makes them most comic to the reader is his sense of a completely different possible explanation for Mr Elton's actions. The operative principle is, in short, an irony that works against the heroine.

This irony dominates the novel. It is contrived through the device of an omniscient narrator who is able to offer an alternative set of values, and it concerns almost always the difference between what the character sees and comes to judgment about, and other potential readings of the incident. It refers then particularly to Emma's habit of pre-judging situations. It is offered by a variety of methods, such as the changes in point of view that – for example – let us, at the beginning of chapter 20, see Jane Fairfax independently of Emma's judging eye. Its effect is not simply to set up another set of *facts* against which Emma's foolish interpretations are judged; we have to wait a while for *those*. What, at the time, we are invited to realize is not that Emma is wrong, but that she might be – that she has pre-judged. In short, then, we are drawn away from a determined interpretation or prejudice about people and events, and towards a sense of possible variety. The irony is thus in favour of empiricism; and the pattern of the book is one in which the events presented before us are capable of more complex interpretation. And because we commonly see through Emma's eyes, and because Emma doesn't see this further interpretation, it is dramatically delayed and becomes the centre of our sustained interest. The devices which assure us that it is there are, among other things, the insistent and critical presence of Mr Knightley, the occasional movements to other points of view, and the revelation of the first part that Emma has been wrong about Harriet Smith and so can be wrong again. This tension between events as they seem and events as they might be – between the pleasing Frank Churchill that Emma sees, and the temporizing and cunning Churchill that Mr Knightley sees – is the dynamic of the book. When Churchill comes to Randalls and talks so pleasantly, pleasing everyone, we wonder, we have been prepared to wonder, whether this is because he is deeply amiable or simply cunning. Events will bear at least two interpretations. But it should be said that Emma suspects this, that her views put to Mr Knightley are views she doubts, and that to some extent she has learned from the Harriet incident. As readers, however, skilled in plots, we are put into the position of being encouraged to entertain our suspicions longer;

there is a devised relationship between reader and heroine, inherent in the ironic note.

The novel closes on a final irony. One of Emma's faults has been her external view of persons, and her willingness to interfere in the destinies of others without being prepared to involve herself. Marriages are to be made only for others. In being forced into true feelings of love, she is released and opened out; love is the final testimony, in fact, of her redemption. She concludes the book by involving herself in the essential commitment of the Austen universe, which is marriage; so she has opened out into tenderness of heart, a tenderness without weakness or sentimentality. If she has still some faults to recant, these will come in time, for the fundamental liberation has taken place; she is no longer the Sleeping Beauty.

And in this way the shape of the novel is fulfilled. It has begun by delineating a variety of contesting moral viewpoints; it ends by clarification, by offering to the reader his way through the variety. We have learned this particularly through our understanding of Emma's faults, and by learning above all how significant, how *fundamental*, they are. For Emma's aloof relation to others, her willingness to treat them as toys or counters, her over-practical view of the good quality, which she sees simply as ensuring for its possessor a good match – these become significant betrayals of human possibility. 'With insufferable vanity she had believed herself in the secret of everybody's feelings; with unpardonable arrogance proposed to arrange everybody's destiny. She was proved to have been universally mistaken; and she had not quite done nothing – for she had done mischief. She had brought evil on Harriet, on herself, and, she too much feared, on Mr Knightley . . .' The social and moral universe I described at the beginning of these comments takes on all the weight of its significance here, for it provides a context in which Emma's faults are not peccadilloes to be regarded with indulgence, but total violations of a whole worthwhile universe. Jane Austen's method is to rouse our expectations and draw on our moral stringency to such an extent that this insight becomes absolutely essential, and retribution is demanded. The agents of retribution here are Mr Knightley and Jane Austen herself, and the retribution, once understanding has come, is genial – the lesson learned by Emma is that of how to commit herself fully and properly in the moral and social act of marriage, an act whose validity she has begun by denying and with which she begins her mature life. And what is rendered for us, then, is the moral horror of values we are awfully apt to associate with Jane Austen herself – snobbery, an excessive regard for the elegant and smart, a practical regard for goodness because it is such a *marriageable* trait. These are the values that are purged. We have been turned another way; we have learned of the duty of the individual to immerse himself in the events about him and to accept his obligations to his acquaintance finely and squarely; we have learned of the value of 'the serious spirit', involved and totally responsible. We have been persuaded in fact of the importance of true regard for self and others, persuaded to see the full human being as full, fine, morally serious, totally responsible, entirely involved, and to consider every human action as a crucial, committing act of self-definition.

W. J. Harvey

THE PLOT OF *EMMA* (1967)

LIKE Isabel Archer, Emma Woodhouse is a heroine who evokes a wide spectrum of critical response, ranging from almost total indulgence and sympathy to almost total hostility and disapproval. But most of us, I imagine, approximate to that medial position of mixed response described by Wayne Booth.[1] His analysis of the techniques whereby Jane Austen controls this complicated calculus of response and commands the varying degrees of moral, emotional and aesthetic distance between reader and character cannot be bettered and need not be repeated. There is one section of his argument, however, where I must take issue with him and this difference provides a convenient starting point for yet another exploration of what must, by now, seem well-mapped territory.

The point concerns Jane Austen's deliberate delay in revealing the truth about the Frank Churchill–Jane Fairfax relationship. As Professor Booth writes:

> The question is always one of desired effects, and the choice of any one effect always bans innumerable other effects. . . . On the one hand [Jane Austen] cares about maintaining some sense of mystery as long as she can. On the other, she works at all points to heighten the reader's sense of dramatic irony, usually in the form of a contrast between what Emma knows, and what the reader knows. . . . The longer we are in doubt about Frank Churchill, the weaker our sense of ironic contrast between Emma's views and the truth. . . . The author must, then, choose whether to purchase mystery at the expense of irony. For many of us Jane Austen's choice here is perhaps the weakest aspect of the novel.

Since Jane Austen's choice becomes the main structural agent and narrative strategy of the novel, this may seem a radically damaging criticism. I think that we can say that there is a humble but valid aesthetic pleasure to be derived from the sheer ingenuity of the plot, from the scrupulousness with which Jane Austen seeds her clues and the neatness with which she bundles up her complicated harvest. Moreover, this neatness-in-complication is important in establishing the comic mode of the novel, in limiting and cooling off passions that might otherwise disturb that mode, in establishing a poetically just world of reversals, rewards and punishments that delight by their very precision. Like *Tom Jones* or like *The Egoist* we can almost say that the plot of *Emma* rhymes in its formal elegance. It is for this reason that I think those critics mistaken who see the they-married-and-lived-happily-ever-after convention as yet another example, conscious or unconscious, of Jane Austen's irony. For this would not only subvert Emma's comic anagnorisis and conversion, which I take to be genuine, but would also make the conclusion of the novel, like that of *The Bostonians*, transcend the established comic mode by virtue of its very open-endedness. But if this is all that can be said in defence of Jane Austen's choice of strategies, then I agree that it is not enough; Professor Booth's criticism would still be valid. Mere ingenuity, mere mystification are not in themselves sufficient; on these grounds we would have to think Michael Innes a better artist than Jane Austen. And the formal, rhyming, closed nature of the novel is not in itself significant except in so far as it gestures to us, as I have said, the appropriate kind of response. I shall try to show later that within the formal, closed world of *Emma* there is indeed a curious and enriching kind of openness to life. But for the moment it is what is enclosed that is important and this is, essentially, the nature of Emma Woodhouse. So it is to her that we must first turn.

Emma's failings are generally diagnosed as being, on the surface, those of snobbery and, below the surface, those of pride. (Hence we notice the unobtrusive but consistent use of a religious vocabulary – *remorse, contrition, penitence,* etc.) Her pride leads her to domineer and to stage-manage, to see the lives of others as extensions of her own ego, to deny them their human autonomy. In this she is like a bad artist, though her medium is human experience. (Hence we notice the relevance of charades and word-games, so appropriate also to the business of mystification, and we are offered as a hint her inferiority to Jane Fairfax as a musician. What Emma does badly with people, Jane Austen does supremely well with her characters.) Hence her punishment is appropriate; she, who delights in using others, discovers that she in turn has been used. Because 'With insufferable vanity had she believed herself in the secret of everybody's feelings: with unpardonable arrogance proposed to arrange everybody's destiny' (ch. 47), she must be brought to realise of Frank Churchill that:

'He has imposed on me, but he has not injured me . . . now I can tolerably comprehend his behaviour. He never wished to attach me. It was merely a blind to conceal his real situation with another. It was his object to blind all about him; and no one, I am sure, could be more effectually blinded than myself.' (ch. 49)

So much is critical commonplace and needs no further elaboration. What is not so commonly recognised is that this fault in Emma largely derives from another failure in her, the failure to control an over-active and perverted imagination. If Emma is an artist *manqué* in human material, then this is the prime cause; but the fact also gains in resonance if we remember that by Jane Austen's time the imagination was well-established as an essential moral agent, necessary for the sympathetic identification of ourselves with our fellow human beings. Jane Austen so stresses this aspect of Emma that she coins a new word, *imaginist*, to describe her. Speculating on Frank Churchill's rescue of Harriet from the gipsies, Emma thinks:

Such an adventure as this, a fine young man and a lovely young woman thrown together in such a way, could hardly fail of suggesting certain ideas to the coldest heart and the steadiest brain. . . . Could a linguist, could a grammarian, could even a mathematician have seen what she did, have witnessed their appearance together, and heard their history of it, without feeling that circumstances had been at work to make them peculiarly interesting to each other? How much more must an imaginist, like herself, be on fire with speculation and foresight!   (ch. 39)

This note is stressed throughout. Emma is 'too eager and busy in her own previous conceptions and ideas to hear [Mr Elton] impartially, or to see him with clear vision' (ch. 13); of Frank Churchill, 'her own imagination had already given her ... instinctive knowledge' (ch. 14); in one of her moments of good resolution she parts from Harriet 'confirmed of being humble and discreet and repressing imagination all the rest of her life' (ch. 17); when she meets Frank Churchill 'there was nothing to denote him unworthy of the distinguished honour which her imagination had given him; the honour, if not of being really in love with her, of being at least very near it' (ch. 25). And so on: any reader can easily compile an impressive catalogue of such instances.

Again, as with her pride, Emma is appropriately punished; she is doomed to live in the imaginations of others, to become part of *their* speculations, desires and misunderstandings. Thus in the Harriet–Elton fiasco, part of her punishment is not merely to suffer the just reproaches of Mr Knightley but also to bear with the witless speculations of Miss Bates:

'A Miss Hawkins! Well, I had always fancied it would be some young lady hereabouts; not that I ever – Mrs Cole once whispered to me – but I immediately said, "No, Mr. Elton is a most worthy young man – but" – in short, I do not think I am particularly quick at those sort of discoveries.'   (ch. 21)

This, and the later revelation of Frank Churchill's engagement to Jane Fairfax, are a neat enough reprisal for Emma's earlier dream of Churchill: 'she had a great curiosity to see him, a decided intention of finding him pleasant, of being liked by him to a certain degree, and a sort of pleasure in the idea of being coupled in their friends' imagination' (ch. 14). And we should notice that when she recognises the perversity of her imagination Emma can turn it into a source of sympathetic strength; thus when she learns of Frank Churchill's engagement she is quick to relieve Mrs Weston of her guilt at having allowed *her* imagination to become over-active.

This perversion of imagination is, of course, both symptom and cause of Emma's most radical failure; her lack of self-knowledge. This is the lesson hammered home at the crisis of her development, a crisis characteristically founded on yet another misunderstanding – 'to understand, thoroughly understand her own heart, was the first endeavour' (ch. 47). Her lack of self-knowledge naturally leads to those punishments I have already described; 'she had been imposed on by others in a most mortifying degree' but 'she had been imposing on herself in a degree yet more mortifying' (ch. 47). But we should notice that whereas her pride and her imagination render her vulnerable to the other characters, her lack of self-knowledge renders her primarily vulnerable to the reader. The way this is done constitutes one of Jane Austen's major comic tactics; it lies quite simply in the fact that Emma consistently attributes to others characteristics which more truly describe her own nature. Thus when Mr Elton conveys Harriet's picture to London, Emma assures her that:

'It opens his designs to his family, it introduces you among them, it diffuses through the party those pleasantest feelings of our nature – eager curiosity and warm prepossession. How cheerful, how animated, how suspicious, how busy their imaginations all are!'   (ch. 7)

The passage expresses, of course, Emma's own 'busy' imagination. Or again, after Elton's proposal of marriage to her, Emma's reaction applies as well to herself as to him:

It was dreadfully mortifying; but Mr Elton was proving himself, in many respects, the very reverse of what she had meant and believed him – proud, assuming, conceited; very full of his own claims, and little concerned about the feelings of others.
                                                                            (ch. 16)

Again, a catalogue of such instances may easily be compiled. Cumulatively these confident moral judgements act as a boomerang with Emma as the unsuspecting target, and this becomes a major source of the novel's irony – an irony which, it should be noted, does not at all depend upon the strategy of mystification. We must thus qualify Professor Booth's charge that Jane Austen purchases the maximum of narrative surprise at the expense of the reader's ironic perspective.

There can be no doubt of Jane Austen's skill and thoroughness in her use of this narrative strategy. Once we know the secret of the engagement we can see that there is hardly a scene involving Frank Churchill that is not loaded with double meaning, hardly a passage of dialogue that cannot be fruitfully read between the lines. This very thoroughness must surely provide one's first reply to Professor Booth – that if we had been let into the secret from the start, then the irony must have seemed so insistent and obtrusive as to have become mechanical and oppressive. Surely the worst way of reading *Emma* would be to go through the novel, ticking off and totting up the ironies?

The problem, of course, is largely one of deciding which reading of *Emma* we are discussing. Professor Booth recognises the problem when he writes:

The sooner we see through Frank Churchill's secret plot, the greater our pleasure in observing Emma's innumerable mis-readings of his behaviour and the less interest we have in the mere mystery of the situation. And we all find that on second reading we discover new intensities of dramatic irony resulting from the complete loss of mystery; knowing what abysses of error Emma is preparing for herself, even those of us who may on first reading have deciphered nearly all the details of the Churchill mystery find additional ironies.

I can no longer recall my first, naïve reading of *Emma*, and I daresay that most readers of this essay are in the same position. But I suspect that Professor Booth assumes a rather too sophisticated first reading to be the norm. I can only report the testimony of scores of students who have read this novel with me for the first time, and their initial responses fall overwhelmingly into two categories. There are those for whom the revelation of the engagement comes as a complete and genuine narrative surprise. And there are those – not necessarily always the more intelligent students – who begin to suspect the truth at various points in the story. But they do no more than suspect and then only when the story is fairly well advanced. (In so far as this can be located at particular points it tends to occur either about chapter 28, by which time the business of the pianoforte has been sufficiently stressed, in chapter 30 where Churchill almost confesses to Emma his feelings for Jane Fairfax, or even as late as chapter 38, the scene of the dance.) Surely what I am terming suspicion – seeing this relationship as one possible outcome, one possible interpretation, but as no more than that – is a good state of mind for a first reading of *Emma*, one appropriate to the world of surmise, speculation, misunderstandings and cross-purposes that the novel depicts? What I am sure of is that were the reader fully aware from the outset of the true facts then the irony would become ponderous and schematic. Why this should not be so at a subsequent reading when the reader has such foreknowledge is a mystery that I can't pretend to explain, though I will offer one or two tentative suggestions later in this essay.

The other reason why Jane Austen made the right choice of narrative strategy is, oddly enough, noticed by Professor Booth himself when he discusses the novelist's control of our sympathies:

Sympathy for Emma can be heightened by withholding inside views of others as well as by granting them of her. The author knew, for example, that it would be fatal to grant any extended inside view of Jane Fairfax. . . . In *Emma*, Emma must shine supreme. *It is not only that the slightest glance inside Jane's mind would be fatal to all the author's plans for mystification about Frank Churchill, though this is important.* The major problem is that any extended view of her would reveal her as a more sympathetic person than Emma herself.

This seems to me entirely just, except at the one relevant point which I have italicized. Here Professor Booth seems to me to have turned things exactly upside down. Surely a full treatment of Jane is not withheld from us in the interest of mystification? It is rather that the mystification is a necessary narrative choice consequent upon the decision to subdue Jane Fairfax. And this is done, as Professor Booth says, in order to spotlight Emma. Let us suppose that Jane Austen had decided to enlighten us from the outset. The situation would then be so inherently interesting as to demand a much fuller and more vivid treatment of Jane herself. If Jane Austen did not meet these demands, we would then be justifiably disappointed and feel that there was a real failure in her powers of characterization. But if she did meet these demands, then Emma's central position would be usurped and the balance of our sympathies distorted. The result might be a good novel but it would not be *Emma*, the novel that Jane Austen chose to write. Thus I differ from Professor Booth in seeing the choice of mystification not as an end in itself but as a means to two greater ends – the subjugation of an otherwise oppressive and facile irony and the discipline of the reader's feelings about the chosen heroine.

So far I have demonstrated, I hope, that Jane Austen's choice of strategy was a necessary one; it now remains to explore what positive advantages, if any, she derived from it. The obvious formal qualities of *Emma* are those of poise, precision, elegance. The danger is that the shrewdness, accuracy and wisdom of the novel may be obscured by these very qualities, that we may be brought back to the 'ivory miniatures' view of Jane Austen. A sophisticated and distant relative of this view, perhaps, is Professor Booth's judgement that 'Jane Austen goes relatively deep morally, but scarcely skims the surface psychologically'. What I hope to show is that Jane Austen's choice of strategy, her technique of mystification, contributes an unusual depth and solidity to the novel and gives it a wonderful kind of openness and resonance within the apparently precise limits of its form. The plot of the novel may rhyme but it does not tinkle.

The world of *Emma* is binary. Around the visible star, Emma herself, circles an invisible planet whose presence and orbit we can gauge only by measuring the perturbations in the world we can see. Thus the tensions that build and break in the expedition to Box Hill are felt by all, but understood only by Jane Fairfax and Frank Churchill. The written novel contains its unwritten twin whose shape is known only by the shadow it casts. For most of the novel the only ambassador between these two worlds is Frank Churchill, and a good deal of his character is conveyed by his equivocal status. If Jane Fairfax suffers from the stresses of concealment and ambiguity, then Frank Churchill revels in them. If he pokes a good deal of fun at Emma, he can also, on occasion, be playfully cruel at the expense of the woman to whom he is engaged. Thus the technique of mystification allows Jane Austen to skim the psychological surface, but also to suggest the depths beneath. His interest as a character, in fact, largely derives from the question-mark that hovers about him; in this he seems to me to be of the same kind and order of characterization – though drawn within much stricter limits – as Chad Newsome in *The Ambassadors*. Beneath the polished surface there remains, perhaps, the selfish lout. At the very end, for example, despite all the explanations (suspiciously elaborate) of his letter, can we be *quite* sure that his decision to come into the open is entirely prompted by Jane's decision to become a governess? At any rate, the death of old Mrs Churchill is for him an entirely happy and timely accident. This is perhaps the most striking example in the novel of that generalization arrived at by Emma when she ponders, mistakenly, on the possible union of Harriet and Mr Knightley: 'Was it new for anything in this world to be unequal, inconsistent, incongruous – or for chance and circumstance (as second causes) to direct the human fate?' (ch. 47).

What Emma recognises is, indeed, a part of real existence and must be given its proper place in this most equal, consistent and congruous of novels. In few other novels does the protagonist seem so much in control, and in reality be so little in control, of her 'human fate'. This is mainly due to the invisible presence of the Jane Fairfax–Frank Churchill relationship, which allows Jane Austen to accommodate the apparent randomness of existence to the precise elegance of her form. *Emma* is finely shaped but it is not what Iris Murdoch would call a 'dry' novel because it allows for the contingent. The shadow novel-within-a-novel enables Jane Austen to embody that aspect of our intuition of reality summed up by Auden – 'we are lived by powers we do not understand'. One of the powers we do not understand is the incredibly complex pressure put upon us by the actions and interests, dreams and desires – the mere existence, even – of our contiguous or remote fellow human beings. It is something we simply accept as there though invisible, just as the private lives and passions of other people are not to be tamed by the domineering egoism of a blind and blinkered Emma. And just as Frank Churchill and Jane Fairfax impinge on the unsuspecting heroine, so they in turn are governed by people and powers hardly present in the novel at all, by the wealth and interest, for example, of old Mrs Churchill. This is what I mean by the solidity and openness of the novel. We happen to be concerned with the particular history of Emma, but we are aware that surrounding her are other destinies, other people going about their private concerns, other stories left untold which might – like that of Jane Fairfax – have been just as interesting as that of Emma herself. And this is not a matter of mere mystification; we do not have to know the truth of the concealed relationship in order to feel its pressure operating within the novel.

All this is more than merely a part of the substance of *Emma*; it is also inherent in our very experience of reading the novel. One of the reasons why Emma retains our sympathy is that all the other characters make similar mistakes about others or about themselves – even Mr Knightley is not entirely lucid to himself about his dislike of Frank Churchill. These frailties are simply part of what it is to be human; as Jane Austen observes: 'Seldom, very seldom does complete truth belong to any human disclosure; seldom can it happen that something is not a little disguised, or a little mistaken' (ch. 49).

This generalization expands beyond the book; we, too, share the frailty of the characters, not merely by being human, but also, in a special sense, by being readers. In other words, *Emma* is a novel which constantly tempts us into surmise, speculation, judgement; the process of reading runs parallel to the life read about. Hence the need for mystification and hence the delayed revelation which shows us how we, too, are liable to mistake appearances for realities and to arrive at premature conclusions. The novel betrays us to ourselves.

We are thus, once again, brought back to the ebb and flow of our sympathies, to what I earlier called 'the calculus of response'. But this is a bad term if it suggests that we read the book as moral auditors, totting up debits and credits of Emma's account. She is an imagined human being, not an aesthetic ledger, and our response to her is correspondingly complicated, shifting and unstable. One of the novel's major achievements is the way in which Jane Austen contrives this delicate, evanescent, moment-by-moment fluctuation in our attitude to Emma. It is perhaps for this reason that so much of the essential work is done by the cut-and-thrust of dialogue. This is pre-eminently language as gesture; Jane Austen knew all about tropisms long before Nathalie Sarraute. Speech *does* as much as it says; it signals assertiveness, entreaty, knowingness (think, for example of the vulgar parody of Emma's egoism contained in Mrs Elton's characteristic use of the pronoun, *We*).

Since this is a quality of the total book and since it has been well analysed by other critics, there is no need to take more than a sample as typical of the whole even web. From chapter 5 I pick up in mid-flight, a conversation between Knightley and Mrs Weston.

'Yes,' said he, smiling. 'You are better placed *here* – very fit for a wife, but not at all for a governess. But you were preparing yourself to be an excellent wife all the time you were at Hartfield. You might not give Emma such a complete education as your powers would seem to promise; but you were receiving a very good education from *her*, on the very material matrimonial point of submitting your own will, and doing as you were bid; and if Weston had asked me to recommend him a wife, I should certainly have named Miss Taylor.'

'Thank you. There will be very little merit in making a good wife to such a man as Mr Weston.'

'Why, to own the truth, I am afraid you are rather thrown away, and that with every disposition to bear, there will be nothing to be borne. We will not despair, however. Weston may grow cross from the wantonness of comfort, or his son may plague him.'

'I hope not *that*. It is not likely. No, Mr Knightley, do not foretell vexation from that quarter.'

'Not I, indeed. I only name possibilities. I do not pretend to Emma's genius for foretelling and guessing. I hope, with all my heart, the young man may be a Weston in merit, and a Churchill in fortune. But Harriet Smith, I have not half done about Harriet Smith. I think her the very worst sort of companion that Emma could possibly have. She knows nothing herself, and looks upon Emma as knowing everything. She is a flatterer in all her ways; and so much the worse, because undesigned. Her ignorance is hourly flattery. How can Emma imagine she has anything to learn herself, while Harriet is presenting such a delightful inferiority? And as for Harriet, I will venture to say that *she* cannot gain by the acquaintance. Hartfield will only put her out of conceit with all the other places she belongs to. She will grow just refined enough to be uncomfortable with those among whom birth and circumstances have placed her home. I am much mistaken if Emma's doctrines give any strength of mind, or tend at all to make a girl adapt herself rationally to the varieties of her situation in life. They only give a little polish.'

'I either depend more upon Emma's good sense than you do, or am more anxious for her present comfort; for I cannot lament the acquaintance. How well she looked last night!'

'Oh, you would rather talk of her person than her mind, would you? Very well; I shall not attempt to deny Emma's being pretty.'

'Pretty! say beautiful rather. Can you imagine nearer perfect beauty than Emma altogether – face and figure?'

'I do not know what I could imagine, but I confess that I have seldom seen a face or figure more pleasing to me than hers. But I am a partial old friend.'

'Such an eye! – the true hazel eye – and so brilliant! regular features, open countenance, with a complexion – oh what a bloom of full health, and such a pretty height and size! such a firm and upright figure! There is health not merely in her bloom, but in her air, her head, her glance. One hears sometimes of a child being "the picture of health"; now, Emma always gives me the idea of being the complete picture of grown-up health. She is loveliness itself. Mr Knightley, is not she?'

'I have not a fault to find with her person,' he replied. 'I think her all you describe. I love to look at her; and I will add this praise, that I do not think her personally vain. Considering how very handsome she is, she appears to be little occupied with it;

her vanity lies another way. Mrs Weston, I am not to be talked out of my dislike of her intimacy with Harriet Smith, or my dread of its doing them both harm.'

'And I, Mr Knightley, am equally stout in my confidence of its not doing them any harm. With all dear Emma's little faults, she is an excellent creature. Where shall we see a better daughter, or a kinder sister, or a truer friend? No, no; she has qualities which may be trusted; she will never lead any one really wrong; she will make no lasting blunder; where Emma errs once, she is in the right a hundred times.'

'Very well; I will not plague you any more. Emma shall be an angel, and I will keep my spleen to myself till Christmas brings John and Isabella. John loves Emma with a reasonable, and therefore not a blind affection, and Isabella always thinks as he does, except when he is not quite frightened enough about the children. I am sure of having their opinions with me.'

'I know that you all love her really too well to be unjust or unkind; but excuse me, Mr Knightley, if I take the liberty – (I consider myself, you know, as having somewhat of the privilege of speech that Emma's mother might have had) – the liberty of hinting that I do not think any possible good can arise from Harriet Smith's intimacy being made a matter of much discussion among you. Pray excuse me; but supposing any little inconvenience may be apprehended from the intimacy, it cannot be expected that Emma, accountable to nobody but her father, who perfectly approves the acquaintance, should put an end to it, so long as it is a source of pleasure to herself. It has been so many years my province to give advice, that you cannot be surprised, Mr Knightley, at this little remains of office.'

'Not at all,' cried he; 'I am much obliged to you for it. It is very good advice, and it shall have a better fate than your advice has often found; for it shall be attended to.'

'Mrs John Knightley is easily alarmed, and might be made unhappy about her sister.'

'Be satisfied,' said he, 'I will not raise any outcry. I will keep my ill-humour to myself. I have a very sincere interest in Emma. Isabella does not seem more my sister; has never excited a greater interest; perhaps hardly so great. There is an anxiety, a curiosity in what one feels for Emma. I wonder what will become of her.'

'So do I,' said Mrs Weston, gently, 'very much.'

'She always declares she will never marry, which, of course, means just nothing at all. But I have no idea that she has yet ever seen a man she cared for. It would not be a bad thing for her to be very much in love with a proper object. I should like to see Emma in love, and in some doubt of a return; it would do her good. But there is nobody hereabouts to attach her; and she goes so seldom from home.'

'There does, indeed, seem as little to tempt her to break her resolution at present', said Mrs Weston, 'as can well be; and while she is so happy at Hartfield, I cannot wish her to be forming any attachment which would be creating such difficulties on poor Mr Woodhouse's account. I do not recommend matrimony at present to Emma, though I mean no slight to the state, I assure you.'

Part of her meaning was to conceal some favourite thoughts of her own and Mr Weston's on the subject as much as possible. There were wishes at Randalls respecting Emma's destiny, but it was not desirable to have them suspected; and the quiet transition which Mr Knightley soon afterwards made to 'What does Weston think of the weather? – shall we have rain?' – convinced her that he had nothing more to say or surmise about Hartfield.

The quiet control of our attitude to Emma in this passage is obvious enough and needs no comment; it is a matter of constant but very minute fluctuations. What I wish to stress is that our feelings for her take their place in a much wider and more intricate human context; Emma the character is very far from being *Emma* the novel. Consider Knightley and Mrs Weston; though they act here, so to speak, as counsel for the prosecution and the defence and though they are generally throughout the novel exemplars of good-sense and right feeling, yet they too share with Emma the burden of being limited human beings, variable and ignorant of the future. Knightley though he names 'possibilities' cannot foresee them all; his opinion of Harriet Smith, for example, will change later in the novel. Mrs Weston unconsciously bears out his point that as governess she was educated by Emma; in the whole of this passage (particularly in the speech beginning 'Such an eye!') she is, as it were, acting

Emma's typical role – persuading and commanding the reactions
of others in the interests of a little gentle matchmaking. She
conceals 'some favourite thoughts of her own' on the subject of
Emma's marriage; these, too, will waver later in the novel when
Frank Churchill temporarily supplants Mr Knightley as the
desirable imagined groom. And always behind the dialogue,
between the lines, hovers Knightley's unspoken feelings for
Emma. Notice, for example, how he transfers his affections to his
brother so that they may be expressed in the safety of obliquity –
'John loves Emma with a reasonable, and therefore not a blind
affection.' Notice, how, in unconscious response to this, Mrs
Weston edges towards the truth: 'I know that you love her really
too well to be unjust or unkind.' Notice how, later, Knightley
advances – or retreats – to 'an anxiety, a curiosity' about Emma's
future; notice even the force of the one word *gently* which
characterizes Mrs Weston's reply.

The passage resounds, of course, with structural reverberations; some of these, like Knightley's 'I should like to see Emma
in love, and in some doubt of a return; it would do her good',
would be strident were they not far removed in time and space
from the things they echo against. Others are more muted; thus
Mrs Weston's 'I do not recommend matrimony at present to
Emma' perhaps gains a reasonance from a passage in the previous
chapter in which Harriet reports of Mrs Martin and her son:

'Not that she *wanted* him to marry. She was in no hurry at all.'
'Well done, Mrs Martin!' thought Emma. 'You know what
you are about.'   (ch. 4)

The point I wish to stress, however, is that the resonances of
structure are reinforced and complicated by the density of the
texture, by the liveliness of a quickly changing sequence of
interesting particulars. This is perhaps why our foreknowledge
of the end does not make the irony intolerable at a second reading;
our attention is so diversified and diverted by the thick web of
linguistic nuance that we do not concentrate single-mindedly on
the ironic results of the mystification. Indeed it may be that the
plot has to be made thus complicated and elegant precisely in

order to contain and control the multiplicity and plurality of the life it presents. Certainly we can apply wholeheartedly to *Emma* Professor R. A. Brower's fine description of *Pride and Prejudice*:

Jane Austen shows an almost Jamesian awareness of the multiple ways of reading a man's behaviour. She conveys her sense of the possibility of very different interpretations of the 'same' action, as James often does, through dialogues which look trivial and which are extremely ambiguous. At the same time they are not merely confusing because Jane Austen defines so precisely the ironic implications of what is said and because she gradually limits the possibilities with which the reader is to be most concerned.[2]

NOTES

1. 'Control of Distance in Jane Austen's *Emma*', in *The Rhetoric of Fiction* (Chicago, 1961) pp. 243–66; [reprinted in this volume, pp. 195–216].

2. 'The Controlling Hand: Jane Austen and *Pride and Prejudice*', in *Scrutiny* XIII (1945) 99.

QUESTIONS

1. 'I am going to take a heroine whom no-one but myself will much like.' Why do you imagine Jane Austen liked her heroine?

2. 'Reading *Emma* and re-reading *Emma* are two quite different experiences.' Discuss.

3. What attitude, on the evidence of *Emma*, did Jane Austen take to the class-system of her time?

4. In what sense, or senses, is *Emma* a 'comedy'?

5. How legitimate is it to regard the settings and seasons of *Emma* as 'symbolic'?

6. Describe the characteristic features of Jane Austen's prose style, and relate them to the over-all effect of *Emma*.

7. 'The first modern novelist.' How far does *Emma* support this claim made for Jane Austen?

8. Describe the relationship between the authorial voice in *Emma*, and the heroine's consciousness. Are we always able to discriminate confidently between them?

9. Discuss Jane Austen's handling of the minor characters in *Emma*, including those who never appear.

10. *Emma* has been likened to a detective story. Describe Jane Austen's distribution of clues.

11. Is Emma a truly changed character by the end of the novel?

12. 'Gentle Jane Austen' – 'Regulated Hatred'. Which description, on the evidence of *Emma*, is nearer the truth?

13. How does Jane Austen use the following characters to define the character of Emma: Mr Knightley, Frank Churchill, Jane Fairfax, Harriet Smith?

14. An earlier reviewer praised *Emma* for preserving 'the unity of place'. In what way does this unity contribute to the novel's effectiveness?

15. It has been said that Jane Austen's reputation has suffered more from her admirers than from her detractors. From which admirers represented in this book are you most inclined to rescue her?

SELECT BIBLIOGRAPHY

The following books and articles are, in the editor's opinion, of particular interest as contributions to the criticism of *Emma*; though, for various reasons (such as limitations of space), it was not possible to represent them in the main body of this book.

Howard S. Babb, *Jane Austen's Novels: the Fabric of Dialogue* (Ohio U.P., 1963).

    After the excellent introductory chapter on Jane Austen's style, the discussion of *Emma* is a little disappointing, but it includes a perceptive close analysis of Knightley's proposal to Emma.

Frank Bradbrook, *Emma* (Arnold, 1961).

    This careful and sensitive short study, designed primarily for students, is particularly informative on the relationship of *Emma* to earlier English literature. For a more detailed discussion of this topic, see the same author's *Jane Austen and her Predecessors* (Cambridge U.P., 1966).

G. Armour Craig, 'Jane Austen's Emma: the Truths and Disguises of Human Disclosure', in *In Defense of Reading*, ed. R. A. Brower and R. Poirier (Dutton, New York, 1962).

    A complicated but subtle analysis of the novel in terms of 'the web of imputations that link feelings and conduct', with particular stress on the complexities of rank in the Highbury milieu.

Joseph M. Duffy, 'Emma: the Awakening from Innocence', in *Journal of English Literary History*, XXI (1954) 39–53.

    This lively and provocative essay minimises the social texture of the novel and treats it as a fairy-tale-like story of the heroine's passage from innocence to experience. Parallel to Mudrick's reading in some respects – 'Emma is given the reward she in no way deserves' – Duffy's differs in holding that Emma attains at least sexual maturity by the end of the novel.

Mary Lascelles, *Jane Austen and her Art* (Oxford U.P., 1939).

By general agreement still the best orthodox study of Jane Austen's fiction.

Q. D. Leavis, 'A Critical Theory of Jane Austen's Writings', in *Scrutiny*, x (1941–2) 61–87.

See my Introduction for an account of this article.

Robert Liddell, *The Novels of Jane Austen* (Longmans, 1963).

This study includes a lucid examination of Mrs Leavis's theory concerning *Emma* and *The Watsons*, and a good analysis of Emma's self-deception concerning Frank Churchill and Jane Fairfax.

Arthur Walton Litz, *Jane Austen: a study of her artistic development* (Oxford U.P., 1965).

'By allowing us to share Emma's inner life without being limited by it, Jane Austen has avoided that dichotomy between the sympathetic imagination and critical judgment which runs through the earlier novels.'

David Lee Minter, 'Aesthetic Vision and the World of *Emma*', in *Nineteenth-century Fiction*, xxi (1966) 49–59.

In *Emma*, 'Jane Austen renders both the nobility and the dangers, the significance and the consequences, of Emma's endeavour to force an aesthetic ideal upon her world' and thus 'made the only peace she thought worth making with the Romantic mind'.

Andrew Wright, *Jane Austen's Novels: a Study in Structure* (Chatto & Windus and Oxford U.P., New York, 1953).

This includes a lucid account of Jane Austen's ironic handling of her heroine's progress, and useful insights are to be found throughout the book.

NOTES ON CONTRIBUTORS

WAYNE BOOTH is Pullman Professor at the University of Chicago, and the author of *The Rhetoric of Fiction*.

MALCOLM BRADBURY is Senior Lecturer in English at the University of East Anglia. He has published two novels (*Eating People is Wrong* and *Stepping Westwards*) and many critical essays.

D. W. HARDING, Professor of Psychology at the University of London, has published many essays in literary criticism, including contributions to *Scrutiny* and *The Pelican Guide to English Literature*.

W. J. HARVEY, late Professor of English at Queen's University, Belfast, was the author of *The Art of George Eliot* and *Character and the Novel*.

GRAHAM HOUGH is Professor of English at Cambridge University. He is a poet, and the author of several works of literary criticism, the most recent of which is *An Essay on Criticism*.

R. E. HUGHES is Professor of English at Boston College, and the author of *Rhetoric: Principles and Usage*.

ARNOLD KETTLE is Senior Lecturer in English at Leeds University, and the author of *An Introduction to the English Novel*.

MARVIN MUDRICK is Professor of English at the University of California in Santa Barbara, and the author of *Jane Austen: Irony as Defense and Discovery*.

RICHARD POIRIER is Chairman of the English Department at Rutger's University, and the author of *The Comic Sense of Henry James* and *A World Elsewhere*. He is editor of *Partisan Review*.

MARK SCHORER, Professor of English at the University of California in Berkeley, has published novels and short stories as well as literary criticism. He is the author of *Sinclair Lewis: a Biography*.

EDGAR F. SHANNON, JR, is President of the University of Virginia. He has published a number of articles on nineteenth-century English literature.

LIONEL TRILLING, Professor of English at Columbia University, has published studies of Matthew Arnold and E. M. Forster, and several collections of essays including the recent *Beyond Culture*.

INDEX

Note: for obvious reasons, references to Jane Austen, *Emma* and Emma Woodhouse are not included; neither are references of any kind within quotations from the novel.